D0917724

VIETNAM'S
SOUTHERN
REVOLUTION

VIETNAM'S
SOUTHERN
REVOLUTION

FROM PEASANT
INSURRECTION
TO TOTAL WAR

DAVID HUNT

University of Massachusetts Press

AMHERST

Copyright © 2008 by University of Massachusetts Press
All rights reserved
Printed in the United States of America

LC 2008043126
ISBN 978-1-55849-692-7 (paper); 691-0 (library cloth)

Designed by Richard Hendel
Set in Quadraat and The Serif Extra Bold by Binghamton Valley Composition
Printed and bound by The Maple-Vail Book Manufacturing Group

Library of Congress Cataloging-in-Publication Data
Hunt, David, 1942-
Vietnam's southern revolution: from peasant insurrection to total war /
David Hunt. p. cm.
Includes bibliographical references and index.
ISBN 978-1-55849-691-0 (library cloth ed. : alk. paper)—
ISBN 978-1-55849-692-7 (paper : alk. paper)
1. Vietnam War, 1961-1975—Social aspects.
2. Vietnam—Social conditions—20th century.
3. Peasantry—Vietnam—My Tho—History—20th century.
4. My Tho (Vietnam)—Social conditions—20th century.
5. Peasantry—Vietnam—My Tho—Interviews.
6. My Tho (Vietnam)—Biography.   7. War and society—History—20th century.
8. Civil-military relations—Vietnam—History—20th century.
9. Vietnam—Politics and government—1945-1975.   I. Title.
DS559.8.S6H86   2009
959.704'31—dc22
2008043126

British Library Cataloguing in Publication data are available.

To

James McMillin Hunt

and Mai Jean Hunt

and to Thuy Hunt

CONTENTS

ACKNOWLEDGMENTS

Not long after I started teaching at the University of Massachusetts Boston, Linda Gordon and others on the editorial board of *Radical America* called my attention to a collection of interviews with "Viet Cong" defectors and prisoners of war, which the Rand Corporation had just released to the public. I wrote an essay for *Radical America* and then an article for *Past & Present* on the National Liberation Front in My Tho province, all the while thinking that these fascinating materials deserved a more extended treatment. In the following years, while turning to other scholarly tasks, I continued to think about them, and in 1997 I started over again with the first of the interviews in the My Tho series and began to write this book.

The history of *Vietnam's Southern Revolution* is therefore entwined with all the projects and relations of my working life. The idealism, intellectual seriousness, and love of teaching among colleagues at UMass Boston and especially among Column comrades gave me a community and a sense of direction that has lasted to the present. In the History Department, I especially want to thank Esther Kingston-Mann, the most imaginative and intrepid scholar to come out of "peasant studies," Woody Smith, a learned and generous colleague, and Maureen Dwyer, who when problems arise invariably knows what to do to solve them. Most of all, I am grateful to UMB students, by now thousands of them, who have taken my classes. I have been moved and enlightened by their striving for an education and a better life.

In 1985 John McAuliff's invitation to join an educator's delegation to Vietnam set in motion a chain of events that shaped the rest of my professional and personal life. In the William Joiner Center for the Study of War and Social Consequences, Kevin Bowen, Larry Heinemann, and Bruce Weigl shared their poems and stories with me and helped me think in a deeper way about the Vietnamese. Informants who know more about Vietnam than I do, and especially Ngo Vinh Long, Nguyen Ba Chung, Nguyen Duc Chinh, Hue-Tam Ho Tai, and William Turley, have patiently answered my questions and saved me from many errors. Among the people I count on are Bill Beik, my *compagnon de route* going back to Sacramento Place; Jim Dittmar, Milt Kotelchuck, Dick Lourie, Mark Pawlak, and Peter Weiler (and Ron Schreiber, RIP) from the oldest men's group on the east coast; Pam Annas, Linda Dittmar and Jack Spence, for many acts of friendship in time of need; and Marilyn Young, respected and loved, and not just by me, for keeping the faith and for her principled scholarship.

Bill Beik and Peter Weiler have read and commented on just about everything I have written, and this book is no exception. Chris Appy, Mark Bradley, Woody Smith, and William Turley provided a close and helpful critique of the entire manuscript, and drafts of chapters were scrutinized by David Biggs, Dick Cluster, Clark Dougan, Jim Green, Jim Hunt, Esther Kingston-Mann, Rochelle Ruthchild, Tim Sieber, Steve Silliman, Malcolm Smuts, Philip Taylor, Paul Wright, Weili Ye, Katherine Yih, and Marilyn Young. They spotted all the flaws, as I knew they would.

At UMass Press, Paul Wright encouraged me through the years, and so did Clark Dougan, an editor who also happens to be an accomplished historian; Amanda Heller and Mary Bellino worked hard to improve what I had written, Carol Betsch saw the project through, and Kate Blackmer did the maps and taught me a lot about map making. Stephen Denney helped me find clean copies of many interviews in the DT series. People in the know were impressed and I was delighted when Jim O'Brien, whose reputation on this and other fronts is exemplary, agreed to do the index.

My parents, Freda and Jim Hunt, are gone, but the memory of their devotion continues to give me strength, as does the constant support of Miriam Hunt, with her passion for books, Jean Hunt, the anchor of our family, and Mas Nakawatase, the brother I gained in 1971. From the beginning, my son Jim has been there right beside me, full of hope and courage as we made our way through many an adventure. So has my daughter Mai Jean, whose loving heart and radiant presence are a joy and inspiration. I keep trying to find the words to say all there is to say about Thuy Hunt, who cares for me always and is always in my thoughts.

ABBREVIATIONS

ARVN Army of the Republic of Vietnam

CL Cai Lay district, Dinh Tuong (My Tho) province

CT Chau Thanh district, Dinh Tuong (My Tho) province

COSVN Central Office for South Vietnam

DRV Democratic Republic of Vietnam

DT Dinh Tuong (My Tho) province

GVN Government of Vietnam

NLF National Liberation Front (Viet Cong)

PLAF People's Liberation Armed Forces

PRC People's Republic of China

SDC Self-Defense Corps

VC Viet Cong

VIETNAM'S
SOUTHERN
REVOLUTION

CHAPTER ONE

A SOCIAL HISTORY OF
THE VIETNAM WAR

Regime changes, military campaigns, and big-power politics hold center stage in the literature on the Vietnam War. Accounts begin with the August Revolution of 1945, which brought the Viet Minh and the Communist Party to power and led to the formation of the Democratic Republic of Vietnam (DRV) and then to the First Indochina War, pitting the Viet Minh against French colonialism. The conflict became a battleground in the cold war, with the Soviet Union, the People's Republic of China, and the DRV on one side and the United States and France on the other. In 1954 the French were forced to withdraw, and partition followed, with the Communist Party ascendant in the North, while the Republic of South Vietnam, also known as the Government of Vietnam (GVN), took charge in the southern half of the country. The concerted uprising of 1959–60 led to the formation of the National Liberation Front (the NLF, the "Viet Cong"), which, with the aid of the DRV, then battled the GVN and the United States in the Second Indochina War. The 1968 Tet Offensive constituted a turning point in the fighting, and the end came in 1975 with the overthrow of the Saigon government, the departure of the Americans, and, a year later, reunification of the country.[1]

What I have attempted here is a different kind of history, with the emphasis on everyday realities at village level, as documented in a remarkable source, assembled by the Rand Corporation. Having been commissioned by the U.S. Department of Defense to study "Viet Cong motivation and morale," Rand interviewed thousands of defectors and prisoners who had been associated with the NLF. Of particular interest is one subset of the collection, the "DT series," based on 285 interviews conducted from 1965 to 1968 in the Mekong Delta province of My Tho. Bordering on a guerrilla base area in the Plain of Reeds and inhabited by a population with a history of activism, the province played a key role in the struggle against the French, the Saigon government, and the United States.[2]

The forty-two prisoners in the DT series were regarded as criminals by the GVN, and many had been tortured by soldiers or police before Rand staffers had a chance to interview them. Knowing that their lives were in danger, they were hardly in a position to speak freely. The other 243 informants were defectors who had turned themselves in to one of South Vietnam's "Chieu Hoi" Centers. *Chieu hoi*, which means "call back" in Vietnamese, was translated as "open arms" by the Americans, who hoped that defectors were "rallying" to the government cause. These subjects, who in many instances had served the NLF for a number of years, were under pressure to demonstrate the sincerity of their conversion to the government cause. In the power-laden interview setting, they too had to watch their words.

In spite of these constraints, the poor, largely uneducated country people questioned by Rand presented a rich commentary on village life in My Tho. The interviews are filled with vivid, often clashing reports, as informants struggle to remember and explain turbulent events. They offer crafty feints and disarming confessions, insights of startling penetration and catechisms echoing one or another party line, expressions of fear and hatred, guilt and sorrow, defiance and bewilderment, and also, in more than a few instances, longing for abundance and harmony in a world to be won. The My Tho testimonies amount to an exceptional projection of history from below; they retrieve from obscurity the vicissitudes of everyday life unfolding alongside the events that are highlighted in the dominant narrative. Interviews were conducted from May 1965 to January 1968 and are especially rich on the period that began with the opening salvos of the Second Indochina War. They serve as a point of departure for a study of the war at ground level from the concerted uprising to the Tet Offensive.[3]

THE PARTY AND THE PEASANTS

Assumptions about the Communist Party and the Vietnamese peasantry stand in the way of such a project. Political parties leave a paper trail and are therefore easy to research, while peasants generate few documents and are difficult to research. Parties devote resources to broadcasting their achievements, whereas agrarian populations find limited opportunities to speak for themselves. Parties have leaders whose names and views are known, while plebeian militants remain anonymous. Cold war commentators, perhaps especially the anticommunists among them, were mesmerized by images of a cunning and relentless enemy and habitually inflated the strength of the Communist Party in Vietnam. At the same time, the term "peasant" connoted ignorance and backwardness, even within the Marxist tradition.[4]

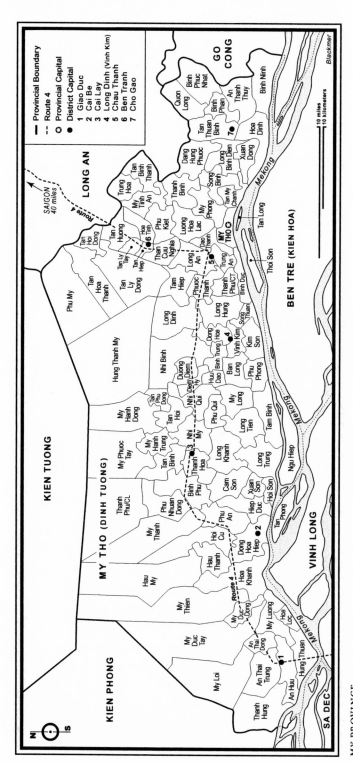

MY PROVINCE

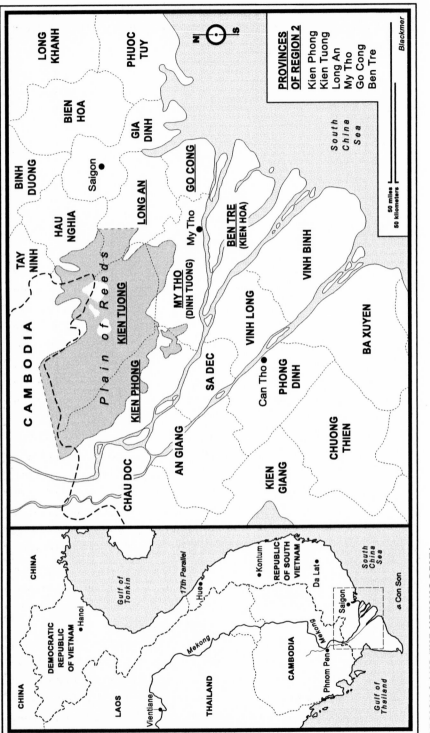

REGION 2 AND THE MEKONG DELTA

Blackmer

PROVINCES OF REGION 2

Kien Phong
Kien Tuong
Long An
My Tho
Go Cong
Ben Tre

At times the class bias implicit in such views is overt, as when Rand consultants David Elliott and W. A. Stewart assert that the Communist Party in Vietnam preferred to recruit among peasants:

> Coming from a lower stratum of society they tend to be less educated than the wealthier village elements, and often less adaptable to formal education. Far from presenting a problem, this situation is one which the VC [Viet Cong] find quite congenial. To implant a few basic ideas on a tabula rasa, relatively uncluttered by conflicting teachings, helps to eliminate confusion and uncertainty, and assures some uniformity in the ideological outlook of VC lower level cadres. To structure reality for less sophisticated minds leaves a more lasting impression, particularly when it is imbedded by incessant repetition, and gives voice to inchoate political urges which have hitherto been unable to find expression.

Elsewhere in the literature the party remains in the foreground, as if that way of thinking were a mental habit authors could not break. By the time he completed his important study of the revolution in My Tho, David Elliott had moved beyond the "tabula rasa" view just quoted. "I have not tried to reduce the whole movement to the Party itself," he declares, then puzzlingly adds, "except when constant repetition of the term 'revolutionaries' makes it more convenient to refer to the 'Party' as the embodiment of the leadership of the revolution." Convenient or not, a vertical axis, with leaders at the top, remains a deeply entrenched framework for understandings of the war.[5]

I begin with the conviction that observing and forming opinions on the uses of power are constitutive human activities and that the notion of a collective blank slate among subaltern populations is a figment. Elites are always telling people what to think and do, and on the basis of their own observations and judgments, people always absorb, reject, ignore, and recast elements of the messages they are hearing. Sometimes this analysis awakens a sense of common purpose and leads to the emergence of popular movements with their own leadership and programs and a capacity to challenge existing hierarchies. At such moments the vertical axis structuring domination must be considered in relation to the horizontal axis made manifest in common understandings and collective action at the base.[6]

In order to give this argument a hearing, readers must look past Ho Chi Minh and General Vo Nguyen Giap and try to see things through the eyes of rural dwellers. Policies conceived in the upper echelons of the Communist Party, headquartered in Hanoi, were transmitted down the chain of command to the Central Office for South Vietnam (COSVN), near the Cambodia border, then to the party's various regional headquarters. (My Tho was located in Region 2, in a cluster of six provinces in the upper delta.) In turn, resolutions were sent to province, district, and village sectors. Members of the party's Central Committee often disagreed about what to do, and in formulating policy they cobbled together policy statements from contending factions. In district and village training sessions, local cadres listened selectively to instructions whose tactical applications were often difficult to discern. Unable to catch a strategic nuance, or convinced that on-the-spot judgments should override policies conceived elsewhere, they made choices according to their own lights.[7]

Though imperfect, party discipline was a vertical axis of exceptional sturdiness, one that played a role in the Vietnam War, as historians have shown. But it would have achieved little if not for the horizontal axis, the agendas and leaderships that took shape at the grassroots level. Village activists were peasants with local roots. In the words of one Rand informant: "These cadres had many experiences in the class struggle's political activities. Since they belonged to the poor class, they had known many hard experiences of the underprivileged rural people. So they based their political activities on the common thinking of the peasants and adopted methods suitable to the rural people's thought and situation in carrying out these activities. That explained why they enjoyed the sympathy and confidence of the peasants." Rural dwellers molded by hard experiences in class struggle gravitated toward leaders who remained attuned to their interests. The consciousness of individuals they chose to follow was shaped by local circumstances as well as by party policy, and when villagers are identified as communists, I assume that one can attribute to them a social as well as a political identity and that the views and aspirations they expressed were derived from the "common thinking" of their class. They needed a nationally organized party, with strategic perspectives not readily attained at hamlet level, but in the sometimes unstable alliance that emerged, the party was also a dependent entity. Without a popular movement, it would have flailed in a void.[8]

In many accounts the southern revolution is identified with the National Liberation Front. But the NLF, which was unveiled in response to a Hanoi initiative in December 1960 and not introduced in My Tho until July 1961 or later, was not the same as the "Liberation Front," which had earlier marched out of the shadows and seized control of the countryside. In 1959–60 that Front led and the party followed. A degree of unity was achieved during the following years, but with escalation in 1965, a gap opened. It was made manifest politically, in resistance to NLF tax and draft policies, and spatially, as most villagers left heavily bombarded settlements and took refuge elsewhere, while cadres and guerrillas remained in hamlet redoubts. The separation was neither complete nor permanent, and in 1968 the party and the popular movement again came together in order to launch the Tet Offensive. Yet even in that moment of immense common effort, not all participants shared the same expectations, a lack of consensus once more suggesting the need for an analytic distinction between the two currents within the Vietnamese revolution.

The Mekong Delta was the most revolutionary section of the country. During the First Indochina War, commonly known as "the Resistance" in My Tho, Communist Party leadership tabled land reform and called on all Vietnamese to oppose the French. In the North, village notables responded to this invitation even to the point of joining the party, while in the South, Viet Minh cadres disregarded united front guidelines and chased away rural elites. In My Tho, "the big landlords saw the handwriting on the wall and fled for the towns," and local militants seized tens of thousands of hectares and distributed them to the poor and landless. By 1954 "the old power structure" in the province "had been irretrievably overthrown," in contrast to the situation in northern provinces, where village hierarchies remained intact, thereby obliging party leadership to sponsor the land reform campaign of 1953–1956. In 1960 the party once more opted for an inclusive coalition, this time against the entourage of President Ngo Dinh Diem and his foreign allies. But activists in the South again showed little interest in cross-class alliances and resumed their campaign to topple "the entire socioeconomic elite which constituted the foundation of the Saigon regime." These events call attention to the revolutionary temper of the popular movement in the area and to the relative autonomy that characterized its relations with the party.[9]

THE SOCIAL TRANSFORMATION

Vietnam's place in the world in the middle of the twentieth century was not determined by cold war dynamics alone. Summing up the global significance of the moment, Eric Hobsbawm declares that it witnessed "the greatest and most dramatic, rapid, and universal social transformation in human history," and to a greater or lesser extent, its reverberations were felt everywhere. Even without revolution and without war, the Vietnamese people were going to be dealing with abrupt and comprehensive changes. In particular, testimonies in the DT series call attention to a restlessness among country people in the period after the Geneva Accords and suggest that the 1954–1960 interlude should not be dismissed as a mere time-out between the First and

Second Indochina wars. During what Rand informants called "the six years of peace," many villagers took to the road in hopes of escaping from the poverty and frustrations of rural life. Exotic items in market stalls disturbed some and tempted others with the promise of a novel kind of freedom. Family structures buckled as one or another parent got sick or died, left in search of work, or found a new partner. Gossips jeered at "concubines" even when the targets of their barbs were restless women looking for ways to live that did not involve being kept by any man. Elders muttered about youthful "cowboys" in an echo of the uneasiness occasioned at the same moment by "juvenile delinquents" in the United States. Indeed, all of this turmoil was part of an international rupture in time and space and behavior.[10]

Beginning with the concerted uprising of 1959–60, local militants declared themselves sponsors and organizers of this unrest, which they hoped to appropriate and speed up according to their vision of a new society. No doubt they valued the "boon of continuity" with the past, but of equal importance was the longing for an escape from feudal backwardness and for an unprecedented future happiness. Activists demanded an end to landlordism and an egalitarian distribution of the means of life and also a democratization of relations between peasants and urban dwellers, parents and children, men and women. They hoped that the Vietnamese people would achieve a fuller sense of their place in the world and of the power they possessed to fashion their own destinies, without reliance on supernatural forces. While drawing freely on themes embedded in Communist Party discourse, their utopianism displayed an unmistakable originality. Land reform alone, and beyond that a proletarian status, would not have satisfied cultural revolutionaries, who hoped to transform all phases of everyday life.[11]

In the war that followed, adversaries of the Liberation Front imitated its call for change and even for revolution. Samuel Huntington's announcement that the United States was bringing "forced draft urbanization and modernization" to Vietnam bluntly stated a rationale that was affirmed, albeit in sanitized language, by many defenders of U.S. escalation. Given these overlapping terminologies and the difficulty attendant on specifying what elements qualify a policy as "modern," I propose to reserve the term "modernization" for reforms that Americans wished to bestow or force on Vietnam and to employ "modernism" to characterize the efforts of the popular movement to block externally sponsored projects and to chart its own route forward. The Rand materials help to pin down the meaning of these competing programs as they were manifested in the lives of villagers in My Tho, who worked to make themselves "the subjects as well as the objects of modernization," who sought "to change the world that was changing them, to make their way through the maelstrom and to make it their own." The American war sucked Vietnam into the maelstrom and imposed all the dilemmas of modern life on those Vietnamese who aspired to change the world.[12]

Readers used to associating modernism with high culture may be skeptical about my deployment of the term. It rests on the assumption that the Vietnamese, and indeed all human beings caught up in the midst of rapidly evolving circumstances, are capable of and cannot avoid reflecting on what is happening to them and on how they can safeguard their lives and futures. I therefore take my distance from scholars who portray the city, with its sophisticated intellectuals, its grand boulevards and back alleys, its pleasures and estrangements, as the exclusive locus of modernity and launch discussion from the perspective of what lies outside the city and, for many, stands as its antithesis. The object is not just to identify who was left out or left behind in an increasingly urbanized Vietnam, but to study how peasants interrogated what it means to be modern.[13]

During the war, when some Americans claimed that the Vietnamese were caught in a crossfire and just wanted to be left alone, that formulation might have been mistaken for an expression of sympathy. But the informants whose stories are recorded in the Rand materials were not mere victims, crouched over their bowls of rice and oblivious to the larger issues others were fighting and dying to resolve. Living along the fault lines of the social transformation, where they were exposed to all its possibilities and dangers, the Vietnamese made a heroic effort to control their own destiny. Today, as sequels of that moment unfold at an ever-accelerating pace, the specific remedies they sought may no longer seem relevant. The more thoughtful of local activists would not have been surprised to hear that Vietnam was going to change enormously in the decades to come. What set them apart was a readiness to experiment, to weigh new departures, and, most of all, a refusal to be pawns of modernization. What follows is a study of their revolutionary modernism.

CHAPTER TWO

AN ITINERANT PEASANTRY

In the years leading up to the Second Indochina War, rural dwellers in My Tho often traveled back and forth between the countryside and the towns, and many were familiar with Saigon, by far the largest agglomeration in the South. In the context of the social transformation, one might assume a state of dependency in the hamlets and attribute this movement of peoples to the power and allure of the city, a core area strong enough to impose its will and ethos on agrarian populations. But evidence in the DT series indicates that country people fashioned multiple readings as they crossed and recrossed the rural-urban divide. When these pilgrims became conscious of the collective strength that resided in their home villages, they and their more sedentary neighbors broke out of the periphery and made a bid to seize control of society.[1]

TAKING NOTICE OF THE EVERYDAY

To get at this topic, I have been obliged to think in a new way about the origins of the Vietnam War. Fernand Braudel warns us not to be mesmerized by the Event, not to lose sight of quotidian realities that form the bedrock of human experience. "Everyday life consists of the little things one hardly notices in time and space," he affirms. "Sometimes a few anecdotes are enough to set up a signal which points to a way of life." In reading through the DT series, I have tried to notice "the little things" that Rand interviewers and interviewees passed over as they talked about the event we call the Vietnam War and that illustrate how the Vietnamese lived in the middle of the twentieth century. Dilemmas of modernity were posed with the greatest urgency in the sphere of the everyday, and the experience of everyday life generated the resentments and yearnings that motivated those who flocked to the banner of the Liberation Front. In what follows I offer the beginning of a social history of the revolution in My Tho, a dimension underlying and shaping the political and military events that up to now have been taken as the crux of the war.[2]

In summing up the session with a poor peasant from Long Hung, a Rand interviewer wrote, "He never had any opportunity to make contact with the people in the GVN-controlled zone and to understand the conditions there." The staffer did not notice that his subject had worked in Saigon for three years as a pedicab driver, in the heart of "the GVN-controlled zone." Informants themselves sometimes failed to notice. A resident of Long Dinh stated that he had lived in the village "from my childhood to the day I was arrested" and that he had "also stayed in Saigon for over a year, from 1961 to 1962, and worked as a bricklayer." Elsewhere in the session he called attention to his enrollment in a GVN training course for rural youth in Saigon in 1959.[3]

A man from Dang Hung Phuoc had worked as a pedicab driver in Saigon in 1954–55. But when asked who would win the war he responded, "I cannot guess who will be the winner, because I have always been living in the countryside and never went to Saigon, [so] how can I guess about Russian and American affairs?" This was a man who may have been involved in the Nam Ky uprising of 1940 and who joined the Resistance in 1946 and the Communist Party in 1950, then was captured two years later and incarcerated in three different jails within the French prison system. He was serving as party chapter secretary when captured again, this time by Saigon troops, in 1965. A militant of long standing, he most certainly had thought about the course of the war. Perhaps the humble tone was meant to suggest that he was a simple peasant and not a revolutionary. Or maybe he too failed to notice, failed to assign any larger significance to, displacements that routinely figured in the lives of villagers in My Tho.[4]

A thirty-three-year-old man I will call the Platoon Leader spoke more freely. When asked by the interviewer what put him at ease, he laughed and replied: "Because I saw that you were sincerely moved by my story when I told you of all the painful experiences I had had when I was a child. If you were a cadre planted here, you would certainly not be affected like that. Out there (in the VC area) amidst all the denunciations there were countless stories that were more heart wrenching than mine." Unlike the Vietnamese who worked for Rand and who belonged to a different "social class," Front cadres would view his tale "as just one of a thousand other stories of misery" and not at all unusual.[5]

So, then, what was this everyday "story of misery"? The Platoon Leader began by saying: "Because he was so poor, my father did not get married until later in his life, and only had one child—myself. As I was growing up, I couldn't go to school, although I wanted to very much. Because my family was extremely poor and didn't have enough to eat, my father kept insisting that I go to work and become a buffalo herd[er] for a landlord in the village when I was only 11 years old."[6]

After much ill treatment ("the beatings and cursings were as regular as rain"), the boy and his family moved to Ca Mau and lived as woodcutters until the moment four years later when the father was arrested by the French, accused of affiliating with the Viet Minh, and imprisoned on Poulo Condore island. His son "never saw him again." An uncle then volunteered to take the boy to Phnom Penh, where he might have a chance for a better life. But once in Cambodia, he was treated like an indentured servant and put to work selling newspapers and shining shoes. In 1950 he escaped and returned home, only to be "crushed" by the news that his mother had decamped to Saigon (where neighbors said she hoped to find a job selling soup). Since he "didn't know the way to Saigon, and because of the war," this teenager, now effectively an orphan, had to stay in the village with his grandfather. In the following years, he joined the Viet Minh, regrouped to the DRV, then returned to My Tho in 1960 and served as an officer in the Front army, the People's Liberation Armed Forces (PLAF). His wife had remarried while he was in the North, and when he got married again, to the widow of a government soldier, comrades objected. Irked by their criticisms, persuaded that the Front could not win the war, and with the prospect of an affluent life in the Saigon zone (his new father-in-law was a wealthy man), he defected to the government side.[7]

The Platoon Leader had come a long way and took pains to distinguish himself from the "ignorant bumpkins" who remained in the Front-controlled sector. At the end of the session, the interviewer commented: "The subject's abilities and comprehension showed how much training courses given to him have changed him. From an ignorant buffalo tender, he has become a very good platoon leader whose comprehension on political matters is really astonishing." After rallying to the GVN, he at first tried to masquerade as a simple peasant. But the charade did not fool a soldier who was bringing him to the Chieu Hoi Center. "I have met many ordinary citizens here," the escort declared, "and I have noticed that when they get to the district, everything is a surprise for them. Moreover, they are reluctant and afraid. Your attitude was completely different. You took it very matter of factly and gave the impression that you were very familiar with life in the towns. That's what made me think that you were a ranking cadre in there." It seemed that the Viet Minh and the National Liberation Front had succeeded in refashioning an unlettered peasant into a self-assured urbanite.[8]

No doubt service in the Resistance and the Front helped to form the Platoon Leader, but his trials and wanderings must also be counted among the forces that changed him. He was already a resilient survivor, toughened by family tragedy, political repression, and years spent away from home when he found the Viet Minh and the Viet Minh found him. Because he was not the only villager who had traveled widely, I prefer to situate his story within the mid-century social transformation that was refashioning everyday life in the delta. A juxtaposition of "ignorant bumpkins" with city sophisticates does not do justice to an enlargement in experience and consciousness throughout the countryside that helped to prepare the ground for the concerted uprising of 1959–60.

RURAL ESTRANGEMENTS

Personal crises of the sort related by the Platoon Leader and the displacements they occasioned were common in the lives of peasants in the delta. The household economies on which they depended were fragile. Most units engaged in subsistence farming, while some family members also worked for a wage in the village or elsewhere or traded in marketplaces near and far. Quarrels between spouses or between parents and their offspring, untimely illness and death, and troubles with the authorities all combined with economic factors to disrupt household arrangements.

In these circumstances, children were especially vulnerable. "Life was very hard for me while I was still a small boy," recalled a man who grew up in a family of day laborers. "My parents, very poor and landless, had to make a living working for others. Every day, they had to get up very early in the morning and leave home for the field, staying until late in the evening. They didn't have time to take care of us and we had to rear ourselves. Since I was the youngest boy, my brother and my sister had to keep me with them all day." In other cases children lost both parents. One Rand informant was orphaned at four, two were orphaned at six, another was orphaned at eight. A Khmer from Tra Cu was orphaned at thirteen, and he and his brother survived by working as servants. A child from Binh Trung was orphaned at fourteen, then followed his older brother to Saigon and became a pedicab driver in Cholon. Another unfortunate was orphaned "very early in life" and was raised by an aunt. "She did not treat me well," he reported. "I wasn't allowed to attend the village school and I still don't know how to read and write." Still another informant recalled that in 1954, "as I didn't have to support anyone because my parents were dead, I decided to regroup in the North." An observer had the impression that most of the village youth who volunteered for the PLAF "were poor orphans."[9]

Other interviewees grew up in single-parent families. A youth from Long Thuan lost his father when he was three, and his mother "had to slave" to raise him and his brothers and sisters. When a man was killed in battle against the Viet Minh, the government refused to pay his wife the "death allowance" to which she was entitled. "This is why I hated the GVN even when I was young," his son explained. The father of another informant died when the boy was two, and he and his many siblings were raised in penury by their mother. He was forced to tend ducks and buffaloes for others, spent only one year in school, and was too poor to marry. "I feel very sad whenever I am reminded of my miserable childhood," he declared. The mother of a Phu Phong resident died when he was thirteen. His father insisted that he leave school and work as a buffalo boy, then arranged his marriage and refused to let him make his own decisions until he was twenty-five. Another child who lost a father earned a pittance as a buffalo boy while his mother tried to support a family of nine on the income from a tiny parcel of land. The father of another was killed by the Viet Minh when the interviewee was twelve; "with great courage," his mother worked as a day laborer to raise him and his siblings through "a series of hardships and misfortunes." [10]

Arrangements that were not disrupted by poverty or illness or imprisonment or accidents of war were often undone by deteriorating relations between husbands and wives. Polygamous males broke up more than one household, as in the case of the informant who kept "two wives" and "courted" village women and who exclaimed "the hell with my family" when asked why he had rallied on his own, without bringing along his first wife and children; or of another man who had two wives in Xuan Dong and two mistresses, both married and both pregnant by him, in neighboring Hoa Dinh. A boy from Vinh Kim was raised by his grandmother. "When I was still living at home," he reported, "I found life very hard. My father had some money but he didn't pay any attention to me. He only thought of the well being of his second wife and her children." The father of an informant from Long Khanh died when the boy was six, and some years later his mother married another man from Long Trung. "But she was only his concubine," he recounted, and the arrangement does not seem to have brought any benefit, as mother and son continued to live in Long Khanh. In a world where the stability of domestic arrangements was crucial for survival, many country people, and especially the very young, were at risk when households fell apart. [11]

Tensions between parents and children also troubled many a household. After failing his school exams, a teenager was beaten by his father and "longed to get away" in order to "lead a new life." He agreed to join the Front because "I couldn't stand my father's treatment any longer." A buffalo boy who was "frequently beaten" by his stepfather was recruited by the NLF at thirteen. "I didn't dare let my father know about my decision [to join the Front]," reported a soldier who enlisted at sixteen, and another recruit stated that his father had disowned him when he opted for the NLF at the age of eighteen. One almost has the impression that the movement adopted rather than recruited these disaffected village youth.[12]

Rand's fourteen female informants told similar stories. Three had lost both parents: the mother of one was shot by government soldiers, and her father succumbed to typhoid fever; the mother of another died in childbirth, the father took off for Saigon, and the girl was raised by grandparents; a grandmother stepped in to care for a third girl, who was orphaned at ten. Five others grew up in single-parent households. A subject explained: "My father died when I was only six or seven years old. When my mother got married a second time she didn't live with her second husband and my step-father couldn't support us. So, our life was very hard." Two of the fourteen refused arranged marriages. One recalled that her grandmother wanted her "to get married to a villager of whom I was rather afraid. He was a mature man who had been divorced and had a few children to rear. My grandmother was very angry at my refusal and kept on insisting that I had to take him as my husband." Refusing a loveless marriage, she fled. "When I was 19 years old," recalled another, "my parents wanted me to marry a man in the village, [but] I didn't like him so I ran away from home." Another escaped a tyrannical mother-in-law. When a nineteen-year-old married a local guerrilla, her father objected. "I was fed up with my father's reproaches," she stated, by way of explaining her decision to enlist in the NLF. All in all, twelve of the fourteen women ran away from home or departed against their parents' wishes.[13]

The Rand materials call attention to chronic family breakdown in My Tho. In order to escape from a countryside where poverty was endemic and domestic arrangements proved unable to secure the livelihood of the inhabitants or to meet their demands for happiness, rural dwellers were ready to try something new. Hoping for a better life, they headed for the towns.

ENCOUNTERS WITH THE CITY

One Rand staffer assumed that peasants never ventured out of their hamlets and were therefore like "a frog at the bottom of a well seeing only a piece of the sky," while another thought that those who were exposed to city life would not be "bluffed by VC propaganda."[14] But stories told by the Platoon Leader and others indicate that villagers had often been to the city and had developed a critical perspective on what they had seen. At least forty-two Rand informants were drawn to Saigon: to attend school; to sell fruit, cabbage, pigs, sugarcane, bananas, and coconuts; to drive pedicabs, trucks, and buses; to hire out as domestics, haulers, chauffeurs, dishwashers, coconut pickers, bricklayers, silversmiths, carpenters, seamstresses, masons, stevedores, mechanics, and traffic light installers; and to work in a brewery, a textile mill, a rice noodle plant, an import-export firm, a coconut warehouse, a recording studio, an oriental medicine shop, and a fish sauce container factory. Others ventured even farther afield: a bus driver's assistant in Dalat, a trucker in Bien Hoa, a carpenter in the Highlands, a man seeking medical treatment in Cao Tho. Still others had been drafted into the Army of the Republic of Vietnam (ARVN) and trained in Quang Trung, near Saigon, then assigned to posts in Kontum, Hue, and elsewhere. In addition to these cases, at least twenty-nine informants had relatives in Saigon: sisters working as a maid or seamstress, brothers driving a cab or a cyclo, an aunt whose husband was a journalist, mothers selling fruit, a father who was a construction worker, a husband employed by a firm, a wife who had lived in the capital city before marriage, a son employed in a post office.

My Tho was no Saigon, but it was unmistakably a city, with schools that attracted village children, medical services patronized by people of all ages, and markets for fruit, sugar, ducks, and other farm products. Some itinerants found jobs there: an apprentice tailor, a bricklayer and bicycle repairman, a cook, a seamstress, and a worker in a dredging company. District capitals were modest agglomerations, but they encouraged a division of labor beyond what might be found in villages. The transcripts make reference to a poor peasant who attended primary and secondary school, a gas station attendant, an apprentice tailor, a tri-wheel Lambretta driver, and a servant in Cai Be; an ice cream vendor in Cho Gao; an apprentice watchmaker and two high school students in Cai Lay; and a man who worked in his cousin's Chinese soup shop in Giao Duc.

A few of the mobile villagers were from well-off households that could afford to send children to an urban school. Typical in this regard was a man born into a landlord family in 1907. After study in the École Normale de Pédagogie in Saigon, he taught elementary school in Ben Tre province, then took a job as a principal in Binh Duc village. But most itinerants were more like the subject who worked as a Saigon bricklayer and whose circumstances were so dire that he was "the only man in the village who did not raise any pigs."[15]

Some urban stays were temporary, as in the case of the teenager from My Thanh village who got a job as a gas station attendant at the Cai Be intersection for one lonely month, then went back home; or the poor peasant from Tan Binh who, as a twenty-four-year-old, was briefly employed in a Saigon brewery. Others developed a taste for movement. A precocious young man from An Thanh Thuy made a living taking coconuts by boat from his home through Long An to Saigon, Bien Hoa, and Phuoc Tuy and also had worked for a year and a half in Saigon as a domestic servant. Another joined an entertainment troupe at the age of seventeen and performed all over Saigon, then periodically returned to sell fruit from his family orchard in Phu An. Then there was the very poor sharecropper who was at home in the marketplace selling sugarcane and stayed in touch with relatives and friends outside of his native village of Xuan Son. His wanderings seem to have been as much for pleasure as for material gain. "I went out of my village at least once every two months," he remarked, "to the GVN-controlled areas to learn about the general situation and to see my friends living there." Curiosity also drove the man who enlisted in the Imperial Guard in Dalat because he "wanted to know more about the country," and the twenty-four-year-old who regrouped to the DRV "in order to be able to see new places."[16]

As these accounts suggest, some itinerants were attracted to the city. A poor peasant born in 1906 went to Saigon in 1933 and got a job with Denis Frères, an import-export company. "Life was then easy," he recalled. An informant who worked as a hired hand in the capital city reported that the experience "was very pleasant and one could do what he pleased." Another envied his mother-in-law, a Saigon fruit dealer. "She was free and happy," he reported; "she had to work only half a day and still had a comfortable life." According to the grapevine, if a man were strong enough to carry up to 100 kilograms, he could make a lot of money as a stevedore at the Saigon docks and could send 2,000 to 3,000 piasters a month to his family. My Tho City made a positive impression on a deserter from the PLAF, who enjoyed "taking a stroll in the public garden near the river" and gaped at marketplace displays of meat and fish. "Going to the theater is great!" he exclaimed. "When I attended school in Cai Lay," remarked an informant from Cam Son, "I found life in the District town and the cities more comfortable than that in the countryside." He hoped to return someday because "in the countryside, even the rich had a hard life. They did not have the conveniences and did not even have soap, tooth brush, lamp, and wardrobe, etc. I wished I could have in the future a higher standard of living but the circumstances brought me the reverse."[17]

Less-traveled villagers dreamed about urban life. A twenty-year-old poor peasant was drawn to "town-girls": "I noticed that they are more attractive than peasant girls. I knew that because some of the town-girls often came back to Tam Hiep during the Tet festivities or to attend the ancestor worship rites." He added that "every bachelor in the Front's ranks longed to live in the towns and to marry a town-girl." Females were also mesmerized. An eighteen-year-old from a sharecropper family imagined "that the people in the city must have a happier life and more freedom, because all the towns-people who came to our village were well-dressed and had so much money to spend. At the time, I cherished the hope of coming and settling in the city some day."[18]

Other migrants expressed more skeptical views. A very poor twenty-four-year-old from My Duc Dong village moved to Saigon with his father, worked as an ARVN truck driver in Bien Hoa, then deserted and made a living paint-ing wooden shoes in the capital city. When the police began to round up AWOL personnel, he returned home, only to find that the NLF had instituted a draft of its own, a step that once more drove him to Saigon. Unable to sur-vive on his wages as a bricklayer and again facing military duty in ARVN ranks, he decamped once more to My Duc Dong, only to be conscripted by the NLF. He twice deserted and was forcibly reintegrated, deserted a third time, then hosted a banquet to celebrate his return to civilian life. "You defected from your unit," local cadres fumed, "and you dare to kill a duck to celebrate your desertion?" Packing his bags one more time, he trudged back to Saigon, but, "because life is very hard in town," decided to rally and enlist in an ARVN unit. That this chronic draft evader was unable to find an alternative to mili-tary service underscores the difficulties for peasants trying to make a place for themselves in the city.[19]

The Rand transcripts suggest that a gulf remained between urban and rural comportments. A Tan Thoi resident who "often came to My Tho" still felt uneasy because "I was a peasant in town and my behavior was not nor-mal." Another villager complained that "in the cities, people wear reveal-ing clothes and form-fit pants" and objected to the formation of strategic hamlets because the inhabitants "had to live in close quarters like in the cities." A twenty-eight-year-old defector did not want to venture out of the Saigon Chieu Hoi Center because he was "afraid of being kidnapped by the 'cowboys.'" District capitals are better understood as villages with a smattering of administrative offices, but even there peasants acted "reluc-tant and afraid," as noted in the interview with the Platoon Leader, cited earlier.[20]

Material difficulties often reinforced this sense of alienation. A man from Phu An frequently went to Saigon to trade fruit and visit his sisters but thought "it was impossible" to gain a livelihood there. "Living on my garden," he noted, "I had enough to eat." A Cam Son resident visited Saigon many times "but didn't succeed in getting a job and settling in town." A twenty-eight-year-old from Dao Thanh recalled leading "a very hard life" as a bicycle repairman and bricklayer in My Tho. A poor peasant from Vinh Kim, who was in his mid-twenties at the time of the Rand interview, had already worked for a dredging company in My Tho, a sugar mill in Cap Saint Jacques, a fish sauce plant in Ca Mau, and a rice noodle firm and a construction crew in Saigon. Employers "liked me a great deal and never spoke harsh words to me," he recounted. "But the thing was that I didn't earn enough money to live on. I kept changing jobs, hoping to make more money, but it was always the same." A young man moved from Long Khanh village to Saigon and became an apprentice silversmith but could not survive on a "meager salary of 800 piasters a month." Fleeing "miserable conditions," he and his wife came back to Long Khanh. "Saigon is certainly very heavily populated," he observed, "but you live with strangers and therefore you feel more lonely than living with your family and friends in the countryside."[21]

Some commentators called attention to the injustice of the urban social order. A seventeen-year-old from My Phong village enrolled in a Saigon school and roomed with his eldest brother, a military policeman. After he had earned a "baccalaureate first degree," his brother and sister-in-law "scorned" his lack of "connections" and poor job prospects. Disgusted with "the division and sectarianism prevailing in the society at that time," he went back to My Phong. A twenty-seven-year-old from a poor family in Binh Xuan was raised in Saigon, where his father worked as a janitor. He dropped out of school when his parents moved to the countryside, "where the cost of living was lower than in the city," and tried to find a job. "I soon found out that life in the city was full of injustice," especially manifest in "the misfortunes and miserable life of the labor class." A possible alternative arose when "during vacation, I returned to my native village and heard the people whisper about the activities of the Front." Soon after, he reestablished himself in Binh Xuan and joined the NLF. A twenty-six-year-old from Tan Ly Tay moved to Saigon with his two younger brothers and worked as an apprentice to a practitioner of oriental medicine. He returned to the village in 1962 and volunteered as a guerrilla "because at that time the Government was drafting young people of the working class into the military while most youths of rich families were exempted from military service."[22]

As these accounts suggest, itinerancy sometimes had a radicalizing effect. A young man was sent to Saigon, where he lived with an uncle and attended school, then later on tried his hand at watch repair and photography.

"When I was living in the city I saw many things that made me feel sorry for the poor," he declared.

> Many rich families in Saigon raised German shepherd dogs which had a better life than the poor who lived under bridges and so on. This pained me. There were many poor families living near my school. Every morning their children asked for money to buy this and that to eat, but they never could afford it. All they could give their children was rice gruel or a piece of French bread, or sweet potatoes. They had to toil to earn their living. Poverty bred greediness and crime. They resorted to stealing or killing people for money.

"I wanted to see a society in which no one would be exploited," he summed up, "in which men would not kill each other for money, and in which no one could use money or power to oppress others."[23]

The mix of wealth and deprivation country people encountered in town, the contrast between cultural effervescence and workplace drudgery, and the unpredictable rhythms in the labor market all honed critical awareness. The effort to make sense of an alien environment had the added benefit of sharpening their appreciation for resources and possibilities in the villages that cities could not match. Exposure to an urbanity that stood in marked contrast to rural folkways also drove home the point that there were alternatives to hamlet routines. Every person of a certain age in My Tho had experienced more than one revolution, and only the most blinkered rustic could have been insensitive to the currents that were reworking everyday life. The different costumes and gestures, sights and smells, work regimes and leisure patterns in the city served as additional reminders that other ways of living were possible. Schooling in the contingency of social arrangements did not make revolution inevitable, but it did help to enlarge the consciousness of a transient peasantry.

Among town dwellers there was no counterpart to this meditation on the urban-rural divide. According to Philip Taylor, they regarded the countryside as "a symbol of tradition, yet one in which they would not like to spend too much time." The delta, they marveled, was a place where "you can just stick something in the ground . . . and it will grow." This was an expression of self-serving blindness among "creditors, process factory owners, and tax agents who benefit from the agricultural wealth of the delta without having to undertake the manual labor or suffer the loss of livelihood and well-being in the economically and environmentally unstable conditions of agricultural commodity production. The wealth of the land is imagined not as a human product for which a substantial debt of gratitude might be owed, but as a natural blessing to the Vietnamese people." At best patronizing, urbanites did not always succeed in masking the disdain that informed their view of the agrarian population. At one moment country life was seen as "quaint," and villagers were portrayed as "simple, forthright and full of charmingly archaic turns of phrase." At the next they were ridiculed as superstitious boors. While itinerancy gave peasants at least a modicum of experience on which they might base a claim to speak for the nation, the myopia of privileged city dwellers helps explain their paralysis when rebellion broke out in the countryside.[24]

THE *RASSEMBLEMENT*

The peasant class was not a static entity. A snapshot view of rural society calls attention to differences between the rural poor and prosperous truck farmers, between the illiterate and the handful who had attended secondary school, between devout and agnostic, old and young, men and women. Pictured over time and with attention to patterns of movement, the social formation appears even more ambiguous. Individuals who left their hamlets often could not predict when and if they might return. Many city-dwelling migrants continued to think of the village as home, but with the passage of time, occasional visits, as for Tet celebrations, became no more than ritual pauses in a new, urbane way of living. Modernization everywhere, and not just in Vietnam, constantly makes and unmakes communities and class solidarities, obliging those caught up in its rhythms to ask again and again who they are and where they fit in society.

Given this evidence, one should be cautious about assuming a direct transition from the Resistance to the National Liberation Front, as if the Viet Minh legacy alone might explain the emergence of a revolutionary consciousness among country people in the 1960s. While there was undoubtedly a link between the two movements, unsettling changes in everyday life during the six years of peace, and especially the multiple reverberations in awareness and behavior that issued out of the rural encounter with urban life, also shaped a new generation of activists. Their concerted uprising ushered in what one informant called a "golden period," filled with debate over the organization of material life, the relationship between religion and politics, the function and control of print communication, the proper use of entertainment and leisure, the roles of youth and elders and of women and men. It also sponsored a remapping of space in the delta. As cities lost their earlier power of attraction, the outflow of migrants trying to get away from the penury and frustration of rural life gave way to an inflow of peasants coming home.[25]

An informant from a wealthy family attended primary school in My Tho, then in 1933, at the age of nineteen, became a tradesman, moving fruit from Ca Mau to Saigon. He joined the Front in 1960, and so did his son. This affluent villager quit the NLF in 1962, was called back, quit again, was inactive for three years, then rallied in order to acquire government identity papers. That a man so well situated, from an entrepreneurial rich peasant family, could have been swept into the movement, even if only for a couple of years, is eloquent testimony to the power of the *rassemblement*, the gathering of the people, set in motion by the concerted uprising.[26]

It was less surprising when poor people came home. After being dismissed by his landlord, an informant from My Tinh An went to Saigon and found employment as a carpenter with Johnson, Drake, and Piper, a U.S. construction company building the Saigon–Bien Hoa highway. With savings from a salary of 152 piasters a day, he moved with his two children to Bien Hoa and built a house that cost 2,000 piasters. When the highway project ended, he took a sequence of odd jobs, then sold the house for 1,000 piasters, moved back to Saigon, and lived with a brother, whose income as a cyclo driver "was barely sufficient for him and his family of six children." It was during this time that he "got wind of the uprising of the Viet Cong." Returning to the countryside was "the direct result of my inability to find a job in the capital city of Saigon and my assumption that I would make an easier living in my own native village now that the Front had given back the lands to me for farming."[27]

A similar impression emerges from the testimony of a man who was classified by the Front as a poor peasant, but who declared that he did not "know anything about farming and worked in the market place" as a barber and tailor. At first portraying himself to Rand as a reluctant recruit, he later indicated that his mother had benefited from NLF land reform and that he heartily approved of "the distribution of wealth to the poor people." The revolution was drawing this seemingly deracinated peasant back to the land in his native village.[28]

The *rassemblement* constituted a development of exceptional interest and originality in the history of southern Vietnam. Peasants of My Tho lived and worked within an orbit dominated by the Saigon metropolis, with its concentration of administrative and political authority, its seductive commodities and styles, its insatiable appetite for the produce of the delta, its huge labor market, which employed and dismissed working people according to a logic that no one could anticipate or control. But Saigon was not invincible. By creating a sense of novelty and progress more gripping than any urban fashion, the revolution shifted the locus of modernity to the villages. According to a witness from Thoi Son, in 1962–1964 rural dwellers "absolutely supported" the NLF, and "even the people who lived in the city were with the Front." In fact, "there wasn't much difference between life in the city and in the [liberated] zone, especially in clothing and in material needs," he recalled. "Coffee shops were filled with people. People came in great numbers to do business. Whenever there was a festival, a lot of people were present." The attempt to end the age-old subordination of rural to urban space numbered among the most ambitious goals of what was a many-sided cultural revolution.[29]

ODYSSEY OF THE ETHNOGRAPHER

These themes are well illustrated in the story told by interviewee no. 233, a witness I call the Ethnographer. He was born in 1936 in Tan Ly Dong. Both his mother and his father, a Caodaist teacher and tobacco trader, were dead by the time he was nine, and two siblings died soon after. He grew up with a grandmother, then with an uncle, who had him tending buffalo, and in 1949 ran away to join the Viet Minh. After a year of service as a liaison agent, he returned to Tan Ly Dong, was employed by another uncle as a buffalo boy, and managed to save 1,000 piasters catching fish and breeding chickens. A relative who worked as a nurse in My Tho brought him to the city, where he rented an icebox and sold ice cream. In 1956 he apprenticed as a silversmith, only to be treated more as a servant than an aspiring craftsman, so he quit and went back to the village. "I'm very poor," his uncle told him. "It is up to you to go and look for yourself the type of job you can do." Now twenty years old, he returned to My Tho and "bought some pieces of musical songs for resale" but was not successful. He next tried working for "a hat-washing firm" and had "almost mastered the trade when the proprietor went bankrupt as a result of his large gambling losses." He switched to a glassware shop run by a Chinese retailer, and when that enterprise also collapsed, he moved to another shop across the street.[30]

At this point the uncle, who feared that he "might live a loose life in the city," called the Ethnographer back home, arranged his marriage to a local woman, and gave him a parcel of land and 500 piasters. A baby was born soon after, but the new husband and father soon found that he had no knack for farming. So he took off again, this time for Saigon, and got a job installing traffic lights for the railway service (40 piasters a day), then another wrapping goods and collecting money in an oriental medicine shop (600 piasters a month, plus meals and extra for overtime). Meanwhile, back in Tan Ly Dong, his wife was spending extravagantly and having an affair with a bus driver. In 1961 the child died, and the Ethnographer was fired from his job at the medicine shop because he was spending too much time studying for night school classes. "I wanted to have my elementary school certificate because we have to have a degree in any type of work," he explained, "and because I wanted to enlist in the Navy or in the Police." Having failed repeatedly to escape from loneliness and poverty, he had reached an impasse. "I reluctantly returned to Tan Ly Dong, completely heart broken," he recalled. "My wife had left me, my child had died, and I only had 1,000 piasters left at that time."

In his village and in My Tho and Saigon, the Ethnographer had twice lost his family and had been a buffalo boy and cultivator, fisherman and chicken breeder, ice cream vendor and silversmith, sheet music peddler and hat washer, glassware salesman, traffic light installer and medicine shop clerk. This orphan and drifter was rescued by the movement and functioned effectively in a variety of roles within the Front. But habits formed during a lifetime of wandering did not readily bend to party discipline. Twice expelled from the Communist Party for illicit love affairs, he periodically retreated into a kind of escapism. "I was not a member of any organization," he reported. "I could go anywhere I pleased. When I came to an area where I had friends or acquaintances, I would stay with them for a while. If I felt like it, I would cooperate with the local village security cadres and work with them. Otherwise, I would join some friends for a drinking party." Nonetheless, until the moment of his rally, he could not let go of the revolution. "We are Bolsheviks," the other cadres declared, "and we are not afraid of shortcomings. Therefore, you should not feel embarrassed." After all, "anyone can make mistakes," and "if we know our own shortcomings and try our best to overcome them, we will become good men." This appeal, from comrades who had shared his "pleasures and sorrows," persuaded him to resume political work. But then, in August 1967, after almost getting killed in a commando raid (not his only brush with death), he defected to the GVN.[31]

I call interviewee no. 233 the Ethnographer because of the keenness and penetration of his extended commentary on village life. In a sample filled with individual displacements, he was the most mobile of the informants and was also, perhaps not incidentally, the most astute observer of everyday life. In his extended dialogue with Rand, he offered both a history of the Front in My Tho and a commentary on the advent of a certain kind of modernity in the countryside, and in the telling drew out the interplay between these two developments.

This book owes a particular debt to one of the threads developed by the Ethnographer. "In the past," he stated, "people in the countryside conceived that when they get married, they should build a big house with all conveniences," such as "wardrobes, chairs, wooden boards, lamps," and other items in line with "traditional customs," as well as "buffaloes and ricefields to give to their children." But, he continued, "people are now for modern life" and are constantly on the lookout "for modern and strange things."

> For instance, if I were rich enough to buy a sewing machine, my neighbor would try to buy one although he was not as rich as I was and he did not actually need it since his children were still very young and were unable to learn how to use that machine and no members of his family were able to use it either. He just bought it and put it in a corner of his house. There are also the families who are in financial difficulties, but they still bought radio sets when they saw that their neighbors had already bought them.

Here one notes the emerging logic of a consumer society, puzzling to its first chroniclers, in which need, strictly defined, no longer controlled spending habits.[32]

Village youth seized on the freedoms associated with these developments. "Young people have entirely forgotten our traditional customs," the Ethnographer observed. Girls "talked freely with the boys," males and females wore "modern clothes" and "were not polite in their speeches and manners," most young men drank alcohol, and "only three out of nine girls in my village still wear their short blouse and their ample pantaloon." Other Rand informants seconded this analysis. During the six years of peace in Quon Long,

> the hamlet young men and women didn't aspire to anything else than having saved enough money to take a trip to the cities either on the occasion of Tet or during their spare time. In the cities, they would spend their money on clothes, and such items as radio sets. At that time they were dreaming of taking a trip to My Tho or Saigon where they would visit the market place, where they would go to see shows, and to go here and there to have fun. That was all they aspired to. The majority of the girls in the hamlet dreamed of marrying a husband and going to the city where they would live in grand style, and would be dressed in elegant clothes.

A similar report came from an informant from Long Tien, where youths enjoyed "traveling here and there as part of their education." They saved money, but only "in order to be able to go to the city at Tet time and do their shopping, buying to their satisfaction."[33]

Leading the way in scorning custom and "buying to satisfaction" were "cowboys" and their female consorts. Calling attention to a man he did not like, an informant said, "He was quite impolite in his speaking, he was naughty, and usually put his hat on his head at a rakish angle like a 'cow boy,'" which the Rand staffer defined as a "term commonly used to designate ill-bred youngsters." This objectionable comportment was doubly rebuked because it came from the city, as when an observer noted, "Teenagers of both sexes are dressing in the way the juvenile delinquents in the cities are doing." Critics reprimanded young people "for their irrespectful behavior and careless speech, their taste for eccentric clothes, indulgence in good living and heedlessness about their family and their own future." Another witness reported that elders "blamed the youngsters for their insolence and immorality." In their opinion, "the youths did not want to settle down. Instead of building a house of their own, they moved from one place to another, leading a bohemian, homeless life. They didn't remember even the anniversaries of their ancestors, or those of Confucius and Mencius. They were like renegades who had abandoned all the good principles of the country in which they were born." Young people who liked to move "from one place to another" were thus a conspicuous presence in the traffic between village and town that was destabilizing society in the delta.[34]

Changes in female comportment appeared especially dramatic. A lost time of modesty and subordination, nostalgically conjured up by men, served as the reference point. Women used to wear their hair "in the old fashion," one informant recalled, while another observed that "in the old days" they were "so shy" and "were only allowed to wear black heavy loose clothes." "Modern girls" took the lead in defying these conventions. "Women in rural areas like to dress and make up like those of the city," another observer stated; "they imitate one another in dressing and have given up their one-time simplicity." Yet another witness declared that during the six years of peace the girls "liked to dress well, especially the girls who always wanted to be fashionable, and always needed money to buy new materials for new dresses," while another also identified that period as a moment when women became interested in "material things and luxury."[35]

This evidence suggests that comparable shifts in taste and behavior were emerging among rural youth of both sexes in the years leading up to the concerted uprising, as a fascination with "modern and strange things" spread across the countryside. In the Mekong Delta of the 1950s, the advent of consumer culture and the accompanying malleability of personal identities that it seemed to make possible formed part of the social transformation of the mid-twentieth century. In the beginning, the freedom to choose how to dress or to style one's hair felt like an experiment in self-transformation, one that prompted thoughts of other departures: to break from stifling patterns of deference, to choose a partner rather than accepting an arranged marriage, or to seek out work different from the farm labor of previous generations. Liberation writ large, as the popular movement was to imagine it, was not an inevitable outcome of these trends. But experimentation among "cowboys" and "modern girls" amounted to a signal that people might be open to the possibilities that abruptly emerged during the concerted uprising.[36]

In 1966, when he took yet another leave from the Front and returned to his village, the Ethnographer found that the people now playing leading roles in the local movement "had all been in 1961 backward youth whom I did a lot to build up. Now they were all in the Village Party Chapter whereas I was an outsider. I felt ashamed and disgusted and had no desire to stay in my village." The tone here and elsewhere in the interview works to distance the speaker from the younger generation in a way that makes him sound almost like an elder, although he was only thirty-one when interviewed by Rand in September 1967. But here is how he remembered the situation in his village six years before: "In the beginning till the end of 1961, the youths in my village were curious about the Front and so they very much wanted to join. They loved to be sent around with loudspeakers to make the propaganda to the villagers or drop leaflets and display flags. They were also fond of displaying their bare chests and wearing pistol belts to show off themselves as heroes. I was among those peculiar youths." The Ethnographer belonged to a "backward" cohort of young people who gravitated toward the movement at the time of the concerted uprising, then "built each other up" into revolutionaries. He began as a "cowboy" (recall his uncle's worry about the "loose life" he might be leading in the city) and never fully shed the habits he acquired during a wayward youth, as reflected in his repeated liaisons with "one girl after another" and fondness for "eating and drinking" parties. In a postscript the Rand staffer notes that "he smoked good cigarettes, drank beer," and "liked to dress well and spend money."[37]

The Ethnographer exemplified changes taking place in the delta in the 1950s. Born into a peasant family and active in a peasant revolution, he had mostly resided in town. "Since my childhood I had known nothing of farming," he confessed, and when given a parcel of land, "I didn't know what to do." If not for the concerted uprising, he might have spent his working life in the Saigon police force instead of an NLF security section. He understood that village youth under the spell of urban culture and not sufficiently "aware of the class struggle" would "drink alcohol, wear cowboys' (hoodlums') outfits and speak impolitely" and therefore "could never be employed to work with the farmers." "True communists" grasped the need to unite fractious youthful cadres and rural dwellers less touched by modern currents. "In addition to our real society," he mused, "there is an 'undecided' society in which there are people who wear an old-style pajama trouser with a modern shirt, or conversely a man who wears a Western style trouser with a pajama shirt." Himself a protean figure, he organized his political work with reference to such behaviors and the hybrid social reality that shaped them.[38]

When the Ethnographer explained that "communism is now inadvertently going in pair with 'undecided doctrine' (lung lo)," he captured the duality and vitality of the Liberation Front. In love with movement, its leaders borrowed freely from Marxist-Leninist doctrine, which they interpreted according to their own lights. They took "dialectical materialism as a guideline for the settlement of their problems. They think that everything in this world never stood at one place but always changed. A human being or a thing experiences the same change of conditions. If a party cadre or member does not think so, he is a backward person." This was a demanding, a modernist credo among militants who were not afraid to plunge into the maelstrom.[39]

CHAPTER THREE

THE PEASANT REVOLT
OF 1959–60

In 1959–60 a movement arose against the Saigon government of South Vietnam. Washington blamed the Hanoi-based Communist Party for fomenting the insurgency, and party leaders in the DRV, who at first feigned noninvolvement, in the end claimed credit for what they called the "concerted uprising." Scholarly treatments have developed a more complex picture of what happened while continuing to assign the party a leading role. Typical is the analysis of William Duiker, who, in an often-quoted passage, affirms that "the insurgency was a genuine revolt based in the South, but it was organized and directed from the North."[1]

In this chapter the emphasis shifts toward the "genuine revolt" in the South. Since communities are always organizing and directing themselves as well as being organized and directed from outside, a satisfactory picture of what is going on is attainable only if internal as well as external factors are made part of the inquiry. Party leaders in Hanoi, in COSVN, and in Region 2 did not have the power to control events at hamlet level, and though closer to the ground, provincial cadres felt constrained by instructions from above and were not always able or willing to heed signals from below. At the decisive moment a "Liberation Front" of local inspiration stepped forward to make a revolution.

STAGES OF REBELLION

The concerted uprising in My Tho did not begin all at once on a particular day. In reviewing the Rand interviews that include testimony on the subject, one finds six informants who state that the revolt broke out in 1959, forty-five who claim that it emerged in 1960, fifteen who identify 1961 as the starting point, and several whose recollections make it seem as if the government was not challenged until 1962 or 1963. Instigators in the hamlets or coming from outside were responsible for the overture. Their nocturnal forays signaled that a rebellion had been launched, with shouted slogans and attacks on GVN symbols and installations. These were usually episodic intrusions—"every now and then," according to one witness—accompanied by destruction of property and sometimes by assaults on individuals, but primarily designed to announce the existence of the "Liberation Front" or "Liberation Forces" or "Liberation Army," as they called themselves, and to tear down emblems of the regime. When challenged, some officials ran away, while others counter-attacked or at least tried to maintain a local presence. The result was dual power, with Saigon nominally in charge during the day, while at night the movement drew converts into its ranks. Sometimes in tandem with the over-ture, more often weeks or months later, rebels tried once and for all to "break the grip" of the regime by killing or expelling local power holders. Mass mo-bilizations then made possible victory marches across the countryside and unarmed sieges of military posts. Eventually the Front gained control over many villages, thus creating liberated zones.[2]

The concerted uprising was the sum total of many hamlet revolts, each marked by its own lurches and delays, so that difficulties arise when one is trying to compile a province-wide history of the event. Hoi Cu, a village with twelve hamlets, is among the most thoroughly documented in the DT series. One informant began the story in 1959; several thought that the uprising started in the first half of 1960; one singled out July 20, 1960, as the key date; and one said that the movement erupted in his hamlet in early 1961. Popular violence succeeded in breaking the grip of the authorities in July 1960 in one account and December in another, while demonstrations and sieges were situated in July by one witness and in December by two others. One infor-mant said that four hamlets in Hoi Cu had been liberated by late 1960; one claimed that five were liberated by June 1961; one noted that the village was entirely liberated in 1961; and one remembered that his hamlet was liberated in 1962. The Hoi Cu case was typical. All over My Tho the uprising unfolded in fits and starts and spread unevenly from hamlet to hamlet over a period of months and years.[3]

Communist Party accounts cannot be squared with this evidence. In Janu-ary and May 1959, the Central Committee decided to step up the campaign against the Saigon regime and in its Resolution 15 authorized local branches in the South to employ a measure of force. But it also stipulated that violence should be in self-defense only, with the emphasis remaining on "political" rather than "military" struggle. Resolution 15 did not reach My Tho until January 1960, after the uprising had begun in at least six locales and probably in others as well. Party leaders in Hanoi then had little to say about the devel-oping situation in the South until September 1960, when the Third Party Congress called for overthrow of the Saigon regime. Arriving in My Tho

sometime in 1961, this declaration must have seemed to many like a reitera-
tion of what had been proclaimed in dozens of villages months and even
years earlier. Similarly, news of the formation of the Hanoi-sponsored National Liberation Front in Tay Ninh province on December 20, 1960, did not
reach My Tho until later, when it came as an afterthought to revolutionaries
who were already deciding on their own what sort of liberation they were
striving to achieve.[4]

The My Tho Province Committee seemed to be getting out ahead of the
party leadership when it affirmed in May 1958 that "killing cruel and wicked
tyrants is correct." But it also rebuked a committee member who had authorized the assassination of a GVN district chief the previous year, and other
province recommendations in 1958 continued to stress "legal" work over
armed struggle. The committee's May 1959 meeting issued a somewhat more
emphatic and perhaps more consequential statement, calling for recruitment
of three "armed propaganda squads" with the aim of "breaking the grip" of
the GVN and supporting "the political struggle of the masses." The slender
military means implied by the three-squad order would seem to point toward
a self-defense strategy, as does the continuing insistence that political rather
than military means should remain paramount. But as events were to demonstrate, the letter of these instructions was not as important as the way in
which they were interpreted at district and village levels.[5]

Province efforts to take control of the popular movement were organized especially around July 20, 1960, the anniversary of the signing of the
Geneva Accords. Party machinery did its best to make that date a launching
point for the revolt, one that would give it a more concerted character, and
official accounts published after the war follow that model. Some affirm
that the movement began on July 20. According to David Elliott, "the official My Tho province account of the revolution does not seem to reflect how
far the insurgency had spread in the first months of 1960. It focuses on the
situation in villages close to the Plain of Reeds revolutionary bases, which
were also the officially designated targets of the first phase of the uprising,
but does not have much to say about villages south of Highway 4, which the
interviews indicate were already hotbeds of revolutionary activity." One
upper-echelon cadre asserted that an extra push on July 20 was required to
help "timid" My Tho communities catch up with vanguard base areas along
the northern border of the province. The party decision to name the "heartland" region the "20/7" zone was meant to underscore that temporizing
peasants of the area owed their participation in the revolution to an external impetus. Taking the point, later commentators forgot about the Geneva

Accords and characterized July 20 as "the date commemorating the Front concerted uprising in My Tho province."[6]

Whenever the Communist Party intervened in force, it was bound to have an impact, and July 20 stands out as an important moment, albeit one of many, in the concerted uprising. Its significance varied from one locale to the next. In some it marked an overture, as in a sector of Hau My where, according to a resident, "the Front began to operate in the hamlet on July 20, 1960," and also in My Hanh Trung and My Duc Tay. By contrast, in the 20/7 village of Long Hung, the overture came in February 1960, and "the most important" step was not taken until November of that year, when the land problem "was solved to the satisfaction of the villagers." This informant also remembered July 20, but only as the date of a meeting, "attended by about 50 people," for study of the Geneva Accords. According to another Long Hung resident, perhaps from a different hamlet, the overture came "at the end of 1960," and the grip of the GVN was not broken until 1961. A My Long witness remembered July 20 as the time when "the Front first made its appearance," then added, "but not until mid-1961 did [its] activities reach a peak." July upsurges in violence were recorded in Hoi Cu, Ban Long, and Hau My, where "it was not until the commemorative day of July the twentieth that the Front started killing its foes." Elsewhere the date was no more than an official-seeming occasion, as in Thanh Phu (CL), where "the Front officially began operating among the people on July 20, 1960, excluding the period when the underground carried out secret propaganda activities." It was the same in Hoi Cu, where rebels had been active since early 1960, going from hamlet to hamlet, making broadcasts through megaphones, beating on drums and "wooden fish," and organizing meetings, and where "the Front officially began to operate in the village at night on July 20, 1960."[7]

An examination of terminology sheds further light on the problem. The Vietnamese phrase *pha the kem kep* literally means "destroying (*pha*) the posture of (*the*) clampdown (*kem kep*)," or "breaking the grip," and is often translated in the Rand interviews as "Destruction of the Oppression." The phrase seems to have been first employed in the May 1959 meeting of the My Tho Province Committee, which called for the formation of armed propaganda squads whose mission was to "break the grip" and "support the political struggle of the masses," not to launch a revolution. It therefore might be understood as a first step toward what would eventually turn into something like the concerted uprising. But in the accounts of Rand informants, "breaking the grip" sounds like a tactic utilized from hamlet to hamlet at different stages of the movement in order to eliminate the government presence in the countryside. Not confined to self-defense, it involved arresting, assassinating, or driving away officials and soldiers. These clashing usages draw attention to a party leadership trying, both in the moment and in its later construction of events, to establish control over the anarchic violence of the popular movement.[8]

"Concerted uprising" is also a problematic term. It is a translation of *dong khoi*, which in turn is a contraction of *dong loat*, meaning "simultaneous," and *khoi nghia*, meaning "uprising." The phrase was intended to underscore that this was a planned and coordinated campaign, a party campaign and not, in Leninist discourse, "spontaneous," that is, not an impulsive eruption from below. By my reading, the revolt was a decentralized, improvisatory affair and therefore might be characterized as "spontaneous." But the words and the phenomenon are also subject to other constructions. One might revisit "spontaneity" by following the example of the *Oxford English Dictionary* and quoting Thomas Hobbes: "That all voluntary actions, where the thing that induceth the will is not fear, are called spontaneous, and said to be done by a man's own accord." In that sense it was a concerted uprising, as villagers remade themselves and their world of their "own accord." The revolution was achieved because, through the swerves and jolts of revolutionary struggle, they demonstrated an uncommon ability to act "in concert."

THE INSTIGATORS AND THEIR FIRST RECRUITS

David Elliott estimates that in January 1960 there were Communist Party chapters in nine of the ninety villages in My Tho province and ninety-two party members at the base, backed by two hundred others in the Plain of Reeds or other sanctuaries. These shadowy figures were scattered and unarmed. In some locales they had managed to hang on through the dark days of the late 1950s, while elsewhere the party presence had been destroyed. In such circumstances a province-wide mobilization, triggered by marching orders from above, was not feasible. The uprising that did occur was the result of an encounter between a small number of instigators and a rural population that was ready to move. In order to explore this complex interaction, a closer look at the individuals involved, the party members and the others, is in order.[9]

Only one of the 285 defectors and prisoners questioned by Rand staffers claimed to have helped start the revolt in My Tho. Interviewee no. 135, the Instigator, was born in 1936 in a middle peasant family in Tam Hiep village. Five months after becoming politically active in 1959 he was invited to a training course, called "the indoctrination on the Concerted Uprising Campaign," seemingly scheduled for five months but actually conducted for only five days. (It was cut short when the GVN discovered the site.) Even before the course he had already heard "that the Party was going to wage the insurrection." In a possibly meaningful aside, he then corrected himself to say, "As a matter of fact this course only dealt with the Destruction of the Oppression." Once the trainees convened, "regulations" were distributed, specifying modes of organization for the coming campaign. Each plotter was to recruit one "backbone element" per hamlet, and in turn that activist was supposed to draw in others, who would form the "Liberation Army forces." The instructor explained why revolt was necessary but "did not present any methods to be followed. He only attempted to destroy the fear of hardships and of difficulties which would rise from the campaign."[10]

"Building this organization took me a whole year," the Instigator recalled, "but it became easier when Ngo Dinh Diem issued the decree-law 10/59," since the repression that followed made the people more ready to rebel. Jumping forward in time, he then stated that local activists received only five days' notice of the concerted uprising campaign, which started on July 20, 1960. "During these five days I had to mobilize the Liberation Army forces in my hamlet to make machetes, wooden-fish, loudspeakers and a kind of bangalore [tube] made with hollow bamboo sticks filled with acetylene." Finally, on the day of the uprising, "every cadre of my rank in Chau Thanh District had to gather to form the 'illegal forces (luc luong bat hop),'" a district-wide group of eighteen persons (about which more will be said in chapter 4).[11]

This report indicates that local activists were planning an "insurrection" in 1959, one year before July 20, 1960. As the Instigator notes, it took him "a whole year" to lay the groundwork. Supporting a 1959 starting point is the observation that preparations began before and became easier after May 1959, when Diem's repressive law 10/59 was promulgated. They could not have gotten the inspiration for such a plan from Resolution 15, which had not yet reached the South, or from COSVN or the regional office of the party, which remained uncertain about what to do. Province cadres were somewhat more ready to fight, but, as previously noted, their call for three armed propaganda squads sent an ambiguous signal.

It therefore seems that tentative province pronouncements were refashioned at the grass roots into a summons to revolt. Like peasants on the eve of the French Revolution who credited rumors that Louis XVI was calling on them to stop paying feudal dues, or Russian peasants who believed that the tsar wished for them to burn manor houses, local militants told themselves that the party had finally opted for revolution. In My Tho the phrase "armed propaganda activities" was understood to mean "armed activities," a less restrictive formulation. "I joined the movement in 1959," the Instigator stated. "When the Party started the Concerted Uprising Campaign, the cadres only said it was a resolution from the Party." This news appeared to be confirmed by the invitation to the training course. "But before it took place," he specified, "I already knew that the Party was going to wage the insurrection." The grapevine was broadcasting a message that higher echelons were not yet willing to transmit.[12]

The account took a further twist as the interview moved on to events in 1960. Here, in the process of retelling, the Instigator leaped over several months of local history and tried to make it seem as if the Tam Hiep insurrection was launched on July 20, 1960, in party accounts the official beginning of the uprising. In order to make his account fit in with that chronology, he corrected himself by specifying that "Destruction of the Oppression," in official usage a form of self-defense only, and not the "concerted uprising," was the subject of the 1959 indoctrination session. But the Instigator had already made clear that insurrection was in the air long before July 1960, and the point is reinforced by another interviewee, who asserted that the Front arose in Tam Hiep in December 1959, when rebels beat on drums and wooden fish, destroyed GVN flags and house plates, burned an information booth and watchtower, and arrested two hamlet chiefs and beheaded two others. According to this account the movement accelerated in May 1960, when "the Front gained control" over several hamlets in the village "during the day as well as at night." Perhaps the Instigator was the one who, in December 1959, appeared at midnight in Tam Hiep, megaphone in hand, but if that was the case he chose not to tell Rand about it. His account obscures the early months of the uprising and his own identity as a revolutionary before the revolution as it was to be portrayed in Communist Party histories.[13]

The Instigator's testimony is therefore not the last word on events in 1959–60. In their commentaries on the overture, other Rand informants indicate that the first acts leading to the resumption of armed struggle were carried out by a handful of people. In fourteen of the cases where numbers were given, informants said that a single individual made the first move; in three interviews, two were mentioned; and according to four others, three to six took the initiative. Sometimes they were village residents, either underground survivors of the dark days or cadres who had taken refuge elsewhere and were now coming home. When strangers launched the revolt, it is almost always specified that they quickly established contact with previously inactive militants or recruited local residents to take over direction of the campaign.

Arriving in the middle of the night and insisting that villagers extinguish lamps and remain inside while they addressed them from the shadows, the intruders seemed on the one hand to fear being identified. But on the other, their comportment was anything but furtive. "The VC came and made a lot of noise by hitting a pole against the tin roof of the watchtower, and pulled it down before withdrawing," recalled an informant from Binh Ninh. The pains taken by instigators to remain anonymous were a kind of charade. An informant from Nhi My declared, "I recognized the voices of some of the guys who lived in the hamlet." Elsewhere the words of the hidden speakers made clear that they were neighbors, familiar with the local scene. By a process of elimination and through the grapevine villagers must have been able to identify most of them. With provocative words and gestures the rebels announced a subversive intent and in the process mocked the authorities and dared more timid neighbors to join them.[14]

Delphic pronouncements from the Central Committee would have confused rather than energized peasant audiences, so it is not surprising that instigators fashioned their own call to arms. In Cam Son a single paladin "talked through his megaphone to invite the people to assemble at some place and said: 'I am the representative of the Liberation Front of the South. I have a mission to break the enemy grip for the people.'" In Duong Diem "they sneaked in to burn down the watch towers" and arrest local officials. In Tra Cu they shouted "Down with Ngo Dinh Diem!" and "Bravo Ho Chi Minh!" In Binh Trung a handful of activists came around midnight "to the hamlet sentry post," where they "used their long sharp sabers to intimidate the watchmen and tied all of them up. They then set fire to the sentry post and the information booth. Afterwards, they entered every household to tear up Mr. Ngo Dinh Diem's pictures and destroy the house number boards. They proclaimed themselves the Liberation Forces of South Vietnam who were rising up." With desecrations and threats and leaflets, like the one that showed President Diem "holding a net in one hand to catch the people with, and in the other hand a Colt 12 to shoot the people to death," instigators were issuing a declaration of war.[15]

When the Front first arose in Vinh Kim, "it said that it would carry out soon a general insurrection and offensive and everyone was wildly enthusiastic about it." No tactical ploy, for self-defense only, the rebellion aimed to "overthrow the regime of Ngo Dinh Diem." According to an informant from My Long, "when the Front first started its insurgent movement to break the grip of the government on the population, the cadres who went on missions or operated in the village called themselves 'Liberation Troops.' It was not until the 20th of December, 1961, that the cadres called the people to a big meeting and officially proclaimed that their organization was the NLF." The name "Front," or "Liberation Front," predominated in the everyday discourse of the popular movement, whereas "National Liberation Front" refers to the structures the party helped to install in 1961 and after. Leaders hoping for a patriotic mobilization of all Vietnamese against foreign intervention preferred a name that emphasized the "national" aspect, in contrast to a movement that took an unqualified "liberation" as its watchword. It was a threat and a promise.[16]

Instigators had issued a challenge, but without reinforcement their provocations would have amounted to no more than a gesture. "The population was then very scared," declared an informant from Tan Hoi. "As soon as darkness fell, they locked their doors carefully and stayed inside very fearful at the least noise." He then reported that on the way home from an evening visit with a friend, "I stumbled into Tam Ban's group then operating on the road. He was shouting through a megaphone." The transcript hints that the informant was already friends with Tam Ban (he had "often come across him in the village") and suggests that the meeting occurred because he wished to "follow the revolution."[17]

This young man hoped to retrace the footsteps of the previous generation, whose exploits remained vivid in popular culture. "I had heard, long before, of rumors saying that the Viet Minh were almost supernatural people," he reported. "Stories were then circulating that they could cross the river without having to resort to a sampan and cook their meals without using fire." He confessed, "Deep down in myself I already was very impressed by them. That's why I followed the guerrillas and joined Tam Ban very earnestly." But the story he told illustrates that the Resistance legacy was not alone responsible for this commitment and that there were additional reasons why, as he put it, "I also wanted to change my way of living." When his mother left his father, he was put in a grandmother's care. "I had to suffer a lot from the rumors still circulating about my mother's behavior," he declared, "and I felt very bitter about my family situation during my younger years." As a teenager he had to work as a buffalo boy. "That's why I didn't know how to read and write when I joined the Front in 1960. My boss paid me only 80 piasters a year with two meals every day. He was a tough man and he bawled me out very often." Circumstances did not improve later on. "I always had to work for others because we were landless.

My life was very hard and even now I always feel bitter when I think back on it."[18]

Given this state of mind, he continued, "I was then longing for a change and I even completely agreed with the Front when it claimed it would try to raise the peasants' living standards and to reduce the gap between the living conditions in the city and those in the countryside. I also thought that the Front people were quite right when they advocated that the man-exploiting-man system should be eradicated in the future society." Hatred of the regime reinforced this affiliation. When local militants called for revolution, "this was exactly what the people were longing for because Diem had made their blood boil for a long time with the forced labor that had been imposed on every one of them." Early in the uprising, at the age of twenty-seven, he joined the movement.[19]

Other early recruits told similar stories. Shaped by an everyday experience of poverty, family breakdown, and trouble with the authorities, they were determined to make a better life for themselves. The interviewee from Tan Hoi did not follow the example of neighbors who "locked their doors carefully and stayed inside," and he almost certainly did not stumble, as if by accident, upon a group of men on the road "shouting through a megaphone." He and others who joined forces with the instigators were all "longing for a change."

EMERGENCE OF THE POPULAR MOVEMENT

The popular movement came together in "study sessions." As an informant from Xuan Son put it, "every night, the noisy sounds of drums and tocsin scared the people very much. But after having studied about the Front, the people then felt secure." Rand personnel called the meetings "indoctrination" rather than "study" sessions, but "indoctrination," which conjures up an image of apparatchiks drilling a captive audience, cannot do justice to assemblies charged with a revelatory fervor. Front watchwords were suited to and forged by the villagers themselves, including the communists among them. An informant from Ban Long recalled that in the early days, convocations were "crowded and enthusiastic." Another, from Long Tien, stated that "during previous years, the hamlet cadres needed only to invite the people through a loud speaker. People gather for a meeting in minutes." A respondent from Hoi Cu noted, "All they had to do was to invite the villagers two hours in advance, and 3,000 to 4,000 persons came for the meeting." In Binh Duc, villagers were skeptical at first and "kept quiet," but then they "became more eager to participate in the discussion of the situation," which "showed clearly that they had agreed to side with the Front."[20]

The give-and-take character of "study" is evident in remarks from the Long Hung informant, who remembered that "the people enjoyed very much the meetings held by the NLF, during which the Front cadres revealed to the audience the Front's platform and its anti-government position. They also corroborated the Front's viewpoint, contending they could no longer endure the Ngo Dinh Diem regime's oppression. They wished that the Front would soon succeed, so they might enjoy freedom soon." The movement took hold because peasants were primed to "corroborate" what they heard from instigators, and because they too had a lot to say. According to a report from Vinh Kim, people "were so fond of attending the village meetings that, sometimes, they were regretful that some meetings ended so soon. During these sessions, they lingered around the meeting places, discussing the Front's policies, the cadres' behavior, and the cruelty of Diem's regime until late at night." An informant from My Duc Tay reported that "the atmosphere in the village was extremely festive and exciting." Entertainment troupes added to the celebratory spirit, as in Hoi Cu, where meetings were "attended by people from many villages," with "plays and music shows staged by the village Entertainment Troupe."[21]

The Front message elicited a near-universal response in the countryside. One observer noted that the movement "incessantly held many study sessions," with cadres "telling the people about the very things they wanted to hear, namely about the national liberation, the general election leading to reunification and peace. Frankly speaking, at that time, we sincerely believed that the Front would surely win. Most people shared my opinion: people of middle and poor farming classes positively carried out their duties and joined study sessions day and night." The same was true of "those rich farmers who had volunteered to remain in the village," the informant added, indicating that revolutionary appeals had an impact even in the most unlikely quarters. Once again, this testimony indicates that Front watchwords were effective because they corresponded to what villagers "wanted to hear."[22]

Subject to peer pressure and little mindful of repercussions, young people were quick to join the uprising. A teenager affirmed that his father was repeatedly embroiled with landlords and usurers in Hiep Duc and ended up in the Resistance. "My life wasn't very easy when I was young," he recalled. "I didn't have enough of anything." In 1961, when he was sixteen, a hamlet cadre recruited him and several others, all from families associated with the Viet Minh. Most of the people in Hiep Duc "had relatives in the Resistance. But the former resistance members had become weak and old, so their children and grandchildren had to carry out the revolution and follow in the footsteps of their ancestors." An informant from Hoi Cu declared: "I was young—the devil-may-care type—and wanted to join the Front to have fun and adventure. . . . Seeing that all my friends in the village had joined and knowing about their gay collective life, I was very enthusiastic and agreed to join the Liberation Youth." Residents from Viet Minh families "were the ones who supported the Front most wholeheartedly when it emerged," he added; "next came the female and male youths in the village who loved new and strange things, and then the Poor Farmers." An eighteen year old from Thanh Hung stated: "I was then a youth and was very excited by the atmosphere the Front had created in the village. The villagers knocked on drums and wooden fish every night, and explosions of firecrackers, which I took for rifle shooting from afar, all these sounds excited my young mind longing for adventures and changes."[23]

Youth cohorts exerted a powerful influence on stragglers. "The majority of the youths were dragged along by the collectivity," reported a woman from Long Hung. "Each time there was a mission," noted an informant from Vinh Kim, "all the youths in my hamlet went along with the VC units. Those who hid in their shelters were pulled out and forced to go along." As part of what might be called a "kidnap narrative" (a device the Americans came to understand was recommended by the NLF to those who might fall into the hands of the enemy), Rand informants sometimes indicated that the Viet Cong forcibly confiscated and destroyed their GVN identity cards. But this measure, at a moment when many in the party hierarchy were still urging cadres to protect "the legal status of the masses," was also an episode within the current of the youth movement, especially among young men. "I was compelled to be in the Front because in 1960 the village guerrillas tore up my ID card, and I couldn't go out to the GVN areas," asserted an informant from Tan Binh, "but after a while I didn't mind it at all."[24]

Within the movement, noisemaking was the weapon of choice. A respondent from Vinh Kim explained that at first, many villagers "were so scared of the GVN they closed themselves in their rooms to knock on the wooden fish." But gradually the tactic spread. Its purpose "was to create a fighting atmosphere among the villagers and to make everyone feel that the people were determined to resist the GVN and very united in their actions." In Hoi Cu demonstrators beating drums and wooden fish "snaked around the hamlets," while fearful government troops and officials huddled "near the highway." Another respondent, from Phu Nhuan Dong, explained: "My confidence stemmed from the fact that every night sounds coming from the knocking on everything that could produce a sound, arose from the dark countryside all around my hamlet. This created a diabolical concert which gave all of us a frightening thrill. It made me think the whole population had decided to stand behind the Front and that the huge manpower would give the Front the necessary punch to overcome anything." The "diabolical concert" served as the anthem of the concerted uprising.[25]

GVN military outposts were the preferred targets of the rebels, who employed tactics more akin to the festive unruliness of youthful crowds than to a military maneuver. "Since a lot of youths took part in this type of activity, the atmosphere became very gay and the youths felt fearless," noted a guerrilla from Vinh Kim. "We made such a deafening noise that the soldiers in the post didn't dare to come out to shoot at us." In a number of such cases the assault took on a siege-like character. In Binh Trung, in August 1962, "the ARVN troops were intimidated by the crowd's propaganda in the daytime, and at night they were frightened by the tumultuous noises of shouting and the beating of tocsins and drums by the peasants and youths. In addition, they were aggravated by the constant firing of the self-defense members. That condition kept dragging on for about five months until the post defenders could no longer endure the strain. They abandoned their post in January 1963." In Hau My "the GVN posts had been encircled for years. In the daytime, all their supply routes were obstructed, and they were harassed by the guerrillas all night. The station defenders were unable to go out to buy anything. They were constantly tense and fearful." Finally, according to a midwife working in the area, "the villagers poured in on the agroville with machetes and sticks." Government Self-Defense Corps (SDC) militia and Civil Guards "were overwhelmed by the people and couldn't suppress the rebellion, and had to withdraw. After they withdrew the people poured in the agroville and destroyed many buildings there. I was then working at the [NLF] district headquarters which weren't far away, and I could hear the clamor of drums and wooden fish. . . . The noise the people made was deafening."[26]

In Thanh Phu (CL) villagers surrounded a GVN post for two consecutive months. "They shouted and made a lot of noises day and night to demoralize the soldiers in the post. Once every one or two hours the guerrillas shot into the post and exploded extremely big firecrackers. The soldiers in the post didn't dare to open fire because the crowd of people was too large." In My Hanh Dong, "as the Front had gotten the villagers to surround [the post] for four successive months, it had been impossible for the militiamen to leave the post." It was evacuated in March 1961. In Xuan Son soldiers "were besieged like a bird in a cage," and by the end of 1960 they "could no longer endure the siege of the guerrillas and evacuated the post." Hamlet by hamlet, a liberated zone was taking shape.[27]

A thought experiment based on this evidence demonstrates that the concerted uprising was as much a peasant revolt as a Communist Party project. Early in 1959 party leaders from the Central Committee all the way down to province level in the Mekong Delta could not agree on a policy to follow in the South, with some advocating a resumption of armed struggle while others thought the opportune moment for action had not yet arrived. Deviating from the temporizing guidelines they issued, district- and village-level militants then called on the people to rise up. When these instigators summoned residents to meetings, many hesitated to respond, and if none at all had shown up, or if the few who were willing to attend had been unimpressed by what they heard, the movement would have stalled, and party elements in favor of postponing the uprising would then have been vindicated. What had begun as a reckless provocation would have fizzled out, leaving a handful of agitators isolated and exposed to government retaliation.

But that is not what happened. A man from Long Hung was perhaps typical of the intrepid souls who were willing to come and hear what the instigators had to say. A sharecropper who was thirty years old in 1960, he had not been active during the Resistance and was not affiliated with the "extremist people" who first announced the emergence of a Liberation Front. But after determining that the ideas of the instigators "squared with the people's aspirations for social justice," he decided to back their campaign and to tell neighbors "to cooperate with the Front cadres in ringing tocsins." Here and elsewhere recommendations were offered, and villagers talked among themselves, with reference to their own conception of "social justice," before agreeing to join. Study sessions were part of a larger dialogue, and when the affirmations from one group "squared with" the sentiments of others, the response was swift and massive.[28]

If rural dwellers had not stood up, the rebellion would have been crushed. In Hau My "the Village Council arrested a lot of people and led them to the province capital." But the government was "unable to smash the movement" because it "couldn't seize the cadres who then led it," presumably because local militants were being sheltered by their friends and neighbors. In Binh Trung the GVN set night ambushes, with disappointing results, because "the NLF had recruited a number of residents in the village," who "informed the NLF cadres of the appearance of the ARVN troops." In Thanh Phu (CL) an ambush at the end of 1960 killed two guerrillas and captured three others. Casualties might have been higher if "a number of Poor Farmer families and the families of the regroupees" had not been "willing to hide the cadres if the soldiers came to check." Soon enough crowds of chanting demonstrators were surrounding and then expelling GVN garrisons, and reports transmitted up the party chain of command were undermining the cautious faction and emboldening those in favor of revolutionary struggle. An emerging popular movement had resolved the debate among high-ranking leaders.[29]

The concerted uprising exploded out of a confluence of circumstances. However tentative, decisions taken by the Communist Party in 1959 opened the door for those who wished to revolt, and the more emphatic pronouncements of 1960 added impetus to the movement. Lonely tribunes deserve recognition for standing up with megaphones in hand and summoning the people to overthrow the regime. The decisive moment came when their overture was reinforced by thousands of rural dwellers. The party had a role to play, as did brave instigators and early recruits. But peasants made the revolution.

THE GVN RESPONSE

In the beginning, rebels possessed two French rifles in Luong Hoa, two or three in Xuan Son, and seven in all of Cho Gao district. In Chau Thanh district, according to the Instigator, they had only "five rusty rifles." An informant from Hoi Cu noted that "when the Front first arose, it was very weak militarily speaking, but it had the people's strength behind it and it was able to expand rapidly." In Thanh Phu (CL) "the guerrillas were empty handed, yet they succeeded in destroying posts and forcing the village council and other GVN agencies to withdraw." The GVN was not steamrollered by a war-making machine.[30]

Victory was also achieved without benefit of the "organizational weapon," credited by Douglas Pike and others for the success of the NLF. In Nhi Binh, "from 1960 to 1962, Front organization in the hamlet was still weak." In Binh Thanh Dong "the Front set up its organizations in the village first in 1961, and it was only in 1962 that these organizations appeared in the hamlet." In Tan Ly Dong in July 1961 "no organizations were yet set up in the hamlets, although at that time there were enough hard-core elements in the hamlet level." The revolution was carried forward by a movement with a modest party infrastructure and no army, but with the participation of enough "hard-core elements" to get the job done.[31]

The government's tentative response, at a moment when it enjoyed an overwhelming military advantage, therefore requires attention. To be sure, some GVN personnel fought back, with looting, arrests, and torture in Hoi

Cu, a wave of arrests in Hau My, night ambushes in Binh Trung, and an attack in Thanh Phu (CL) that captured and killed several guerrillas. By contrast, all of the officials in My Tinh An "simply fled and lived in the nearby military posts." In Tan Phu Dong residents followed government instructions and sounded the alarm. But when soldiers did not arrive, the people "argued that the NLF activities were legal, and that the GVN did not dare to fight against them. Gradually, the people sided with the NLF." Soldiers also failed to respond to signals announcing the presence of rebels in Duong Diem and in My Hanh Dong, where "the village authorities' opposition to the daring activities of the Front proved to be very weak indeed." The GVN alarm system made no sense at a moment when the "diabolical concert" was more than sufficient to put the government on alert. The problem was that authorities did not seek out instigators who were daring them to retaliate, a failure that convinced villagers that the Front had assumed sovereign ("legal") power in the countryside.[32]

The authorities were afraid, but fear was not the main problem. Police and soldiers simply did not know what to do about a challenge that seemed to be more than a disturbance and less than a revolution. In Vinh Kim they "shouted at the people, threatened them, and asked them if they had seen any VC." Hamlet and village officials "did not have any reaction worth mentioning," recalled an informant from Hau My. "They worked in the hamlet in the day time and at night they came to the stations to sleep. When a section of road was dug out or power lines were cut off, they usually went to the hamlet, along with armed Self-Defense Corps soldiers or Civil Guardsmen, and directed the inhabitants to fill up the dug out sections of road, then they explained what had happened and advised the people not to follow the insurgents." One might imagine the reaction among peasants sleeping in their own beds when officials who fled at dusk returned the next day and "explained" to them what had happened in the village during the night.[33]

Even in a regimented society such as South Vietnam during the six years of peace, local officials had to deal every day with situations that might be interpreted as threats to public order. At a time when governmental misconduct could plausibly be blamed for more than one fatality, policemen must have wondered if the grief-stricken wailing of mourners in a funeral procession amounted to a protest against the regime. In wine shops they spotted idlers of mean estate whispering among themselves, as if hatching a plot. They heard mutterings and rumors and observed crudely scrawled graffiti on the walls without being able to determine the gravity of the antigovernment sentiments they seemed to express.[34]

At first the concerted uprising befuddled officials because the instigators were so few in number, their appearances were episodic rather than ongoing, and the uproar they caused could not easily be distinguished from low-level static already agitating the countryside. Even an assassination here and there might be construed as an isolated incident, for, after all, a few officials had been killed in previous years, while the overall situation remained stable. The disjointed character of local revolts, each advancing at its own pace, may have further confused observers, who could not readily identify the "concerted" character of the movement. Dual power, with its night-day coexistence of the rebels and the authorities, could be interpreted to mean that GVN representatives, who normally functioned only during "office hours," were still in control.

Ominous yet amorphous, the specter arising in the darkened countryside did not appear to have any organizational framework or military capacity. No one knew how to respond when villagers banged on pots and pans in the middle of the night. In An Thanh Thuy "the VC came to the village bringing along several effigies that had on red turbans and belts, and they planted them along the roads." Soldiers "opened fire fiercely." And yet the targets were mere dummies; no medals would be forthcoming for troops who had riddled them with bullets. Unsure how to respond, many officials must have hoped that the rural population would eventually calm down and that the problem would go away.[35]

The Saigon party line helped to undermine resistance. When held and tortured in a government reeducation camp, an informant was taught that under communism, "injustices were organized and institutionalized, and exploitation became policy, therefore man was no longer a human being, he became a machine or an animal whose sole aim was to produce to his maximum capacity." These teachings suggested that an enemy attack would occur when faraway leaders barked out a command and serried ranks responded in machinelike fashion, as would an invading army. The notion of communists as machines also circulated within the party, which cultivated an image of itself as an engine for making revolution. Groping to uncover the secrets of the enemy, authorities seized, as they often did, on a conceit embedded in party discourse, one that betrayed more than a little wishful thinking, and elaborated on it in dangerously misleading ways, so that peasant militants were seen as robots.[36]

When the revolution came, it took the form of a popular uprising that owed more to rural custom than to Mao or General Giap. Noisemaking had been heard in the countryside long before the cold war, and bands of young people surrounding government outposts were employing tactics closer to a charivari than to a conventional siege. How much easier it would have been to fight back if the challenge had been a communist plot. Uncertainty was dispelled as rebels moved to break the grip. When militants "entered the houses of these officials to arrest them," recalled an informant from Thanh Phu (CL), "only those with genuine rifles came in. Those with fake rifles stood outside to lend support. The people who were arrested and their families couldn't distinguish between the real and the fake rifles; they were frightened and told others that the Front was strong and armed with many different kinds of weapons." As a result, "it was the families of the people who were arrested themselves who unwittingly made propaganda for the Front and made it appear more powerful than it actually was." Those who were surprised and overwhelmed needed an excuse for their failure; thus "the Front was said to have a wide network everywhere, a great strength, very powerful forces." The uprising was still largely unarmed, and so here again, authorities were misreading the situation. Nonetheless, a realization of their peril now spread through the GVN milieu. But it was too late.[37]

A Leviathan had taken possession of the countryside, a revelation and a portent so uncanny, so "strange, exciting, and new," that speakers had to push against the limits of everyday language in order to describe it. "Joy" reigned in the countryside; the atmosphere was "extremely festive and exciting" in My Duc Tay; Cam Son was "the merriest village in the liberated area." "The revolutionary movement was rising so high" that a near delirium had taken hold. People were "wildly enthusiastic," "inflamed," "bowled over," "drunk with enthusiasm," "so extremely excited." A "solemn" atmosphere prevailed at meetings, with flags, banners, slogans, and other emblems of popular sovereignty "hung in the tops of trees." To officials, the Liberation Front seemed a monster with heavy tread, its approach signaled by a deafening clamor. The rebels were no less astounded, as the southern revolution touched off a violent chain reaction overwhelming everything in its path. It was a mighty force that the United States would strive over long and bloody years to crush.[38]

CHAPTER FOUR

CONTESTED UNITIES OF
THE GOLDEN PERIOD

Fresh from its triumphs in 1959–60, the movement entered a "golden period." According to an informant from Thanh Phu (CL), "revolutionary fervor increased every day, and the Front was winning everywhere." Contributions from the population obviated the need for a formal tax system, and volunteers competed for selection to newly formed military units. "Students left school to ask to be Liberation soldiers," recalled a cadre from Thoi Son. "We didn't push the enlisting movement, but even so, many people volunteered to be soldiers." As part of the *rassemblement* brought about by the concerted uprising, "people who lived in the GVN zone, when they reached the age of military service, would run away with the Front." In Nhi Binh, "since there were too many volunteers and there were not enough places to house them and weapons to be issued to them, a number of those youths were not accepted."[1]

Warfare could not dampen the celebratory mood. "Shellings and encounters were rare" in Binh Duc, and casualties remained low in Xuan Son, where villagers turned out to "cheer the guerrillas when they came back from a shooting at the nearby outpost." In Binh Trung entertainment teams "flooded the village with songs and music." According to an informant from Ban Long, the liberated areas were "absolutely secure." In the midst of mass enthusiasm, the labor required to fight a people's war was readily mobilized. "During the two years of 1962 and 1963," noted a witness from Binh Duc, "it was easy to gather about 80 civilian laborers whenever we had some hard work to do." Villagers in Quon Long came to regard Front militants as "national heroes," and in Nhi Binh, "wherever the cadres went, the people invited them inside their houses in a solicitous manner and gave them food to eat out of real sympathy for and confidence in the Front."[2]

Combatants in the PLAF shared a different kind of experience, marked by battles lost as well as won, by homesickness, material deprivation, and physical danger. Yet even there one finds evidence of optimism and deep commitment. Interviewee no. 215 recalled that "the morale of the fighters in the company was very high because they were constantly indoctrinated by the cadres to bolster their morale and to make them willing and ready to sacrifice their lives. They seemed entranced with fighting and didn't pay any attention to the length of the war. They didn't worry as to when the war would end, and only thought of achieving victory." In elite sapper units there were always more volunteers than needed for high-risk assignments. Those who were chosen "had the honor of attending their own solemn commemorative ceremony, because they might get killed while on mission, before setting out to perform their task." When citing him further along, I call the informant in this case the Soldier. For him and his comrades who staged their own funerals on the eve of battle, pride in service and hope for victory seemed to override the fear of death.[3]

Voiced in an interview context controlled by people who were working for the defeat of the revolution, these nostalgic recollections of the golden period deserve to be taken seriously. At the same time, it is worth noting that they were offered retrospectively, in 1965–1967, by witnesses who were trapped in the nightmare of escalation and who may have been tempted to idealize the paradise they had lost. And indeed, closer examination of the transcripts indicates that while villages had been liberated, liberation writ large, as the militants imagined and longed for it, had not yet been achieved. Having broken free of government control, they came to grips with the far more complicated task of sustaining their revolution.

The prospect was dimmed first of all by memories of violence and premonitions of future strife. Villagers could not forget occasions when landlords and officials had aggressed against them, and more than a few still burned with a desire for revenge. The movement had also claimed its share of victims, and rural dwellers continued to fear assassins who had acted in its name and who continued to hold positions of authority within the Front. Many hoped that an ideal world waiting to be built would heal old wounds and that the inclusive public space created by the movement would encourage debate and open imaginations to new possibilities. But as people discussed what to do next, potentially incompatible claims began to emerge, once again signaling that revolutionary solidarities might not hold.

TAKING LIVES

From the beginning, while they strove to inspire peasants with visions of a bright future, rebels of the Liberation Front also threatened, humiliated, and launched murderous assaults on those whom they saw as enemies. To justify these actions, Front cadres pointed to the cruelty of the government and argued that the people had a right to defend themselves and to punish wrongs committed by soldiers and officials. In this vein the Instigator described a helicopter assault in 1962 that clamed many victims and ended with ARVN soldiers cutting out the gallbladders of the dead and wounded. "Human liver has always been considered to have some kind of curative effects for a given disease and therefore can be sold with great profit to the Chinese in Cho Lon," he explained. Some of the dead were so riddled with bullets that they could not be identified. "Out of despair," their relatives "writhed on the ground lamenting, crying and cursing like mad. Even the onlookers seemed not able to stand the extremity of their pain and joined the frenzied mob in violently cursing Ngo Dinh Diem and his family."[4]

Accounts of atrocities help to explain why the popular movement resorted to violence, but they do not resolve the moral issues posed by its aggressions. According to the Instigator, the "illegal force," which he helped to organize, compiled lists of targets, and on July 20, 1960, four of its members assassinated a number of enemies. The aim was "to destroy every GVN organization in the village by arresting or killing every GVN follower." He further affirmed that the Front "had completed investigations on all these men" and that "the village officials' fate depended on the villagers' denunciations. If the majority of them thought A had been cruel towards them, A would be killed. Those who had not been cruel received better treatment." But it seems obvious that roving assassins, arriving at night in villages inhabited by people they did not know, must have misidentified more than one victim. Lists of suspects could not have been completely reliable, given that the underground unit of eighteen militants, operating in a district containing thirty villages and tens of thousands of inhabitants, was obliged to rely on local informants of varying probity.[5]

In such circumstances some were tempted to define crimes against the people in broad terms. Village notables were singled out, perhaps because of specific acts against the revolution, but also out of class hatred, as in Kim Son, where the targets were "well off farmers" who "used to be great pals of the village officials, because they had money." Others were killed because of sexual transgressions, such as the chief of a military post who "went alone into the hamlet to flirt with the girls" or "those who had adulterous relations with regroupees' wives." In Thanh Phu (CL) a moneylender beat up a debtor, and when the victim later became a "VC leader," he ordered the execution of his assailant. A Rand interviewee characterized this as a murder committed "out of personal hatred," but no doubt the perpetrator told himself and others that he was punishing a tyrannical usurer.[6]

In the context of the overture, it was often not possible for villagers to make sense of the bloodshed. Individuals were summoned from their homes in the middle of the night and assassinated, and their corpses were left in the fields. In some instances people simply disappeared and were not seen again, as in Binh Thanh Dong, where a man was "led away at night and he never came back. Rumor had it that he had been killed by the Front." One morning in Phu Nhuan Dong the body of a fisherman was found in a sampan. The victim "was reported to have been killed while he was fishing at night," and neighbors thought, but could not be sure, that insurgents were responsible for his execution. People were often left to wonder if a murder had been a nonpolitical act of vengeance committed either by one of the rebels or by a simple citizen. In cases when government authorities responded aggressively to the rebellion, they too claimed lives, and no doubt in the chaotic first phase of the uprising, homicides by cadres were intermixed with those perpetrated by GVN forces and with aggressions by unattached individuals seizing on the occasion to settle private scores.[7]

According to an informant from Duong Diem, "everyone was afraid that the Front would suspect them, because they didn't know what constituted a crime in the eyes of the Front and what didn't." He added that the villagers "were all afraid, but they didn't know exactly of whom or of what." An observer from Binh Ninh recalled, "We were afraid they might come to behead us one day just to settle certain personal grudges, which we were not aware of." In the densely woven fabric of rural society, a significant number had worked for the government, as interfamily heads, hamlet chiefs, or village council members, or had been militiamen or ARVN soldiers. "I also got anxious about my own fate," explained an informant from Thanh Phu (CT), "because I had enlisted in the French expeditionary corps before." Relatives or acquaintances of government personnel also had reason for concern. In Cam Son, a revolutionary bastion, "everyone in the village had somewhat collaborated with the GVN or had been in touch with GVN officials, so they were afraid."[8]

In Hoi Cu militants tried to gain control over the political fallout associated with clandestine homicides by "informing" the people after "GVN officials and supporters" had been executed. "The Front did this to spread terror and to show off its strength to the people to frighten them and to win their respect." Elsewhere, nighttime executioners pinned indictments on the chests of victims, as in Ban Long, My Phuoc, and Tam Hiep. After the enemy grip had been broken, the four-man assassination team was demobilized, and "people's courts" were assigned the task of sentencing miscreants and witnessing their punishment. In Cam Son cadres brought officials before crowds of villagers "with their arms tied together. They denounced their crimes and forced them to bow down to the ground and beg the people's forgiveness. They only killed a GVN official who had extorted money from the villagers when the GVN had ordered the building of agrovilles or strategic hamlets." As a result, "their prestige grew."[9]

A number of Rand informants testified that people's-court verdicts were prearranged by cadres, with the aid of backbone elements in the crowd who could be counted on to raise their voices at the appropriate moment, either for or against the defendant. Still, mass meetings did convey a sense that assassinations were based on recognizable definitions of what was criminal and that there was a dossier purporting to establish the culpability of the victim. Front personnel did not always play by the rules, but the transcripts suggest that a notion of NLF "constitutionalism" took hold, according to which the accused had the right to hear and respond to the case against them, with the verdict coming from the people, and with the proceedings cleared by higher echelons.

Complaints about abuses indirectly call attention to such principles. When a cadre in Dong Hoa Hiep ordered two nocturnal assassinations, an associate declared: "I never heard him try to explain these killings to the villagers. I felt that he had taken this liberty of killing the people without consulting the higher-ups." In response to homicides in Duong Diem an informant reported: "I heard the people say that these were arbitrary, that victims were arrested or killed out of personal hatred, because if they had really been guilty, the Front should have brought them to a people's court to let the people decide, as the Front had declared on many occasions." In My Thanh, after two individuals were executed, "the people said among themselves that: 'The Front didn't act very fairly,' because it had gone ahead and killed the men and then read the accusation later; thus the men didn't have a chance to defend themselves."[10]

Many informants testified to the innocence of individuals who were executed, but in a surprising number of cases they declared that at least some of the killings were just. "The more the people in the countryside were trampled on, exploited and oppressed, the more the Front profited from it to expand the movement," asserted a rallier from Thanh Phu (CL). "When the Front emerged, it played the role of the exterminator of the tyrants and corrupted officials, and so it terrorized and killed the GVN officials who had a record of despicable and horrible acts toward the people." A witness from Hoi Cu whose father had been shot by the Viet Minh and whose uncle had been shot by the Front claimed that "what the VC wanted was to make everyone pay credit to their power" and that "they didn't care about what was right or wrong." But then he turned around and asserted: "The villagers' opinion vis-à-vis those who were arrested by the VC was not unfavorable to the VC. If there were innocents among them, there were also many of them deserving such treatment."[11]

Villagers condoned the execution of officials more readily than of security agents, whose covert activity was, by its nature, hard to document. "Most of the people thought that it was all right for the Front to kill those who were working for the GVN," declared an informant from Ban Long, "but that it was wrong for them to kill those they merely suspected of working for the GVN." Villagers hated "very strongly" the police chief in Hau My, and when a mine claimed his life, "the news of his death pleased every one of them." Self-Defense Corps men in Trung An were "very wicked," and whenever the villagers heard that one had been killed, they said: "So much the better! That's one less to worry about!" In Cam Son the Front executed a corrupt and extortionate official, "the most wicked man in the village," and villagers "were quite pleased to see the Front capture and kill the Civil Guards." A cadre "witnessed some of the villagers throwing stones at the Front's prisoners. Some wanted to beat them, but I had orders to protect them." In Long Hung, according to an observer, local militants arrested but did not kill GVN personnel. As a result, "the people felt that the Front was working for them against dictatorship and oppression" but also persisted in thinking that "the village officials rather deserved the death penalty."[12]

Most of the defendants were GVN officeholders or people thought to be spies or secret agents. Those found guilty were shot or stabbed, or, in the majority of cases, beheaded. A few informants attested to a large number of executions during the concerted uprising: twenty each in Hau My and My Hanh Dong, thirty in Hoi Cu, around a hundred in Long Hoa. These high numbers are not seconded, and are sometimes contradicted, by other witnesses from the same villages. Other informants put forward single-digit estimates, most commonly one or two victims, and in a number of instances they said that no one was killed, though it was usually added that rumors of killings elsewhere frightened the people.[13]

With respect to moral issues posed by revolutionary violence, the "body count" is not the crux of the matter. The reality was that everyone had witnessed an execution or knew of someone who was executed or had heard of such cases in adjoining hamlets. The rural population was well aware that insurgents were prepared to kill anyone who stood in their way. This understanding most certainly weighed in the balance when individuals hesitated between support for the Front or neutrality, and it must have loomed large in the minds of those who in other circumstances might have been tempted to speak out against the movement.

Even if one were to assume that all villagers thought all its executions were justified, the measure of revolutionary violence would not be complete. Arrogating to itself the right to take the lives of others, the Front assumed a moral burden that no citation of exculpating circumstances could lift. Militants convened people's courts in order to secure the complicity of the villagers, but the transcripts make clear that some of the individuals who cheered the news that hated enemies had been punished reacted with less ferocity when summoned to witness executions. Onlookers in Hoi Cu "got nightmares at night." When two youths were sentenced in Binh Thanh Dong, the local Front leader "coldly seized a machete and cut off their heads," even as they begged for mercy. "It was a chilling spectacle," recalled an observer. In Thanh Phu (CL), a man accused of spying for the GVN was hauled up before a crowd of villagers, where he "shouted and insulted the cadres." After four or five thrusts with a machete did not kill him, "he struggled free and then ran all over the hamlet, he was covered with blood from head to toes. The guerrillas ran after him and stabbed him many times before he fell on the ground." One of the cadres "ran to his body, cut off the head and threw it in the hole that had been dug." Although the guilt of the victim may not have been in question (instead of mounting a defense, he "shouted and insulted the cadres"), "the people were frightened, and some of them became unconscious."[14]

These accounts indicate that there was a gulf between the bulk of the village population and the individuals who stepped forward to serve as executioners. Among the most unforgettable Rand informants was a village guerrilla from An Thai Trung. He first killed a man caught alerting the GVN that PLAF troops were in the village. When the death sentence was announced, the assassin "jumped up to" the accused "and stabbed him in the neck." The mother of the victim "fainted at the sight," while the man's five-year-old son pleaded, "Don't kill him! Don't kill my father!" A second victim had shown the GVN where three mines were planted; he was beheaded "with a large machete (ma tau)." A third unfortunate, the hamlet chief, sentenced in 1965, was strangled and then buried immediately afterward by the executioner himself (and not by the dead man's surviving kin). "The first time when I killed," he admitted, "I was a little bit scared, a little bit shaken," but "for the next two times, I was not scared any more. Now I have become used to it. I love to fight and I love to kill. If I were given a platoon I would completely destroy all Front bases at An Thai Dong and then would be willing to stay right there." Two weeks after the interview he stole a weapon and escaped from the Chieu Hoi Center. Rand staffers thought he might have returned to the NLF, but it seems equally possible that a person of such sanguinary temperament ended up in the criminal underworld.[15]

The Instigator offered sketches of four other executioners, all members of an assassination team that formed part of the district "illegal force." One, who had dispatched over fifty victims, was no longer connected to the Front "because he is hated by the people." Another was serving as the executive officer in the district local force, a third was in charge of providing security for a province base area, and the fourth had been appointed a platoon leader in the 514th Battalion. Wherever they went, men of this sort frightened others, as in Hau My, where residents did not forget the case of a neighbor who was punished in 1961. According to a witness, "the killers are still present in the village, and every villager knows who they are." The chief of the village security section may have been one of the executioners. "He is very cruel and therefore he is much hated," affirmed another informant. "Some months ago, he executed four villagers charged with spying on the Front's activities." Along the same lines, the deputy secretary in My Phong was feared "because so far he has killed about six men."[16]

Rand materials indicate that many cadres were liked and respected and that they shrank from violence. In Thanh Phu (CL) no one volunteered to serve as executioner, and the party chapter was left to assign the job to one of its members. "I witnessed an execution once," recalled a cadre, "and it was so frightening that I almost lost consciousness. The man who was given the task of killing the victim was shaking with fear. He closed his eyes and hit at random. He had to hit the victim up to ten times with his machete before the latter died." In Phu Qui an informant testified that the execution of his uncle was ordered by a cadre who then "made believe that he was not in favor of it by pretending to criticize the murderers and by wading into the creek to pull my uncle's corpse out of it." The implication was that the cadre was "highly politically minded (chinh tri cao)" and that he acted in bad faith. But it seems equally plausible that this militant was not alone in trying to soften the impact of revolutionary terror, and that others who took responsibility for acts of violence did so with reluctance.[17]

Still, even the most gentle souls among the activists were part of a movement that had claimed for itself a license to kill and shared a collective discipline with executioners, whose actions they condoned. In the transcripts, hints of personal qualms among cadres are balanced by references to executions that sound like vendettas. The Thanh Phu (CL) witness who said that no one volunteered to serve as executioner also declared: "After killing these people, the cadres left a condemnation note on their bodies. The cadres absolutely forbade the neighbors to help these families conduct funeral services. The families of the victims were left to themselves and had to bury the dead themselves. No one helped them or went to the funeral." In My Phuoc Tay cadres "did not allow the deceased's relatives to have the corpse. They buried the deceased and kept her grave a secret to her kinsmen. They even leveled the grave at the ground."[18]

As for the general village population, they lived in a harsh world of landlordism and dictatorship and would not have joined a movement that did not dare to smite their enemies. But they could hardly have been unmoved by scenes of anguish and death. The transcripts make clear that executions spread grief and rage among peasants with some connection to the victims, such as the man whose two brothers were assassinated and who "cried profusely and ever since he cursed the Front whenever he got drunk," or the son who wept when describing how his mother had been killed. "I wish I could exterminate them and I will fight against them as long as I live," he vowed. "I will come back to Cai Lay to cooperate with the local authorities to kill them." For others with no direct connection to the dead, the killings left terrifying memories.[19]

Frantz Fanon argues that popular violence "is a cleansing force," one that frees the perpetrator "from his inferiority complex and from his despair and inaction; it makes him fearless and restores his self-respect." Other commentators reproach fainthearted scholars who are too squeamish to acknowledge the festive ambiance prevailing among crowds that kill. According to Regina Janes, "removing the promenade removes the celebration and denies the perpetrators of violence their pleasure." These declarations afford no purchase on the Rand materials, which do not mention carnival-like rejoicing over the downfall of enemies. When blood was shed, people fainted or fled from the scene. Others, though distraught, remained convinced that executions were just and necessary. For them, militancy combined with guilt over brutalities that could not be separated from the objectives they sought to achieve. Perhaps some onlookers gained a measure of satisfaction from "reduction-of-prestige" sessions, in which people who had brought them suffering were forced to grovel and beg forgiveness. But no Rand informant claims that revenge killings were cathartic or that raining down curses on now helpless former officials brought peace of mind to the accusers. It may have been different for the assassins, who discovered that they "liked to kill." The fear and revulsion these men inspired indicates that their sentiments were not typical.[20]

At the same time, violence in My Tho was unmistakably a peasant violence. Villagers remembered when landlords ruled and peasants lived in conditions of "virtual slavery." Asked by an American researcher if tenants ever requested favors, a local notable was "prompted to rise and leave the room; he then reentered mimicking a tenant approaching his landlord—kowtowing with his chin almost to the floor, a servile smile on his face, and a chicken or duck as a gift in his arms." Reduction-of-prestige rituals were ugly affairs, but it is not surprising that crowds appropriated for themselves an authority previously employed by others at their expense and forced adversaries "to kneel down before the demonstrators, bow to them many times, and promise never to repeat such offences in the future." Beheading was also an inversion, as the movement commandeered a power belonging to the state and embodied in the guillotine, which had been utilized by the French and by the Diem regime after them. Even when peasants were horrified by bloody scenes, executions won "respect" and "prestige" for the Front, which by such means took for itself an attribute of sovereignty.[21]

One might assume that the Communist Party was the architect of revolutionary violence. But in 1959–60 higher echelons in the party did not want southern militants to unleash a red terror against the GVN and, indeed, did not want a revolution in the South. To rein in the use of force at the grass roots, steps were taken to ensure that "only the provincial-level Party could authorize executions." But in practice, "at least two-thirds and possibly four-fifths of the executions were never sanctioned, as local village organizations meted out their own justice." For better or worse, killings in My Tho were the work of village populations and the local militants who served as their leaders.[22]

SEQUELS TO VIOLENCE

The bloodshed of the concerted uprising was followed by a relatively tranquil phase, during which the movement adhered to the principle of "heavy education, light punishment (*nang giao duc nhe trung tri*)." Coercion seemed unnecessary at a time when just about everyone was finding a reason to participate. According to an informant from Xuan Son, poor and very poor peasants "joined the Front in great numbers," and middle peasants were also favorably disposed, while rich peasants were "fence sitters," and landlords who opted to remain in the village "had no choice but to resign themselves to the situation." Even "gamblers and criminals followed the Front in order to atone for their past crimes." Degrees of commitment varied from the most fervent to those who went along because they "had no choice." But still, movement unity must be counted as a significant achievement.[23]

While some government officials were executed or fled or resigned and tried to blend into the population, a surprising number went over to the revolution. To be sure, several were never more than marginal supporters of the Front, such as the GVN sentry in Thanh Phu (CT) who was apprehended by the rebels in 1961 and feared for his life. The transcript does not reveal how he managed to win release or what he did over the next several years. He was drafted by the PLAF in May 1965, bargained his way into a position as a village guerrilla, then rallied in 1967.[24]

Other villagers associated with the government went on to participate more emphatically in the movement. "I was then working as the Civil Records Registrar of the Village Council," an informant declared when asked about the concerted uprising, "and I was very scared too. I didn't dare to continue to sleep at home and took refuge in the Village Police headquarters." He was caught, blindfolded for six days, then freed, but placed under house arrest and subjected to reduction-of-prestige. "I felt very ashamed when, from the villagers' ranks, some people came out to curse me. My emotional life was then very hard. I felt wretched. None of the villagers were willing to talk to me except a few of my closest relatives. My wife had to undergo bitter criticism from the villagers for my past service to the GVN." This ordeal hardly sounds like a model of clemency, yet the informant's further testimony indicates that his impression of the Front was rather favorable. Though himself a target of NLF sanctions, he granted that villagers "hated very strongly" one prominent victim of VC terror, and his later employment as a teacher in the liberated zone, the Front's investment in him (a three-month training course for medics), and six months as a health care cadre suggest that he was trusted by the militants. It is not clear why he rallied.[25]

Several unlikely recruits ended up in the Communist Party. "The villagers were very afraid," said a rich peasant who had been in the GVN Combat Youth and who was placed under house arrest during the concerted uprising. By August 1962 he had gained admission to the party and eventually rose to district level within the Front. Another informant was conscripted by the GVN in 1957 and then worked for the hamlet Republican Youth. "Because of these activities of mine," he recalled, "I was then very scared of the Front." He ran away, then decided to return home. "I was placed under arrest once, and the village cadres asked me to write down all my past activities. I had to tell them that I had been forced by the villagers to work in the Republican Youth group because they elected me to be the clerk in this group, and that I had just worked for two months. I argued that I hadn't done anything against them either. After they listened to me, they freed me and, from then on, they left me alone." He was put to work first as a teacher and later in the Propaganda, Culture, and Indoctrination Section, then rose to district level and joined the party in 1964.[26]

At least sixteen Rand informants whose relatives had been executed by the Viet Minh or the Front ended up in the movement. One such individual came from a Protestant rich peasant family. His mother died in 1942, when he was seven days old, and his father was executed by the Viet Minh in 1946. Still, he asserted, the Front "clearly fought for independence and national reunification. At that time I was very enthusiastic. I liked risky adventures and had a deep hatred for injustice. So when the cadres explained to me, I volunteered to go and fight against the enemy." He joined a village guerrilla squad in 1961, was promoted to a "special mission branch" in 1962, and attended a four-month recon-sapper course in 1963, where he was one of the seventy trainees to complete the program. (The other thirty were sent home because they were "not courageous enough.") It makes sense that a wealthy Christian whose father was assassinated by revolutionaries would eventually defect, as he did in 1967 (for reasons not explored in the interview). More surprising is that a man with that sort of background had joined the movement and performed conscientiously enough to be recruited into an elite sapper unit.[27]

The family of another informant had reason to hate the revolution, and he himself claimed to have been conscripted by force into the PLAF. But a later response makes clear that others blamed him for choosing to enlist: "Well, do what you like," his father admonished, "but don't forget that your grandfather and your uncle were killed by the Viet Minh." A man from Xuan Son rose to a village-level position in the Labor Youth, even though his grandmother had been executed during the Resistance. Another, who worked hard to get into the party (he was finally admitted in 1964), claimed that his brother had been buried alive by the Viet Minh. When asked how he could become a communist after that sort of atrocity, he responded, "I liked to sing very much, so I rather enjoyed being with the [Viet Minh Culture and Arts] Group."[28]

A twenty-four-year-old informant told a no less jarring story. He claimed to have been a GVN hamlet chief in 1960 and a secret agent in 1961, when his reports led to the capture of three Front cadres. After being released from jail, one of the three blew his cover. He was arrested by the guerrillas, then was released and promptly resumed spying for the government. After a tour in the Saigon militia, he was induced to change sides once again and to enlist in the PLAF regional force. His father, suspected of being a GVN agent (a charge the informant denied), was executed by the Front in 1964. The final unexpected twist in this bizarre story is that he eventually became a party member and deputy platoon leader in the 261st Battalion.[29]

Some informants who affirm the innocence of persecuted relatives hint that there might have been grounds for the suspicions they aroused. The uncle of one was accused of spying and was executed by the rebels. "I know that my uncle didn't do anything like that," insisted the informant; "he only hung around the security agents to drink with them." Other explanations are puzzlingly lame. A Rand staffer asked a man whose association with the movement went back to 1961: "If your father was killed by the VC, why did you join the Front? Didn't you resent the VC?" The subject responded: "I lived in a Front-controlled area, and I was forced to join it. The VC threatened that if I moved to the GVN area, I'd be thrown into jail and beaten up. So I had to join the Front, although I really didn't want to." This insistence on the coercive power of village unanimity is plausible, but the informant's response to the Rand query, which revolves around a non sequitur (moving to the GVN area was not the issue), is incongruous and troubling. He seems unaware that Rand staffers knew the Front in 1961 was not forcing villagers into its ranks.[30]

The tangled feelings of individuals caught up in the revolution also emerge in the account of a man whose brother, a policeman, was executed in 1960. "My family, of course, hated the VC very much," he declared. "Since we were afraid that the VC might kill me too, we had to submissively obey the cadres." In order to avoid conscription into a PLAF main force unit, he agreed to become a village guerrilla in 1964. After two months his mother got sick, and cadres allowed him to transfer to the hamlet militia. He was, in short, a "Viet Cong" only by the most generous definition of the term. At the same time, his testimony is complex. "At the outset," he observed, "the cadres who often got in touch with the villagers were highly esteemed and respected." As the war heated up and Front labor, tax, and recruitment demands grew heavier, "the friendly atmosphere that existed in the first days between cadres and villagers began waning," but even then the worst he could say was that "the villagers' attitude toward the cadres became completely indifferent." It seems, then, that for a time this informant found a way to reconcile himself to the movement, in spite of his brother's violent end.[31]

Some villagers whose family members had been slain must have chosen activism in order to distance themselves from the taint of counterrevolution attached to the victims, while others may have reasoned that assassins had acted on their own and not on behalf of the Front, whose cause could therefore be embraced with a clear conscience. Every villager of a certain age had lived through a chaotic period during which mortal enemies took turns in power, so that survivors were likely to have acted in ways that would have seemed like a betrayal to one side or the other. Trying to make sense of a troubled history, people may have concluded that their loved ones had made wrong choices and then, tragically, been forced to pay for them.

But whatever the rationale, the conclusion seems unavoidable that hatred of the perpetrators who had persecuted individuals and their families sometimes gave way to a grudging respect and then to a sense of shared purpose. These troubling stories challenge outside observers to think hard about the uncanny ambiance and transformative power of the southern revolution and, indeed, of any revolution. In the beginning, the movement seized on people's imaginations so urgently that memories of heinous acts temporarily receded. Many seem to have hoped that guarantees of a new world would be honored and that a way would be found to provide restitution to victims and atonement for their assassins. It remained to be seen if these promises could be kept.[32]

UTOPIAS OF THE POPULAR MOVEMENT

Rand transcripts indicate that in My Tho revolutionary more than patriotic motives drove the movement. When asked to identify the most appealing Front promise, an interviewee replied, "I was a very poor farmer, so what I liked most was the land distribution." Another very poor villager was told that "the Front aimed to reunify the country and to chase out the Americans who were trying to take over Vietnam. After the victory, the poor peasant would own land to till and would never again be oppressed." Choosing among these aims, he said, "The thing I liked the most was the Front's promise to give me land." A third very poor peasant agreed. "I was then longing for a change," he asserted, "and I even completely agreed with the Front when it claimed it would try to raise the peasants' living standards and to reduce the gap between the living conditions in the city and those in the countryside."[33]

Many villagers classified by the Front as "poor" expressed similar sentiments. "What I liked best about the political indoctrination (hoc tap)," stated one man, "was the hate campaign against the landlords and class struggle because I wanted to struggle for the rights and privileges for my class, and I wanted to be the master of the countryside (nong thon)." Another confessed, "I, myself, hate the landowners, bullies and wicked persons. As a matter of fact, I hate my own landowner." A third declared, "During the six years of peace I had seen for myself that the rich did oppress the poor. Therefore, I joined the Front to help the poor class to which I belonged." In 1961, recalled a witness from Xuan Son, the Front "promised that it would seize the lands from landlords and reactionaries and distribute them to the poor people. That's why two thirds of the people in the village looked at the Front as their leader and enthusiastically supported it." Another villager "believed that the Front's policy was to fight in order to liberate the poor farmer class, and that of the GVN was to support the capitalists." Stating in extreme form a preference shared by many, he concluded by saying, "The least important aim, in my opinion, was reunification of the country."[34]

More comfortably situated villagers saw matters in the same light. A middle peasant thought that the Front was "fighting for democracy in order to get back the land from the landlords and the petty bourgeoisie so as to redistribute it to the poor who didn't have land to work on. That is the thing I liked the most about the Front's aims." A second peasant of middling rank expressed the wish that "we (I mean the working and poor farmers classes) would be masters of our own country and would be slaves to nobody." When asked, "Which aims of the Front as explained to you by the cadres appealed to you most?" an informant responded, "I liked the policy of land reform most of all." Classified as "petty bourgeois" by the NLF, this militant shared the revolutionary aspirations of his less well placed neighbors.[35]

Many activists believed that the movement was fighting a two-front war against internal and external enemies. "The Front had risen up to liberate our class and the country," stated one poor peasant, while another declared, "I liked the idea of chasing the Americans out and fighting against landlords the most." A sharecropper was told "that I was poor because my family had been exploited by landowners and therefore I had to fight both landowners and Americans who were in league with them." According to another villager, "the Front said that the feudal landlords (dia chu phong kien) and the Americans were the obstacles to national independence, therefore we should fight against them," while another cited cadres who affirmed that "the South was being taken over by the landlords, bourgeois, and American imperialists who were in collusion with one another. Therefore, the farmers had to unite to oppose the landlords, [for] only in this way would they be able to protect their ricefields and orchards." Here and elsewhere local notables were pictured as the primary target, as when the Front charged the Americans "with imperialist aims. In the people's eyes, the imperialists are regarded as the defenders of the native landlords' interests. Since most of the people hate landlords, they abhor the Americans."[36]

Militants sought dignity as well as economic security. In explaining his decision to affiliate with the Front in 1960, an informant stated:

> I left my family to fight and bring rights and material benefits to the people, to my family and also to myself. If we achieved success, my family and other families in my village would share in the prosperity and happiness. There wouldn't be any more differences between classes—there wouldn't be anyone too rich or anyone too poor—and all social injustices would be corrected. No one would have to work as servants for others—no one would be insulted and humiliated by their masters. That was my goal.

Another said that he joined the movement in search of "glory," defined as "the ability to make a revolution in order to liberate the people, and to prevent landlords and wealthy farmers from crushing me down. That's what I liked." Still another declared, "I felt much encouraged when the Front emerged because under the Front's control, poor farmers aren't despised by the rich as they were before." Another "liked most of all the distribution of wealth to the poor people. I saw that the poor people were the slaves of the rich, they had to work as servants and hired laborers for the rich. I loved the poor people and was convinced that the rich class was exploiting the poor class." Material benefits counted for all of these informants, and so did dreams of a world without insults and humiliations.[37]

Mindful of the concerns noted here, a cadre went on to predict:

> When national reunification is achieved, Communism will be established. Then we'll advance to universal communism. Your life will be very happy. There will be no rich and no poor. If someone in your family gets sick, he'll be taken care of by the doctors and you won't even have to pay for the medicine. You'll be paid for your work and you'll have enough to eat. After the harvest, everyone will put their paddy together in a common store. When you need paddy to eat, you'll just go to the store to get the grain. You won't have to live in the fear that you might starve one of these days.

In the same spirit a middle peasant declared: "Yes, I did think about the building of a new society where there was no exploitation between man and man, e.g. where I did not have to hire my labor to another person and he did not have to hire his to me, where there were no landlords, and the people were free to work and free to enjoy." In this avowal, the immediate issues raised by a class struggle analysis give way to a more lyrical register, as everyday language strains to keep up with the longing for a future in which people would be "free to work and free to enjoy."[38]

Going further, others spoke of the revolution as an epic struggle stretching back over the course of human history. According to one informant, "the Front said that the landlords from whom the poor people rented the ricefields were exploiting the people. The Front said that the ricefields were a natural gift and that they were not the products of anyone's making, and that the landlords had relied on the imperialists to acquire their vast land holdings." Claiming nature as an ally, a militant declared that "in the formation of the earth, land didn't belong to anyone. But since there have been people who were shrewder than others, knew how to exploit others, and to seize their land, the man-exploiting-man system was born under these circumstances. The Front, therefore, had to stand up and redistribute land to the poor." Another cadre asserted: "Land cannot be private property. Land is given to mankind by Nature and the Front is about to distribute it equally to everyone. There will no longer be rich and poor."[39]

The revolution also encouraged country people to expand their vision in another direction, from the village to the nation and then to all of humanity. A poor peasant from My Long pictured "a World Commune," a "paradise on earth" in which "nobody would oppress other people. No one would be poor and miserable and people would live in plenty." Another poor peasant voiced similar sentiments:

When I heard that socialism would grant rights and material benefits to everyone, and would bring material well-being to the people, I was bowled over and thought that socialism was a right doctrine. I found it very appealing because I wanted to see the world living under universal Communism. When universal Communism was achieved, there would no longer be any national boundaries, and all people in the world would live as brothers. I liked this very much. I was poor, and I liked the idea of bringing material well-being to all the people—all the poor liked this idea.

Although this witness cannot be assumed to speak for everyone, it is worth pausing over his estimation that "all the people" shared the same hope.[40]

The effort to specify means to achieve these lofty goals began with land reform, which many Rand informants saw as a goal and an ideal. "For a peasant, being able to participate in controlling the countryside is the highest aspiration," a villager declared; "all of them longed to have land to till." A female poor peasant declared, "I think land distribution is really a good deed, and thanks to it, the poor will get richer and nobody will have to steal and to rob for their living." It was widely thought that after the revolution "people would enjoy harmony and equality," and "there would be no rich and no poor people."[41]

At the same time, a troubling contradiction lurked in the recesses of this fervent egalitarianism. Given the ratio of arable land to population in My Tho, household parcels were bound to be small and to provide no more than a subsistence income, a worthy, even a revolutionary objective, but modest when measured against the soaring aspirations inspired by the concerted uprising. "At present, the NLF takes special care of the poor and very poor farmers," said an informant, with the aim of helping them "to become middle farmers who can earn enough to subsist on. However, they cannot become rich farmers since these people will in turn plunder the poor classes. Therefore, the NLF policy is to elevate the poor and very poor farmers to become middle farmers, and this will be the highest class of the society." At times striking a utopian chord (he hoped "equality can be maintained for ever"), the speaker also seems uninterested in and even alarmed by the prospect of abundance. Fear of poverty and the threat of exploitation ("plunder") come through vividly, leading to the insistence that "nobody can become rich." But that line of analysis also discouraged consideration of ways to attain "riches" more imaginatively conceived. A village without landlords, a republic of smallholders, was an ambitious but also a disconcertingly static program, one that seemed to imply a ceiling beyond which human desire would not be able to advance.[42]

Language sometimes reflected this tension. According to a cadre from Hoa Dinh, land transfers would provide the beneficiaries with "good food and good clothes (an sung mac suong)," a perfunctory Rand translation which might be interpreted to mean enough to eat and to wear, no more than the necessities of life. But the Vietnamese phrase an sung mac suong conjures up images of a cornucopia of food and splendid clothes, of the sort one might find at an extravagant Tet celebration or in a rich household. The speaker was anticipating and would not settle for anything less than a life of ease and plenty.[43]

In pursuit of that dream, some militants imagined a future away from the paddy fields, where survival depended on heavy labor, more suited to a beast of burden than to a human being. When people complained that "we work as hard as buffaloes," the water buffalo stood for unremitting toil, and, more generally, for any kind of mind-dulling labor. "I struggled to advance in the movement, and I wasn't struggling and making sacrifices to stay forever in the village," announced an activist from Thanh Phu (CL). When promotion to district level did not materialize, he quoted friends who used to say: "No matter how much a buffalo tries to wear down his horns, he will always remain a buffalo. No matter how zealous we are in our tasks, when we die there will only be a few joss sticks on our tombs, and the commemorative ceremony will last for a few minutes. What significance does all this have?"[44]

The same desires and frustrations were found among PLAF fighters. The Soldier came from a poor peasant family in My Duc Tay. He joined the Front at the age of sixteen "on July 20, 1960, that is to say, the day when the Front called on the people to arise and destroy GVN control," and served in a guerrilla unit for one year.

> I got a little bored because, for the whole year, we didn't do anything of any importance—we stood guard on the roads, or stood guard during meetings to maintain order, or we planted grenades and mines—so I volunteered to join the Front big units when the Front launched an intensive campaign to make the youths enlist in its forces. My ambition in enlisting in the big units was to get promoted and to progress in my work, because I thought that if I stayed in the guerrilla unit, I would work like a buffalo for the Front all my life without any hope in the future.

Other combatants shared this concern. When promotions were slow to come, the Platoon Leader blamed his poor education and the fact that "all the 'yes men' advanced faster than I did." His resentment was shared by other soldiers who worried that in spite of their efforts, they too would "always remain a buffalo."[45]

While control of the land appealed to many, it did not fully satisfy the wider ambitions animating the movement. Whereas some wanted a countryside filled with household plots because that innovation promised to give everyday life a more fixed and stable character, fixity was just what others did not want. "All men want to go around and get to know more and learn more things," affirmed a combatant. "I knew I might get killed if I kept fooling around with weapons. But each day I remained alive meant that my knowledge was furthered by what I saw on that day." Initially assigned roles as privates in the People's Liberation Armed Forces or as hamlet-level cadres in the NLF's civilian sector, many hoped for promotion to upper levels in the PLAF or to village, district, or province echelons in the Front's quasi-government. Their expressions of dissatisfaction with low-level postings indicate that the problem would not be solved simply by turning cultivators into cadres and soldiers. What was really at issue here was the hunger for education, for travel, for challenges and self-realizations that were no less keenly desired for being difficult to anticipate in any concrete way.[46]

At first the movement program seemed to incorporate the varied hopes of the rural population. When asked to spell out his desires for the future, one informant declared: "I had to endure danger and hardship and to sacrifice myself, in order to be able to have land, to live an advanced life, to get more learning, to have a house, to practice my occupation and to enjoy a special regime to be provided by the revolutionary government in the future." In this statement one observes a coexistence of concrete elements (a parcel of land, a house) and more abstract yearnings, for "learning" and an "advanced life." It was a synthesis that almost certainly was not going to remain intact. But during the golden period the utopianism of the popular movement succeeded in blending diverse and potentially clashing desires, and this richness was the source of its strength and mass appeal.[47]

A second unresolved issue had to do with the different agendas of the Communist Party and the popular movement. Party leaders saw fierce class consciousness among village militants as a problem rather than an asset, because they anticipated that rural notables seeking refuge in the GVN zone were bound to alarm the urban bourgeoisie with their accounts of revolutionary terror in the countryside. The party worried about the "political underdevelopment" of the peasantry and the "fragility of a spontaneous peasant movement" and argued that a "united front against Diem and U.S. domination" would lead toward the "national democratic revolution" that seemed most suited to the moment. They set up the National Liberation Front with the hope that it would allow for "greater control over the southern developments, lest events there greatly alter the Party's priorities." By keeping "social issues" off the table, a patriotic front would serve as "an antidote to the existing and potential radicalism of the southern Party and masses." Uneasy allies, the party and the southern revolution did not share the same "priorities."[48]

Villagers gained in confidence and imaginative reach through exposure to linguistic and conceptual systems they encountered in party colloquies, but local militants did not borrow indiscriminately from the ideas presented in training courses and study sessions. Internationalist watchwords struck a chord, but stage theory notions typical of vulgar Marxism, such as the idea that revolution would eventuate in a "national democratic" polity, are little heard in the transcripts. Informants who advanced to higher echelons in the party sometimes voiced enthusiasm for collective agriculture, but they understood that such plans did not have a wide appeal in the countryside. Indeed, the party anticipated and looked forward to the day when the peasantry would evolve into a modern proletariat.

There was an overlap between such views and the aspirations of villagers who did not want to spend their lives like buffaloes in the fields and who had earlier taken to the road and then joined the Front in search of new identities. But the fit was not exact. Drawing up blueprints for utopia amounts to a renunciation of utopian striving, because the exercise will invariably be shaped by mental habits formed in the imperfect world of the present and cannot help taking the form of new structures and disciplines, serving a notion of order as the architects understand it. In David Harvey's words, "utopias of spatial form are typically meant to stabilize and control the processes that must be mobilized to build them." Activists who were in love with movement showed little interest in diagramming a precise end point for the journeys they had undertaken, and they were not fighting for the right to work in a factory or a collective farm. They took as a starting point ideals of abundance, equality, and communal solidarity that grew out of everyday village life and that were then projected globally, in the form of a "world commune," an anticipation charged with feeling even though its contours could not be precisely defined. It was a utopianism suited to peasant revolutionaries of a modernist temper.[49]

CHAPTER FIVE

THE POPULAR MOVEMENT AND
THE GENERATIONAL DIVIDE

In 1964, at the age of twenty, interviewee no. 182 joined the Front. Her mother was shot during an ARVN sweep, her father died of typhoid fever, her fiancé was killed in combat, and two younger siblings "had to make their living by themselves" and had "moved elsewhere." After serving as a liaison agent, a first aid specialist, and a clerk typist, she rallied to the GVN in March 1967. But her affiliation with the Communist Party appears to have remained intact in the Chieu Hoi Center, where, she reported, there was a difference between those who "served in the Communist ranks," who "have a sense of judgment" and "think about their actions (biet suy nghi)," and the shirkers and imposters who were "rude" and "can't be trusted."[1]

The interviewer was not entirely satisfied with the session and concluded by saying: "The subject was a pretty young girl, who looked like she did not know much about anything. She turned out to be rather intelligent and knowledgeable about the Front." The problem was that "she was very cooperative at first when the interview was focused on life in her village, but the moment the interviewer started asking questions about the District Party Committee and the Front's plans and policies, she became very uncooperative." It helped that "her favorite topic was marriage, and knowing this, whenever she became too uncooperative, the interviewer switched to that question to mellow her and usually succeeded in doing so." It seemed that "she was a great fan of the VC" and that "it is hard to understand why she left the Front. The reasons she gave for her rally did not sound very convincing."[2]

The Rand investigator was too hasty in assuming that "life in the village" was a tangent. Interviewee no. 182 had been an enthusiastic participant in the cultural revolution sweeping the countryside during the golden period and had a lot to say about that campaign, a central component if one wishes to understand "Viet Cong motivation and morale." I think of her as a Rebel with many causes. While the interviewer impatiently waited for discussion to turn back to other, presumably more important topics, she brilliantly analyzed the protocols and rhythms of cultural change. Her account began with village rituals. "After worshipping their ancestors," she noted, peasants used to bring offerings of their "best food" to the houses of "the landowners and the rich so that the latter would feel better disposed toward them and help them when necessary. They also used to bow to the sky whenever something happened to them." She went on to assert:

> The bourgeois and the rich used to say that the poor were those that were not blessed by heaven. But when the Front came, the cadres told the people that this was not so, and that the people were poor because they didn't have land to till and that the well-off farmers were rich because they had land to till. The cadres said their economic conditions weren't due to heaven's blessings or the lack of it. The people understood that heaven had nothing to do with their life and they stopped going to the pagoda and shrine to pray for a betterment of their conditions. They knew that if they worked hard and if they had land, they would become better off.

Here landlordism and the propitiation of supernatural forces are both indicted as symptoms of backwardness and obstacles to liberation.[3]

Household relations were also hierarchically structured. Before the revolution, parents "had absolute authority over their children. If they wanted to marry their children to anyone they could go ahead and do it, and they wouldn't even have to ask their children to see if they would want to marry that man or that girl." But after the concerted uprising, arranged marriages and other oppressive customs came under attack, and when children, "from the oldest to the youngest," acted defiantly, "the parents could only criticize them and they couldn't insult them or beat them up."[4]

While the Rebel was proud of changes brought about by her peers, she also called attention to the complexity of issues raised in debates over the politics of family life:

> There was no conflict, because everyone realized that they were living in a new society and that they had to change their attitude. The parents understood that they had to give their children more freedom, and the children understood in which respect they could do as they pleased and in which respect they had to respect and listen to their parents. Some of the parents were irritated by the fact that their children listened to them less, others were resigned to it because there was nothing they could do to change things.

The tone in this commentary is both blunt and nuanced. Elders had to realize that "there was nothing they could do to change things," while children were enjoined to recognize that new freedoms went along with figuring out when "they had to respect and listen to their parents."[5]

The Front was not going to launch a "great proletarian cultural revolution" like the one mounted by "Red Guards" in China. Activists in My Tho pushed for reform of village folkways, but they also remained grounded in the local milieu and did not stop listening to neighbors who persisted in seeing value in received practices. Inviting, and indeed insisting on, the participation of the entire population, the movement created a public space with room for zealots and skeptics, for ringing affirmations and stubborn refusals, for compromises and changes of mind. When custom was questioned, when people lost their temper and insults flew, communities of uncommon verve and plasticity did not fall apart. From such exchanges emerged the hope that injustices rooted in the past could be isolated and destroyed without losing the contribution of ancestors who had managed to create legacies worth retaining.

Among the many issues opened up by cultural revolutionaries in My Tho, this chapter focuses on the generational divide. The struggle involved more than a simple dispute between young and old. One camp took up the defense of tradition, as defined and championed by village elders, in opposition to youthful activists who criticized what they called "feudal" custom. Then there were the "cowboys," another grouping of young people, whose desires had taken shape in the emerging consumer culture of the six years of peace and who often quarreled both with their movement peers and with the older generation. Finally, men and women who had served with the Viet Minh remained on the scene and embodied a distinctive notion of what it meant to be an elder. As these groups collided and overlapped, quarrels over how to move forward simmered without resolution. At the same time, all of the disputants lived in the same communities and could not avoid everyday encounters. Debates were sometimes hurtful, but they also held out the prospect that creative outcomes, not yet envisioned by the participants, might eventually emerge.

ELDERS AS A SOCIAL GROUP

In early 1967 Rand staffers began to ask informants to identify the most "respected" people in their villages, and, as a result, the transcripts include descriptions of sixty-two highly regarded individuals, drawn from forty-eight villages. Two of these persons whose religious affiliations were mentioned were Caodaists, five were Buddhists (including one female, the only woman in the set), and one was a Catholic priest. One was identified as a "farmer," five were described as poor, four as middle peasants, and five as "rich" or in terms that indicated relative affluence. Two NLF cadres and several Resistance veterans gained a mention, and sixteen of the respected persons were identified as former government officials.

This section of the interview provided an opening for informants to send a message about the overall quality of GVN personnel. Thus a former official in Tam Hiep was singled out in the following terms: "He was honest and had integrity. He wasn't greedy and didn't extort bribes from the people when he was on the Council. He didn't threaten the people and wasn't arrogant toward them," qualities that, given his station, came as a surprise and therefore merited special recognition. In the same vein, an official in Long An was praised because "in spite of his position he was just and fair." As for the former policeman in Vinh Kim who was "well educated and wise," he turned out to be a Viet Minh plant.[6]

Respect was not the same as the deference accorded to individuals at the top of the political and economic hierarchy. Two informants from Nhi Binh declared that the village secretary was the most "powerful" person in the village, then went on to single out other residents as the most "respected." A rallier from Quon Long stated, "Besides position and authority that inspire nothing but fear among the people, the villagers sincerely respect and love virtuous people and intellectuals (from Chinese and French studies)." One informant from Thanh Hoa said that virtue, education, and age were more respected than wealth and power, while another distinguished "virtuous and learned people," who were "esteemed and respected by the peasants," from those whose "power and riches" qualified them as "important" persons.[7]

Most of all, "respect" was associated with very advanced age. Forty-year-olds in My Tho were considered "old," while the term "elder" was reserved for people over sixty. Thirty-four of the sixty-two respected people were identified as elders, and a number of others would probably have qualified if their ages had been given. The prestige that went with old age was often buttressed by Confucian credentials; fourteen respected persons were described as Confucians or experts in Chinese studies. Several owned libraries, like the man from Thanh Hoa who "had many old books on the teachings of Confucius and Mencius arranged in piles on the altar in his house."[8]

While some elders were learned, others were not. When asked who was the most highly regarded man in My Hanh Trung, an informant named a seventy-five-year-old man whose stature had nothing to do with his "level of education." He was trusted "because he was sincere, and because he is always true to his word and never fools anyone." Elders in Nhi Binh argued that "although they are illiterate and not indoctrinated by the Revolution they have so far managed to safeguard the village and hamlets thanks to their conservatism, and their determination to follow all the teachings of long-venerated wise people of the country and abroad." These "teachings" were based on values purported to be of great antiquity. They could be found in texts, but people who had resided in the village for many years were also well positioned to understand and explain them to others. "Old age, as they reason, can only be bestowed by God. Not everybody can live until he becomes very old."[9]

Respected people fulfilled a variety of functions. Informants praised individuals who helped their neighbors (assistance to the poor was especially noted) and offered sound advice, including the choice of auspicious days for launching a business deal or building a house. Many were skilled in resolving disputes, as in the case of the man who "reconciled the discontented husbands with their wives." A Confucian scholar and a Catholic priest were experts in "Oriental medicine," and another Confucian was identified as an "herbal doctor." Two respected villagers were matchmakers, two were dinh (communal house) administrators, and three were active in the upkeep of pagodas and other religious places.[10]

Thirty-two respected individuals were singled out because of the role they played in organizing and presiding over festive occasions such as weddings and funerals, a function that put them on a fault line within village culture, one that was dominated by village notables. "Rich families had big celebrations, and poor families had simple ones," remarked a rallier. "The villagers competed with each other to give lavish banquets," another explained; "the more lavish the banquet, the more face gained." With their abbreviated guest lists and meager fare, gatherings arranged by families of limited means were often humbling experiences for the participants. Celebrating was no less problematic when one was the guest and was expected to bring gifts for the host. According to an informant, "such practices would embarrass those who are poor and who have no money to give and would discourage them from attending those events." Even a modest offering, such as a packet of tea, might be beyond the means of some. In another of its aspects, festive life imposed servile obligations. "On feast days, religious holidays and Tet," noted a rallier from Hoa Dinh, "tenant farmers had to bring rice and ducks to the house of the landlord. Then they had to clean the house and the altar for the landlord and spread mats out for them. Only after they had taken care of everything at the houses of the landlords, did they go home to take care of their own household chores." Rich people "only thought of themselves and didn't do anything to help the poor," this observer concluded.[11]

Another informant recalled that before the revolution all the officials, who themselves were "old people," organized festivals with the aim of reinforcing the authority of village power holders and encouraging traditional values within the peasantry. To legitimize such occasions, they sought guidance from elders, who "were asked how to hold ceremonies in the Communal Temple according to the proper customs." Elderly villagers who allowed themselves to be co-opted by local notables would be thrown on the defensive when the victorious revolution demanded changes in local folkways.[12]

A GROWING GENERATIONAL DIVIDE

Old people were unnerved by assaults on tradition and testified that youthful cadres were "tough and rude," "conceited, haughty and arrogant." Militants answered in kind. "The young people, especially the cadres, accuse the old of selfishness, narrow[ness], and lack of enthusiasm in carrying out missions assigned to them." Worse, "the young, especially the young cadres," said that "the old useless people who take refuge behind the shield of 'traditional ethics'" were only trying "to safeguard the ways of life of wicked landlords." Partisans of cultural revolution "look down on the old persons and regard them as antiques, as backward, feudalists, and so on."[13]

The concerted uprising emboldened youthful activists and obliged elders to measure their words. Breaking from past practice, revolutionaries told one another that "the youths were the pillars of society" and were best qualified to assume positions of leadership in the countryside. So it was not surprising that "the old and the young generation are always engaged in a tense but not openly expressed conflict," as one informant put it. "As the leaders of the village are all youngsters, the old people dare not do anything against them." An entire practice of civility seemed to be giving way. "Most youths still respect elderly people," one witness noted. But still, in conversations with elders "they gesticulate when they speak and sometimes they curse, too. Of course, the old people cannot tolerate such irrespectful behavior, but they do not voice their dissatisfaction because they realize that the youths are now endowed with power."[14]

Family dynamics were also affected. "Between old and young," an informant asserted, "or, in other words, between old-timers and those of the new line, there now is a serious gap which is not, however, openly expressed. The old feel that their authority in the family as well as in the society has diminished excessively. At home their children refuse to obey them without a lot of arguments. In the society, every important function is in the hands of young people (the cadres) who not only disregard the old people's ideas but also force the latter to accept theirs." Another witness noted that "parents and uncles still have influence over the children, however it is no longer absolute as before, because the children are now subjected to the influence and leadership of the Front." Activist youth were "taking quite a fancy to new high sounding words such as new democracy and social reform" and were "always thinking of reforming everybody around them, members of their families as well as their neighbors. What their parents and other elders in the family say is, in their opinion, just outmoded and no longer fits in the revolutionary pattern." Sizing up the "new society" from the perspective of the older generation, an eighty-six-year-old woman declared that a number of elders had "lost their bearing" as power shifted into "the hands of the younger generation, but they don't dare to oppose the latter, except by becoming uncooperative in a mild and secret manner."[15]

Custom in festivals as well as in the household came under assault. According to the Rebel, the goal of the movement was a society in which people "no longer had to live in constant fear of the rich, they no longer had to kowtow to them, and they no longer had to offer the rich the choicest food they had on the anniversaries of the deaths of their ancestors. They now were able to treat the rich like their equals and they could maintain their prestige vis-à-vis the rich." When youthful militants married, she further explained, parents and elders lost control over the proceedings, and instead all the wedding guests voted to determine which representative from the Front would preside. In the same spirit, everyone present was encouraged to participate, and so "the families of the bride and bridegroom express their opinion, followed by the guests who also express their opinion." The bride and groom bowed to the altar of the homeland and not, as was the custom, to parents and elders, and pains were taken to assure that "both parties have been free to agree to the marriage" and had not been forced to accept an unwanted mate. In short, the new ceremony was "more egalitarian and fairer" than the old.[16]

In an effort to remake festive ritual, cadres focused on winning over the young. But "if after all their efforts to indoctrinate and persuade their parents failed, then the future bride and bridegroom had to do as their parents wished. The cadres still came to the wedding ceremony, but they didn't have any role to play in it." Resistance proved most stubborn among "the old people, in the 60–70 age group," who "did not like the new customs and refused to marry their children in that manner," while "younger parents, from 40 to

50 years old," were more ready to compromise. Negotiations between brides and grooms on one side and parents on the other often resulted in a mix of new and old arrangements, with parents who gave way on other points most likely to "insist on the bride and the bridegroom bowing to them, to the grandparents and in front of the ancestors' altar." The overall trend was in favor of the movement, and, as a result, among recent weddings, "only one or two brides and bridegrooms still wore traditional *ao dai* and bowed to the elders." The Rebel's assessment may have been overly optimistic. But the least that can be said is that "old customs" no longer went unquestioned in the village.[17]

LIMITS OF A GENERATIONAL COUP D'ÉTAT

While the Rand transcripts sometimes make it seem as if the concerted uprising brought about a generational coup d'état, one also senses among informants an uncertainty about how to portray a situation in which the old deference no longer prevailed and no one was sure what new relations ought to look like. Among complicating factors one might note the interplay between the cadre ideal and the moral code that assigned primacy to the elders. Village militants made much of their loyalty to the poor and put themselves forward as resolvers of disputes, just as did the elders. Both factions also prized learning, but of different sorts. Whereas elders looked to the Confucian masters, a more modern kind of political understanding commanded attention within the movement. Villagers tried to mediate by drawing a line between public and private life. In Long Trung "they respected old age, but as far as policy was concerned they followed the Village Secretary and his Deputy." In Phu An, "on political matters, people listened to the Village Committee. On family matters, they listened to old people." But this compromise was undermined by the insistence among cultural revolutionaries that "family matters" were also political.[18]

In one respect the Front's emphasis on the primacy of the young worked to the advantage to the older generation. Both cadres and elders swore allegiance to virtue, but it was a fealty that cadres had to balance against the requirements and temptations that went with the authority they exercised. At a time when principles were constantly being eroded by judgments of expediency, a disinterested perspective took on a heightened importance. Thinking along those lines, villagers seem to have concluded that it was in their interest to have access to respected persons both in and outside the movement. Indeed, the widespread persistence in treating "respect" as a category distinct from the revolutionary ethos demonstrates the need to treat social practice in its own right, often overlapping with, but remaining independent of, what was going on in the political sphere.

A second complicating factor emerged from the interplay between youthful cadres and their "cowboy" peers. Front policy involved a balancing act, one that depended on the youth while also condemning the lifestyle that many associated with the younger generation. One informant "heard the cadres say that the Americans were the aggressors who used their decadent culture to demoralize Vietnamese young men and women and who organized cowboys (delinquents) to corrupt and destroy the Vietnamese society." New recruits were warned that they should not imitate a "luxurious depraved and delinquent way of life" of foreign origin. In 1965, when PLAF recruiters were desperate for conscripts, exemptions were granted to ten youth in Nhi Binh who drank, "led an idle life," and "did not show any respect to aged persons," and who, if mobilized, "would only derange their organizations." Two years later another witness made a similar point in claiming that unaffiliated youth were not drafted because they "were debauched and undisciplined, and they couldn't stand the rigid discipline of the Labor Youth."[19]

At the same time, the Front could not insulate itself from youth culture. In principle, militants accepted a regimen that demanded austerity while continuing to chafe at its application. They liked "to drink and joke whenever they can afford to do so," one informant noted. They were "paying great attention to the style and the quality of their clothes, spending all the money they received from their relatives to buy felt hats, wrist watches, and fountain pens. No one any longer heeds the Party's prohibition on using 'American' goods." Their motto was "Let's have a ball, but get the job done (Choi boi xe nat, cong tac lam tron)." Choi boi xe nat is stronger than "Let's have a ball"; it might be translated "When there's a chance to party, let's tear it up." A similar emphasis is found in the balancing phrase, cong tac lam tron, which means, loosely, "Do the job right" rather than just "Get the job done." Cadres remained embedded in the "common thinking" of their age cohort as well as of their class, and the tastes and manners they shared with peers outside the movement grated on the older generation. But their determination to "do the job right," which was couched in moral terms of unmistakable authenticity, was equally real and could not be summarily dismissed.[20]

These factors help explain why relations between youthful activists and their elderly neighbors played out with shadings from one community to the next in response to local circumstances and personalities. According to an observer from Vinh Kim, people in the liberated zone had to be circumspect about approaching the most respected person in the village, because cadres wanted them to "ignore" local traditions. But, he added, they nonetheless sought out the man, apparently without interference from the Front, since he knew how "to hold the ceremonies with much dignity and little expense." In Thanh Hoa "even the NLF cadres did not dare to show an insolent attitude or bad manners" toward the village elder, who, in the eyes of the informant, led "an exemplary life." [21]

A different nuance emerges in My Tinh An, where "cadres highly respected the old people because they had a lot of experience. Nevertheless, cadres never sought the opinions of the old men regarding the policies of the Front. They simply came to visit them or have a cup of tea with them." Such visits themselves could be problematic. In Hoa Dinh "the people complained a lot about the attitude, behavior, and language of the young cadres." They declared: "These young cadres are of the same age as our children and grandchildren. But when they come to our houses, they are very rude. The moment they come into our houses, they put their bags on the table right in the middle of the house, then they pour themselves tea, fold their legs on the chairs and start teaching us about life. They don't even wait for us to invite them to sit down or give them tea. They even drink their tea before we do." The atmosphere was also constrained in My Long, where activists did not think one of the village elders was "an important person," even though he had served in the Viet Minh. The best that could be said was that "courtesy greetings are exchanged whenever they meet him." [22]

According to an informant from Hoi Cu, "there were still five or seven notables left in the village," one of whom "had been active during the Resistance." The old notables "were like parents, uncles or aunts to us, so the young people all respected them," which explained why "the Party Chapter saw them often to discuss things and to win their sympathy." "Tea invitations" provided occasion to ask the "old notables" to help mobilize support for Front tax and draft policies. In this case, where "respect" prevailed, the emphasis was instrumental, with cadres telling elders what was expected of them. The tone was again cordial in Long Hung, but with a different twist:

> The most venerated people in the village were old intellectuals, who were helping the broad masses to respect the old traditions and customs. They reflected the image of virtuous scholars of the ancient time and, as such, were considered good examples for the villagers to follow. They also were genuine patriots who did not work for the foreigners during the French domination. They were usually consulted by the villagers on such important occasions as funerals or marriages. The reason for this practice was

that all these old people, disciples of Confucius, were very well versed in ritual ceremonies, as well as in the selection of lucky days for the celebrations of these important events.

In Long Hung, as in Hoi Cu, elders were "venerated," but they were also cast as "genuine patriots" and therefore "good examples for the villagers to follow," and even as useful sources on "old traditions and customs."[23]

The competition between young and old in My Tho was often wounding, but the transcripts convey a sense that tempers cooled somewhat in village lanes and over cups of tea. Cadres held the levers of power, but perhaps they sensed that there was authority on the other side and also that old age, far more surely than landlordism or superstition, was part of the human condition. For their part, even the most disgruntled elder could not overlook the courage and idealism of the iconoclasts, which compared favorably with the delinquent frivolity of the cowboys. The Ethnographer summed up the generational conflict by saying that the young and the old "often hurt each other because their ideas were different on important matters." Bruised feelings were inevitable, but so were the connections that occasioned them.[24]

One informant suggested that young and old "did not clash seriously," then added that they "seemed to live apart from each other and the youths no longer looked up to the old people with much respect." The result was that "it was almost impossible for them to cooperate." Approaching the problem in a more concrete register, an informant from Xuan Son reported: "The youths in the village liked to talk politics when they attended banquets or when they sat around drinking tea or when they conversed with each other about their daily work. They talked about the world situation, socialism, Russia and China. The old people didn't like to listen to this sort of thing because they thought the youths didn't even know what went on in the village let alone the world, Russia and China." This commentary invites readers to picture a festive occasion, with young people talking about "the world situation, socialism, Russia and China," while old people at an adjoining table muttered their disapproval. There is a separation here, but as the first informant put it, the two groups only "seemed" to live apart. On the contrary, they resided in the same hamlets and attended the same banquets, and each listened in on what the other had to say. As long as participants shared a discursive space, the proper balance between young and old and between the world and the village, in short, the outcomes of the cultural revolution, remained open for discussion.[25]

THE VIET MINH VETERANS

A fifty-four-year-old veteran of the Resistance had the impression that "the old political cadres were moderate. During indoctrination sessions, they assessed and analyzed the situation to see whether war or peace would be most advantageous to the Front. They found that no matter how long the Front continued fighting, it wouldn't gain anything, and so they were for peace." By contrast, "the young cadres, who joined the Front much later, thought that Russia and China were as well armed or even better armed than the United States and the GVN, so they were for war. They believed that Russia and China would help the Front and the North to defeat the GVN." The informant added: "I think that if the war goes on, the entire human race will be drawn into the struggle, and there won't be any chance for the human race to survive if atomic bombs are used. This is why I want peace." His account suggests a tension between the idealistic internationalism of the young and the caution of the elders, who were skeptical about war as a political instrument and about the support that could be expected from China and the Soviet Union.[26]

This vignette indicates that both sides in the debate had something to contribute and something to learn and sounds a warning against the tendency to think of elders as exemplars of a tradition abstracted from historical reality. A closer look at "the old political cadres" allows for a fuller analysis of the generational divide. It centers on the twenty-eight Viet Minh veterans in the Rand sample. They may have come from slightly more prosperous families and have received more formal education than other informants (the differences were not pronounced), but their stories indicate that life in the movement had impoverished most of these militants. One of the wealthiest among them, classified as a "bourgeois," found himself in 1956, after a decade of activism and just before a three-year period of incarceration in Saigon jails, reduced to giving guitar lessons, which did no more than provide "enough to keep us going."[27]

The veterans were not "frogs at the bottom of a well." At least seventeen of the twenty-eight had spent a significant amount of time outside their villages. Six had regrouped to the North in 1954 (and offered a complicated picture of life in the DRV). Included among them was the Platoon Leader, who, as we have seen, had also been to Phnom Penh. Another veteran had lived in Saigon and sojourned in France for two years, nine others had also resided in the capital city, and one had managed a tailor's shop in Cai Be district town. Hardened revolutionaries, they had paid a price for their political activism. Twenty-four of the twenty-eight were party members, compared to

43 percent of the total sample, and twelve had been imprisoned by the GVN in the 1950s and early 1960s, four of them more than once. Six of the twelve with jail records were captured again after 1965, as were seven others; those thirteen constituted a significant minority among the forty-two prisoners interviewed by Rand.

Face-to-face with Chieu Hoi and other Saigon personnel and with Rand interviewers, the Viet Minh veterans responded variously. One who had helped the government apprehend several of his ex-comrades exclaimed, "I couldn't care less," when asked about the morality of his switching sides. A Rand staffer characterized him and the Platoon Leader as "mercenaries" who defected because they thought "the GVN could provide them with greater rewards and benefits." A reasonable surmise, this view is also uncharitable in the way it passes over the difficulty of choices posed during the war, especially for high-ranking cadres, who would not be allowed, as were more humble defectors, to escape into the anonymity of the GVN zone. Apostasy was in many instances the only route to survival.[28]

Several among the veterans appeared weary after long years of struggle. An informant born in 1925 and active in the Viet Minh from the time of the 1945 August Revolution quit the movement in 1958 and never affiliated with the NLF. He suffered during the dark days of the late 1950s and defected when the government tortured his father as a way of forcing him to surrender. This trauma sapped his will for further struggle, and a similar exhaustion is apparent in the accounts of others who had managed to remain active. "I'm old and about to die," said a fifty-four-year-old who was captured in 1966 and who suffered from chest pains caused by the collapse of his shelter during an artillery bombardment. Even the interview seemed to tax a fifty-one-year-old informant, who protested, "My words are now running out and I have nothing else to say any more."[29]

Some of the stories told by veterans convey a sense of unhappiness and disarray. "I was an old resistance fighter," one informant began. After becoming active in 1945, he served as a village cadre with the Viet Minh, then lived in his native village of Long Binh Dien during the six years of peace. In 1960, according to his account, he quarreled with his wife over money matters. "My son, siding with his mother, reported to the authorities that my friends had persuaded me to join the Viet Cong and that because my family was opposed to my joining them, I had raged around the house and had beaten my wife." Demoralized, he "went home and swallowed two packets of rat poison." After recovering, he moved to Thanh Binh, his wife's village, and joined the Farmers' Association. Urged on by his wife and son, he resigned in

April 1965 and rallied soon after, perhaps in a final effort to keep his family from disintegrating.[30]

Born in 1926 and raised in an indigent family, another veteran also comes across as a troubled individual. In 1953 he decided to join a French commando unit, but then was arrested by the Viet Minh and taken to the Plain of Reeds "to do production work." After the Geneva Accords, he went north with the other regroupees, then returned to My Tho in 1963 and was assigned to a province demolition company. He left his unit in 1966, then sometime later decided to rally. In the thirteen years between 1953 and 1966 he did not earn a single promotion. Quarrelsome and possibly alcoholic ("We drank till we couldn't see straight"), he was ill-suited to life in the PLAF. Among his many complaints against the Front, perhaps the most vehement centered on its failure to hold regular *kiem thao* sessions for review and self-criticism. If people "couldn't find out what their weak points were in order to develop them," there would be no mechanism to make "their good points known" and to have "their bad points corrected." Only in this way, he concluded, could they "advance in the movement." Insightful in analyzing the mechanisms that were supposed to promote self-development, he criticized the Front for its failure to impose a discipline he was unable to summon on his own.[31]

By contrast, several captured veterans were among the most intransigent of the prisoners interviewed by Rand. Born in 1936 and soon orphaned, one informant reported that he had served at the end of the Resistance, regrouped to the North, then returned south in 1965 as an officer in an artillery unit. Sick with malaria, he was captured in October 1966. "If I am released," he announced, "and if the Americans still invade the South, I will do my duty as a young man to protect my country." Another veteran also refused to recant. Born in 1923, he joined the Communist Party in 1950 and worked for the Viet Minh as a clerk, then was arrested during the six years of peace and, after his release and further service as a village cadre, was captured again in 1967. "The NLF only has two ways, death or life, and it will fight to the end," he proclaimed. "In the time to come when I am released, if the Party recruited me again, I will be more aggressive."[32]

The overall contribution to the Front of militants who had previously affiliated with the Viet Minh is difficult to gauge, but the evidence suggests that they formed a modest but significant presence within the movement. Given their references to jail terms, poor health, deteriorating family situations, political controversies, and general fatigue, perhaps one should be surprised that as many as 28 out of 285 Rand informants reported a link with the

Resistance. Most built respectable and sometimes distinguished careers in the Front. Two rose to the NLF's regional echelon, one worked at province level, four made it to the district, eleven served in villages, and two ended up as hamlet cadres, one of whom held the important position of chair of the Civil Affairs Section. Seven Viet Minh veterans took up positions in the PLAF, including two platoon leaders, two deputy company commanders, and a lieutenant in an artillery platoon. One veteran observed: "There are still old cadres operating. They are those who have been operating without interruption from the Resistance through the years of peace until now. They are the elites and they assume positions of leadership. But their number is small."[33]

In spite of personal sacrifices and long years of service and the evident qualities of the individuals interviewed by Rand, the veterans seem to have played only a limited role in the concerted uprising. One may have been an instigator in 1959–60; another served as a backbone element in a "printing and publishing" cell in Doc Binh Kieu village, Kien Phong province; and a third joined in 1960 and was quickly assigned to a district-level position in 1961. Six regroupees were in the DRV, four veterans languished in GVN prisons, and a fifth, just out of jail, declined to get involved until after the GVN grip had been broken. Several others were in their villages but said nothing to Rand about participating in the revolt. Two were living in Saigon, and another had defected in 1958. Most seem to have rejoined the movement in 1961 or later.

When youthful cadres in Hoi Cu asked a seventy-year-old Viet Minh veteran to talk about the past, he responded: "Conditions during the resistance differed greatly from those of the present time. At that time we had a government, and it was easier for us to work then than it is for you now because we had a machinery of government. I think that the road to victory is still very long, and I'm afraid that if I tell you about the difficulties you'll be discouraged." This commentary forms part of a wider meditation on the relationship between the Viet Minh and the Front. It signals a transfer of power from one generation to the next (the speaker's daughter was the NLF village secretary), and insofar as the reference to coming "difficulties" would have seemed out of place amidst the enthusiasm of the golden period, it hints at misconnections between the two generations of the southern revolution.[34]

Many other observers noticed that "conditions" in the 1960s "differed greatly" from those of the 1940s. The "Bao Dai government" created by the French in 1949, and regarded by many, including Bao Dai himself, as a charade, made no impression on Rand informants, who remembered the First Indochina War as a struggle between the Viet Minh and the French. To them it seemed different from the second war, a three-cornered struggle involving, in addition to the NLF and the Americans, the Republic of South Vietnam. According to one informant, "the Viet Minh had a government and an administrative machinery to help the people and to maintain constant contact between different levels in the administration." Along with this assumption of a state-like sovereignty came a tendency to map the terrain as if a clear line separated the two camps. In 1947, recalled a veteran, there were "two distinct zones," one organized around military outposts controlled by the French, and the other claimed by the Resistance.[35]

But whereas the Hoi Cu veteran thought that the "machinery of government" made for "easier" administration, other informants argued that the two-zone conception had been an illusion. One reported that "the Viet Minh absolutely forbade the people to buy and use various items from the cities, such as fabrics, medicines, kerosene, bicycles, motorbikes, and so on. This was why the people were extremely miserable and lacked all sorts of things." Another veteran noted that the Viet Minh "killed the people through its economic blockade against the enemy." Activists of the 1960s were also prone to mercantilist thinking, which rested on the notion that there was a frontier between the NLF and the GVN when in reality the economic activity on which everyone depended crossed political boundaries on a daily basis. Still, a number of observers praised the Front, which "benefited from past experience" and did not try to seal off the borders of the liberated zone. "Before, the Viet Minh forbade the people to sell their products in the cities and killed those who disobeyed this order," explained an informant old enough to have witnessed Resistance policies firsthand. "Now the Front lets the people sell their products freely in the GVN areas."[36]

As in the preceding citations, several informants criticized Viet Minh terror. "Drawing experience from the 9-year Resistance," one declared, "the Front emphasizes indoctrination more than punishment, to avoid losing prestige as the Viet Minh did during the Resistance. The Viet Minh had the motto: 'It is better for us to kill one innocent person than to release one reactionary by mistake.'" Another affirmed: "I heard people say that the Front differed from the Viet Minh. The Viet Minh's policy was 'it's better to kill an innocent man than to let a guilty man go free.' The Front's policy is more discriminate."[37]

In addition to these criticisms, some informants disapproved of what they took to be the Viet Minh's united front approach, which enabled landlords to secure a place in the movement and led to the exclusion of the poor. "Before, landlords and rich people were appointed to represent the people in administrative affairs," stated a young man (born 1941). "But now the Front doesn't allow these elements to do so. Right now only the middle, poor, and very poor farmers are very active and assume leadership." The same criticism was made by two veterans, both of whom specified that the Viet Minh policy changed in 1949, when landlords and wealthy farmers "gradually disappeared from the local government scene."[38]

On religious questions, critics turned around and scored the Viet Minh for its failure to follow united front principles. "There was no freedom of religion then," one informant asserted, "but now the Front accepts the existence of other political parties and is for religious freedom." The costs of this intolerance were underscored by another witness, who remembered that "the Viet Minh tried to destroy the religious sects in a brutal manner, and in so doing pushed these religious sects into joining ranks with the French Expeditionary Forces." The upshot seemed to be that Viet Minh overtures to landlords had been an error, eventually perceived as such and corrected, and that succumbing to the temptations of sectarianism had also been a mistake.[39]

Some interviewees thought that feminist principles impacted the Front more than the Viet Minh. When a Rand questioner asked, "Did the Front use the alluring women tactic in its troop [proselytizing]?" a veteran responded: "Yes, the Viet Minh used it during the war against the French. We sent women out to marry soldiers in the posts in order to have them help in destroying these posts." He then affirmed: "At present, it is no longer used because the Front thinks that this degrades womanhood. We've stopped using this tactic since 1960." In the same vein the Ethnographer declared, "Women have taken part in more political activities at the present time than during the resistance period."[40]

These citations do not amount to the last word on the Viet Minh, which in other contexts was often praised by Rand sources. But they do underscore the key point, that conditions in the First Indochina War "differed greatly from those of the present time." Passing the baton from one generation to the next was dictated by an understanding that the world was in flux and that thought and action had to move with it. Given this frame of mind, it is not surprising that youthful revolutionaries "set forth the slogan: 'To each period, its cadres,' because the people who were old would be too weak. They had either been in prison, or they were with the GVN and they didn't have the prestige among the people. The Party, therefore, had to choose the young unskilled cadres who still had the trust of the people." After the concerted uprising, an evaluation of each resistance cadre in the Front resulted in the dismissal or demotion of some. "Purge" would be too strong a word for a campaign that left in place a significant number of veterans, but there is no mistaking the shift of power from one generation of activists to another.[41]

By way of explanation, an informant said that "the old time cadres aren't as energetic as the young cadres" and "their health is no longer good, and so they can't assume positions of leadership." But he also noted that these perhaps sensible judgments were put forward in a "very arrogant" fashion by "the new cadres." It is not surprising that "the veteran fighters often bitterly expressed their dissatisfaction, saying they belonged to the 'ugly' class," employing a "slang expression to designate a kind of fruit which is neither good enough to be eaten, nor bad enough to be rejected."[42]

Even more wounding was the presumption that jail time, which might have served as a badge of honor, tended to arouse suspicion. "I have rarely found any cadres who, after having been imprisoned and released, continued working as eagerly as before," remarked a veteran. "Most of the young cadres who had not been arrested doubted the strength of character of those released cadres," he went on to note, "and thought they must have disclosed various organizations of the revolution after having been imprisoned and tortured." Whether true or false, this suspicion had a demoralizing effect, and "the released cadres then felt weary, and once they were suspected by the young cadres, they did not feel like dedicating themselves to their work any more."[43]

Several of the veterans had compromised themselves by naming names or volunteering as prison trustees. "When I was arrested," confessed one informant, "I made some statement during the interrogations. Consequently, ten other persons were arrested and the VC underground organization in my village was completely destroyed. I was forsaken when I was later released and returned to my village." He remained inactive until 1966, when the Front subjected him to harsh criticism. "They also encouraged me to live a new life, try to take part in all activities, and strive to fulfill my duties in order to be able to regain my Party membership," the informant recalled. He remained bitter, perhaps especially because the rebukes he and others had endured were "made public throughout the country."[44]

THE COMMANDER OF HOA DINH

These issues are vividly illustrated in the account of interviewee no. 116, one of the most wily and fascinating of Rand informants. Part Chinese (his grandfather fled to Vietnam after participating in the Taiping rebellion), the Commander was born in 1913 into a landlord and Catholic family in Hoa Dinh village. His father served as a village official under the French, and, after completing two years of high school, he joined the French forces in Saigon. In 1938 he was shipped to France with an artillery battery for two years and formed a negative picture of the standard of living there. "I knew that since they were so poor they only came to our country to oppress and rob us," he said, "and I couldn't stand this." On returning home, he lived by selling coconuts and trading tobacco in Chau Doc. In the August Revolution he helped train Vanguard Youths, then, during the Resistance, was promoted to company level in the Viet Minh armed forces.[45]

Demobilized with kidney stones in 1951, the Commander was arrested by the French, then escaped and rejoined the Viet Minh, where comrades held him at arm's length, given his admission that he had agreed to spy for his captors, "because," he stated, "I wanted to have more freedom in order to escape." Discharged in 1952, he went to Can Tho and survived on 1,000 piasters a month by singing, giving guitar lessons, and growing watermelons and peas. In 1956 he returned to Hoa Dinh, where local militants ordered his assassination because they thought he was still working for the government and doubted his claim that he had come only to buy medicine for one of his four wives. But sympathetic local cadres refused to carry out the order. He was arrested several times in the late 1950s by the GVN, then came back to the village in 1960, agreed to organize resistance to ARVN sweep operations, and soon after was appointed village secretary.

Another informant interviewed by Rand stated that the Commander "was the Front leader of Hoa Dinh Village and helped to destroy the GVN administrative machinery there." Once in charge of the village, "he was all powerful and even had the power to arrest and kill people whom he accused of being opposed to the Front. Compared to the other party chapter secretaries who assumed responsibility later on, he was the most capable one. He had a relatively good level of education, he was persuasive and eloquent, and he was the most powerful man in the village." But, it was claimed, the party secretary "didn't have a virtuous revolutionary character. He was lewd and had many illicit love affairs." He also "accepted a bribe of 20,000 piasters" from the former GVN hamlet chief, who "had been condemned to death by the villagers." In addition, "the rich families in the village had to pay 10,000 piasters in taxes to him, even though they were supposed to pay only 5,000 piasters." When in 1962 higher echelons launched an investigation, he quit the Front, went to Saigon, and made a living transporting fruit from Can Tho to the capital city, where Rand found and interviewed him in 1966.

This tangled narrative raises many questions. A man from a Catholic landlord family who had collaborated with the French and who led a polygamous and philandering personal life might seem an unlikely candidate for revolutionary activism. Yet the moments in the interview when the Commander tried to minimize his political activity ring false. He joined the movement at the time of the August Revolution and stuck with it through the dark days of the late 1950s. When the concerted uprising was galvanizing the countryside, a person with his education, talent, and experience (he had been all over the South and even to France) could have fled to the city with the prospect of a quick adjustment. But instead he returned to Hoa Dinh. He had risen to company level in the Viet Minh army and to the position of NLF village secretary, a combined military and civilian record of accomplishment unusual among Rand informants. It is likely that he was one of the instigators who launched the concerted uprising, and, at the least, he was a willing participant as the revolution again gained momentum.

Given the fragmentary evidence in the transcripts, one cannot solve the mysteries posed by the Commander's story. Critics said he took bribes from suspects who should have been punished by the Front, while his version was that he tried to block the depredations of another cadre who killed people out of "personal hatred." "All the other former Viet Minh people had surrendered to the Security Police," he averred, and "in the end I was the only one left and was made Party secretary," a statement perhaps intended to minimize his political commitment in the eyes of the Rand interviewer. It is a puzzling claim, since he was trying to live down links to the French and compromising behavior while in jail.

The story told by the Commander sheds light on the problematic status of "old Resistance cadres" in the movement launched by the concerted uprising. Those who had lived through earlier stages of the revolution developed political skills and accumulated a wealth of experience, and it is not surprising that when they expressed a desire to reenlist, such offers were initially accepted. But their survival was the product of adaptations that were bound to compromise them in the eyes of a new generation of village activists. Everyone residing in the countryside before 1945 must have had some dealings with the French authorities, and the same might be said of villagers and the GVN during the six years of peace. The Communist Party exhorted militants to stand fast, but prison conditions were likely to break the will even of the most steadfast revolutionary.

Rand transcripts do not tell us if the Commander promised to serve as an informer for the French only as a way of facilitating his escape from jail or if he came back to Hoa Dinh to buy medicine rather than to spy on the movement. Youthful comrades with shorter and "cleaner" personal histories to explain away would have encountered similar difficulties in sorting out truth from falsehood and were bound to be suspicious. It should also be noted that older cadres were more embedded in a "feudal" past. The Commander's bland reference to his four wives did not endear him to a new cohort of activists touched by feminist currents. His troubles with the Front are emblematic of the difficulties encountered by an older generation of revolutionaries, who would not have been human if they had never wavered while making their way through a difficult time in Vietnamese history. It was tragic and also not surprising that the Front extended them a less than enthusiastic welcome.

Given political and generational tensions, one might just as well place emphasis on the rapprochement between the Resistance veterans and the Front. Incarceration, torture, and the shaming inflicted in the GVN's Anti-Communist Denunciation Campaigns, with their forced confessions before captive audiences and demeaning rituals such as the tearing up of the Communist Party flag, were designed to break the will of the militants. And yet many veterans survived these trials with political commitments intact. The transcripts provide only occasional evidence of apostasy among them, few were counted among GVN officials and sympathizers during the six years of peace, and, if the Rand materials are to be credited, they were almost never the targets of NLF terror.

A number of veterans followed the example of the man from Hoi Cu and retired to their homes, dignity intact and seemingly with an understanding of the circumstances that required them to step aside. Others, especially the younger veterans, could not separate themselves from the movement. Born in 1931, an informant from Cam Son joined the Viet Minh in 1952 and served as a guerrilla and a liaison agent. He remained active after the Geneva Accords but had to seek refuge in the Plain of Reeds in 1957, then was incarcerated for three years in a GVN prison. The guards "used to kick me while passing by," he recalled. "I was just an animal in their eyes. They amused themselves by running an electric current into my body through my genital organ." When he returned to Cam Son, "the way the hamlet policeman treated me infuriated me again. As a rule, I had to present myself to him, and his first act was to curse me."[46]

The son of a teacher, raised in a family owning a decent-sized holding, this man was married with three children. "I was not dissatisfied with my life," he admitted, and given his earlier trials, one might guess that he would not want to take further risks. On the contrary, he welcomed the concerted uprising. "I was greatly needed by my family, therefore the day I made up my mind to join the Front, my mother and my wife wept profusely," he recalled. "But

I wanted to find a reason for my existence." Hatred of the GVN figured in his thinking but was not the dominant aspect. "I did not know much about communism," he explained. "I followed them because I felt that the society needed a revolution. I was young and was willing to fight for an ideal, and the Front, in my eyes, represented the ideal indeed."

Relations between Resistance- and Front-era cadres were troubled, but a common revolutionary vocation seems to be the dominant tendency. At the time of the concerted uprising, young men and women were the most likely to step forward, while more prudent villagers took time to calculate the odds before joining. The revolt exposed many who had been in or close to the government orbit, and some paid with their lives for the compromising choices they had made or were publicly shamed and ostracized. But even that unlikely sector of the community produced its share of activists. One should therefore not be surprised that people with long histories of political activism wished to rejoin the movement and that local militants, albeit grudgingly, moved over to make a place for them. Unanimity built on the assembling of so many different sorts of people was fragile. But the victories achieved through concerted action overrode doubts, softened the memory of past injuries, and kindled hopes that all might find a reason for their existence.

CHAPTER SIX

MODERN GIRLS AND
NEW WOMEN

Undaunted by rising violence, interviewee no. 253, a woman I will call the Feminist, joined the movement in 1965. The transcript reveals her as a person of exceptional discipline and ambition. Unschooled and self-educated ("I learned to read and write by myself at home"), she looked forward to a time when a woman no longer "blindly" followed "the desires of her husband, children or relatives" or confined herself to household chores. Movement feminism spoke to her aspirations. "I was taught the duties and responsibilities of a woman in a time of national danger. First of all, if a woman wants to be regarded as equal to a man, she must take charge of her responsibilities toward the people and carry out the activities of a man, if necessary!"[1]

Pronouncements of this sort resounded throughout the countryside, where it was generally understood that the Front aimed to give "equal rights to both men and women" and to help women "liberate themselves." In the words of another interviewee: "They had to struggle to obtain equality with men, to abolish the system of 'daughter-in-law' (the wives were the slaves of their husbands' families), to abolish the system whereby the men were respected and women despised, and to liberate themselves from the oppression of the men." The result was the emergence of what one observer characterized as "the New Women in the New Rural Society," whose "thoughts, arguments and actions mirror the strong influences of the new ways of life."[2]

The experience of women in the southern revolution is a history of victories and defeats. Cultural revolutionaries singled out parental control over children and the larger organization of society around the deference owed to elders as manifestations of "feudal" backwardness. In turn, this campaign raised questions about a deeper layer of belief, associated with commemorating the death anniversaries of forebears in the male line, a custom that favored males over females as well as elders over youth. At first villagers clung to ancestor worship rituals, the Rebel explained. But after having been "indoctrinated by the Front, they gradually discarded them." Then, perhaps reminding herself that she and other iconoclasts were getting ahead of themselves, she offered the more qualified judgment that in any case people were making "less of a fuss" over such practices. Later in the interview the tone was still more cautious, as in her remark that "the cadres couldn't indoctrinate the people to do away with these anniversaries altogether, because these were the occasions when the people thought of their ancestors." The hesitation one detects here was portentous. Without an aggressive campaign to redefine the power of men and women in the family and in the world, the popular movement could not fully realize its mandate to create a "new rural society." The purpose of this chapter is to show how "new women" tested the limits of revolutionary modernism.[3]

A SOCIAL PROFILE

Rand's fourteen female informants were similar to the male subjects in class background, formal education, and religious preference but different in their youth and relative freedom from domestic responsibilities. An eighty-six-year-old woman was by far the oldest of all the interviewees, male or female, and two other women were in their thirties. But seven were teenagers, and an additional four were twenty-four or younger. Whereas most of the men were husbands and fathers, nine of the women were single, two were married, one was divorced, and two were widows. The widows were the only ones who had borne children. The husband of the eighty-six-year-old had passed away in 1917 and her son had died in 1947, and the other widow had placed her only child with a grandmother. These findings suggest that young, unmarried women without child care obligations were both the most likely to respond to the emancipatory promise of the movement and the freest to join its ranks.[4]

Just as "cowboys" and youthful male cadres shared certain traits, "new women" resembled the "modern girls" of an emerging consumer society in their outspokenness and indifference to propriety. While the first wave showed a tendency "to argue about a lot of things," the second liked "to argue about everything." In a manner recalling its ambivalence toward "cowboys," the Front wanted these women to be fierce combatants against the government and the Americans and demure everywhere else. According to an informant, "during the six years of peace, the women in Xuan Son village were interested in material things and luxury. They gambled and engaged in frivolous activities and never thought about politics. At present, however, the women have changed for the better. This is due to the tight control of the Front—its indoctrination and criticism. The women carried out a struggle for equality between the two sexes." A similar point was made by an observer from Long Tien, who noted that women "used to dress in a very showy manner, but all they knew was to take care of their home and do house work. Now they are in rags, but they have come out of their home and launch themselves into political activities to compete with the men." Enjoined to put aside show and frivolity and to struggle and compete against male privilege, women were asked both to respect and to topple received notions of their place in society.[5]

An attempt to compromise between the traditional and the modern could not help lapsing into what the Ethnographer characterized as an "undecided" posture. Conservatively inclined villagers were ready to countenance female militancy if women activists remained "virtuous," as in the case of the "inter-village sector cadre in charge of women's affairs" in Hoa Dinh. Twenty years old and single, she "wore her clothes and hair in the old fashion. She didn't wear thin clothes like the modern girls and behaved nicely." A teenager working in an NLF textile factory on the Cambodia border adopted a more "modern" style. "It certainly was dangerous for me to go through the district town, since I didn't have any legal papers with me," she noted in recounting a trip home on leave. "I also thought that my passage through the town would not raise any suspicions, because I had a hair-do which made me look like a town girl."[6]

Born in 1949 and orphaned at ten, this informant had been raised by a grandmother, then worked for several years as a baby-sitter for a tailor in My Tho. In 1964, when her grandmother insisted that she marry a divorced man with several children, she refused and chose "a more exciting life" with the Front. After several years in the factory, she quit in February 1967 and went to My Tho, then moved to Saigon and got a job as a dishwasher. This, then, was a young woman who had acquired a feel for the urban scene in My Tho and eventually left the movement for the city, a choice that probably figured in her mind from the beginning.[7]

She was not the only "modern girl" to pass through the movement. Before joining the Front, one of Rand's female informants had traded fruit and another had attended school in My Tho, and two others had worked as maids in Saigon, while several convey a sense that they would have left home and village even if there had been no revolution. The father of one objected when she married a local guerrilla in 1964. "Your good for nothing husband is a VC follower!" he raged; "they are all vagabonds." Soon after she ran away and enlisted in an NLF medic-training course. In March 1965 her husband rallied, an example she followed three months later. For her the revolution was an interlude, and her post-NLF choices—she was working as a cook in My Tho and planning to learn dressmaking and settle in Cho Gao—are perhaps the ones she would have selected earlier if there had been no Front to join after the quarrel with her father.[8]

A sixteen-year-old from a very poor family affiliated with the NLF against the wishes of her father, became a liaison agent, then arranged a transfer to an entertainment team. She rallied a few months later. Surprisingly, given her age and brief activism, the comments she offered on Front policies and activities were extensive and sophisticated. One gets a sense of a young woman easily drawn out of village routine, the sort of person who probably would have decamped for the city no matter what. Her final words were: "I am planning to apply to go to the Saigon Chieu Hoi center in order to learn to be a dressmaker." Eager to experiment, she was another pioneer in waiting.[9]

LIFE IN THE FRONT

Female recruits figured prominently in NLF health services and also performed in entertainment troupes and worked as teachers in the Front elementary school system. Because government observers tended to assume that women were incapable of political commitment, they were well suited for liaison work. When a message had to be transmitted over a long distance, an older woman "would be asked to carry the letter on a bus or taxi. There was no great fear of these women being arrested." The same reasoning prompted assignments to intelligence-gathering teams. According to an informant, "there were many young girls who worked as military informers for the Front, which did not employ the youths for this task because the youths move around with more difficulty than the girls."[10]

The fast track for female militants went through the NLF Women's Associations. According to the Feminist, "all activities that required the stimulation of personal feelings, in order to motivate morale or to arouse the sensible instincts of the people, were taken charge of by the Women's Association." Some male interviewees belittled this activism, as when one remarked, "Women cadres worked for the Revolution for sentimental reasons and so they didn't have any ideological stand." But during the golden period organizing work must have been both gratifying for women and likely to earn promotion. Indeed this phase was identified in several interviews as the high-water mark of the Women's Associations, when propaganda was a movement priority and women activists were the most numerous of the propagandists.[11]

Female informants responded variously to their assignments in the Front. Five served as liaison agents carrying documents and letters and escorting cadres from one locale to another. For some this task devolved into a tedious back-and-forth along the same path delivering the mail (one interviewee characterized it as boring), while elsewhere, as in the account offered by the Rebel, liaison work was made to sound like an important and satisfying contribution. Health-related sectors also recruited five women, an assignment promising to impart a complex, interesting, and socially valued skill. It also required studious application, which may have been beyond the capacity of one recruit who was expelled from a training session after getting into a fist-fight with another student and who may have been better suited to "demolitions training," the slot she was occupying when captured.[12]

A twenty-year-old, who was single and from a poor family, enlisted in the Front in November 1964, seemingly after running away from home, and was assigned a position near the NLF rally point at the Phat Da ("Stone Buddha") Pagoda in Hung Thanh My as a clerk in a quartermaster outfit. The only woman in her unit, she was lonely and afraid as the area came under increasing pressure and decided to defect after only eight months in the movement. "They told me to join the Front to live in glory," she declared, "but I have not experienced anything of this sort. They repeatedly promised to send me to study nursing, then did not keep their promise." The Rebel's stint as a clerk-typist in a district office was similarly disappointing. "I liked my work as a first-aid woman," she remarked, "but I didn't like to work as a typist at all."[13]

The discipline another interviewee encountered in a Front textile factory was similar in some respects to what a worker would have found in a Saigon mill and had the further disadvantage of being located on the Cambodia border rather than in a bustling city. She judged her work there "unproductive and insignificant." The four informants who joined NLF entertainment troupes appear to have valued the experience, as did the one teacher in the group, a woman from a single-parent sharecropper family who joined the movement when she was seventeen. "I didn't have anything to complain about during all the time I worked with the Front," she declared. The interview is full of detail about her work as a teacher.[14]

The Feminist was dissatisfied by her initial, "mediocre" hamlet-level assignments, but responded with great energy when promoted to the village association executive committee, where she "carefully examined all reports submitted by hamlet cadres, [and] studied all directives day and night in order to produce good results." This was a woman who from the beginning was uninterested in traditional female roles and had turned down several marriage proposals. From her days trading fruit in My Tho City she was familiar with the urban milieu. As a town dweller, she asserted, "I could not have a sufficient level of education to earn a relatively adequate material living, as those who have lived there long before. I am able to earn my living only as a worker or a servant in a rich family. Thus, my wages can be used only to support myself. I am unable to support my family and to build up my own future. Do you think that I can be a servant until I get old and die? It was also due to my hope of living a better life that I participated in the revolution." When promotion to district level was not accompanied by an invitation to join the Communist Party, on the grounds that her brother had ties to the GVN, she resigned from the Front. "I was in the condition consistent with the saying that goes, 'you'll remain a buffalo although you have tried to sharpen your horns.'" Like the male informants who resented being cast as beasts of burden, she was not willing to accept a routine assignment. For her and other women who left the movement, it remained to be seen if a job as a maid or a dishwasher would prove more rewarding.[15]

A thirty-year-old prisoner had grown up in a single-parent household presided over by her mother, a fruit seller, then married at seventeen. Her husband enlisted in the Viet Minh, was captured by the French, and, after being released, died from an illness contracted in prison. Treated like a servant by her mother-in-law, she left home to join the Front in 1961, was invited into the Communist Party, became Trung An village party secretary in 1962 and chair of the executive committee of the district Women's Association in 1964, then was suspended for four months as a result of a love affair with another cadre. After being reinstated, she was captured in August 1965. Reference to the affair sends a warning that life in the Front, even for a dedicated revolutionary, involved pitfalls. But the account offered by this informant, who fled from an abusive mother-in-law in order "to struggle against feudalism" and to "build up a just and democratic society," draws attention to the appeal the movement exercised on a population of women looking for a "better life."[16]

TESTING GENDER BOUNDARIES

Women in the movement challenged everyday conventions, called into question the division of labor on which household economies depended, and threatened a sexual order dominated by men. According to the Ethnographer, feminist watchwords lent bite to disputes over the politics of housework. "Recently, when I attended a banquet," he reported, "I found that when the young men told the young women to wash the dishes or to take their meals in a secondary house and not in the main one of the host's family, they replied, 'there is now equality between the two sexes. How dare you tell us to wash your dishes and to take our meals in the secondary house whereas you sit in a large one? That's unfair!'" Placing the dispute in a wider context, he added, "In addition to those stories, the women now often take the equality of the two sexes slogan as their weapon to struggle against the men."[17]

Disputes also erupted in public spaces. Popular culture afforded women a license to speak bluntly on neighborhood affairs, but when the Feminist and others departed from the conventions of village gossip and appropriated movement discourse, critics were quick to object. "Personally, I have no idea about the ordinary women," declared an informant from Binh Xuan,

> but the women cadres whom I often met on my various missions and those who worked in the Province Medical Section seemed to have lost all the charm of the fair sex. In my opinion, women cadres have actually become masculine and ridiculous. They all liked to argue and use grandiloquent "revolutionary" words such as "we must consolidate our spirit to overcome all kinds of hardships, we must strengthen our ideology and fight for the final victory, etc." I never liked women cadres, so I had no girl-friends among them.

Ridicule served as an instrument to discipline women who presumed to intervene in political discussion and, by implication, to claim rights of citizenship.[18]

Men were not alone in taking offense. The eighty-six-year-old informant asserted that female cadres "lead ridiculous ways of living, which are completely out of step with the traditional manner. They were educated by the Front and so they have that manly way of talking and behaving. They liked to use terms that I had no idea what they meant, lived with the male cadres, and don't care about cooking and housekeeping. As soon as they open their mouths, words such as: construction, criteria, struggle, etc. . . . come out." Here again, women who talked about politics were made to seem "ridiculous," with the added complaint that they did not "care about cooking and housekeeping." Wives and mothers left the village to go to market and on other errands and then came back without attracting any notice. But unattached female activists, who seemed to be leaving home for good, alarmed many observers. By renouncing assigned roles in the family economy, they destabilized an agrarian system that depended on a customary division of labor, with females taking responsibility for child care, many kinds of agricultural work, and coordination of household finance and market affairs.[19]

This nonconformity is illustrated by a comment on a pair of village cadres in Ban Long. "Both of these female Party members were local people, single, came from the poor class, joined the Revolution from the beginning, about

30 years old," and both "were very enthusiastic in their activities." The speaker then added that villagers "liked and respected these two female cadres because of their comportment and their virtues, but sometimes they ridiculed and mocked their manly way of living: they were away all night long, going here and there, talking to everyone without caution and care like the other women." The behavior of the two militants was deviant, in that women "about 30 years old" were supposed to be married with children. But neighbors had to admit that they seemed "virtuous" and therefore refrained from attacking them unrelentingly (only "sometimes" were they "ridiculed and mocked"). Fearless and idealistic, "new women" made people nervous but were not easy to dismiss, even, one might imagine, by men who "had no girlfriends among them."[20]

As this last remark suggests, sexual overtones were especially disquieting. "Virtue," rigorously practiced and obvious to all, was required of female revolutionaries in order to temper the disapproval of a skeptical village population, and even then a warrant for activism was not always forthcoming. According to the Rebel, "when a girl left home," neighbors "suspected that she ran away with her lover and they didn't believe that she had gone away to join the Front." Onlookers noted that women were on the move "day and night." They no longer paid attention "to housework and live[d] together with men cadres unabashedly." Castigated for their "manly way of living," they were also blamed for living and working—and possibly sleeping with—their male comrades. That political work was done under cover of darkness appeared to attract rather than deter these renegades, who seemed impervious to the usual constraints and carried on "regardless of the late hours and without minding public gossip." Many worried that women revolutionaries would overturn a system based on sex only within marriage and would demand a license to enter into "illicit affairs."[21]

A popular movement challenging parental and communal authority in the name of "liberation" was bound to provoke these reactions. The Front was drawing people out of households and deploying them in spaces where established mechanisms of control could not reach, while at the same time urging its recruits to cast off feudal fetters and demonstrate the authenticity of their revolutionary calling. Male cadres in the civilian sectors of the NLF held positions that gave them power over others, including the power to seduce and coerce. Assignations were always possible for soldiers quartered on the population, especially in the early days of the Front, when many women looked on PLAF combatants as desirable partners. The atmosphere within the movement was even more charged. Activists had to cling to one another in order to fight and to survive, and that intense sharing of hopes and risks was bound to promote intimacy between men and women (as well as among men and among women). Sexual relations outside of marriage were a fact of life in the Liberation Front.

But even the most audacious iconoclasts shrank from the prospect of an untrammeled sexuality. Married men who had left home to serve in the PLAF or in other far-flung sectors of the Front worried about what might be done to their wives and what their wives might do while they were gone, and the village population was certain to be offended when received moral standards were flouted. Intrigues and liaisons and even platonic courtships threatened to divert militants from their assignments and undermine the collective effort required to fight a total war. Since men remained dominant in society and seized a preponderant role within the Front, a laissez-faire approach left women even more exposed than they were in everyday life, where patriarchal norms offered them a limited, but not insignificant, measure of protection.

With these considerations in mind, the Front insisted on chastity for women while also requiring a similar restraint from men. The line on polygamy was unequivocal. "We were told that the Communist policy didn't permit the men to have many wives," reported the Rebel, "and that husbands should treat their wives as equals—the men shouldn't abandon their wives for other women. It was said that any cadres who took many wives violated the teachings of the Communists, and harmed the revolution in the eyes of the people." Even marriages between activists were discouraged, "because it was feared that after a male and a female cadre decided to get married, they might both defect to the GVN to lead an easier life (*giat tay nhau len con duong trang nhua*). The district was afraid that, if many couples did that, there wouldn't be anyone left to carry out the tasks of the revolution." When male cadres with pregnant girlfriends asked the Front for permission to marry, they were often rebuffed on the grounds that the potential bride came from the wrong social class or was somehow connected to the GVN. By blocking virtually all possibilities, even conjugal, for intimacy, the NLF left its militants no alternative to abstinence.[22]

This policy met with widespread resistance, as when conspiracy among men veiled unsanctioned behavior from potential critics. The Instigator "knew perfectly well" why the Labor Youth group was not functioning effectively but did nothing about it. The two responsible organizers were his best friends, and both "had mistresses living in Tam Hiep" and "spent most of their time in this village. Being great lovers, they worried about their girl friends more than about fighting." Though a married man, the Instigator was himself involved in an affair with a woman who was the cousin of one of the labor youth organizers and had been courted by the other, and so he sympathized with and covered for the two men. As for his own affair, he anticipated that a fellow district cadre who had "two wives," and another who "just abandoned his first wife for a younger girl," would not dare accuse him of promiscuity.[23]

At the same time, privacy was a luxury in the villages. Couples were interrupted having sex, or an unwanted pregnancy betrayed them, or quarrels between men over a woman or between women over a man caused enough of an uproar to bring the scandal to light. Communist Party solidarity worked against non-party individuals accusing party members but also provided leverage when party activists of subordinate rank wished to take on their superiors. In the end, relentless criticism even got to the smooth-talking Instigator, who was driven to rally with his "second wife."

Party chapter secretaries were the most powerful village-level Front officials, but they could not act with impunity. When the secretary in Hoi Cu was accused of having an affair with a member of the Women's Association, he "denied everything." But intraparty adversaries were undeterred. Because the couple had been caught in the act, their "crime was clear as day," and the accusers were further emboldened by the thought "that one of them might be appointed as Party Secretary to replace him and the others would be promoted in the future." The secretary was purged from the party.[24]

Another secretary, this time in Binh Duc, "was disciplined by the Party chapter because he slept with a girl in the village and she became pregnant." In Phu Qui the secretary "was demoted because he took a second wife who was a GVN sergeant's widow." The Cai Lay District Committee found out about the affair when the secretary's "second wife came to blows with his first wife." While his spouse was in labor, the secretary in Thanh Hoa "profited by the occasion to slip into the bed of his younger sister-in-law." When she cried out for help, "among those curious persons who rushed to the scene, there was a District Committee member who happened to pass by the village and was an eye-witness to the incident." The offender "was dismissed from his Village Secretaryship and expelled from the Party."[25]

Common villagers were also likely to condemn "lewdness." When one district cadre caught another in bed with his wife, the "criminals" were summoned before a people's court attended by five hundred villagers, where they "admitted their guilt. The people demanded death sentences for both the adulterer and the adulteress." Cadres endeavored to wring a less severe sentence from the assembly, which, in the end, settled for depriving the accused

man of "all official functions." The anecdote calls attention to strongly punitive attitudes within the general population toward adultery, seen in this instance as a capital offense. However much Front leaders may have wished to
protect comrades, they knew that villagers "showed contempt" for guerrillas
who "seduced the village girls"; that when "wanton love affairs were known
to the people," they "spread many rumors which were very harmful to the
Front's prestige"; that militants guilty of adultery lost "the confidence of the
people."[26]

The punishment gradient adopted by the NLF began with criticism and
warnings, then, when offenses were repeated, involved some mix of demotion, removal from positions of authority, or suspension from the Communist Party. An informant noted that "if one courted girls or had immoral love
affairs, one would be expelled from the Front after the third violation." A
guerrilla in Quon Long was demoted "because of a wanton love affair with a
rallier's wife" but remained in the party. The head of the Farmers' Association in Tan Hoi was demoted because of "bad personal conduct. He had just
taken a second wife and his two wives quarreled with each other too often."
Another cadre "had a concubine" and was therefore "farming as a common
villager after he was kicked out of the Front."[27]

Party chapters often reintegrated people who were guilty of moral lapses,
in part "because they still needed them due to the lack of manpower." But
while the movement stretched rules in order to staff its many operations, a
flexible policy also grew out of compassion for human error and confidence
in human redemption. Incorrigibles "would be subjected to ever-mounting
criticism and would feel dissatisfied with the Revolution and would seek to
defect from the Front and the people." But if a man guilty of "illegal love
affairs" should "repent," then "he can become a good individual." In line with
this policy, a district cadre who was caught sleeping with a villager's wife was
reduced to the rank of a "plain citizen" but was later reinstated in a lower-level
position. Another district cadre testified: "I met a woman during a meeting
and had an affair with her. Because of this, I was suspected of being a bad element and was purged from the Party. In December 1964, I was re-admitted in
the Party with a probationary status."[28]

Elsewhere, contradictions embedded in the Front approach, with its "ever-
mounting criticism" of behaviors that refused to go away, drove people out of
the movement and sometimes into the Chieu Hoi program, as in the case of
the Instigator, discussed earlier. The party secretary in Hoa Dinh "excelled in
military activities" and "was excellent in organizing the Front" in the village.
But then he got involved in "an illicit love affair." His wife became "jealous

when he was carrying on with the other girl, and because of the noise his wife made about his illicit affair the Party Chapter found out about it." News of the scandal spread even more widely when it emerged that the "mistress" was pregnant, and as a result the secretary "lost his prestige with the cadres and the villagers." Higher echelons "criticized him and transferred him upward" to province level, perhaps with the hope of reintegrating and reassigning him at a later date. But after returning to the village, he left his wife and two children and rallied with his "second wife." [29]

One might hazard that in such cases U.S.-style modernization was undermining polygamy. The women who followed male ralliers into the GVN zone were thereby promoted out of their status as "second wives" in polygamous families and became modern wives of husbands who no longer wanted to live with their original families. It was the Chieu Hoi version of a "divorce," albeit without alimony, child support, or other protections for abandoned women and children. [30]

THE OTHER WOMEN

Men subjected to the Front's regulation of sexuality were publicly shamed, demoted, and in some cases hounded to the point where they sought refuge in the GVN zone. The Soldier reported:

I joined the Front when it first arose. I belonged to the basic social class, I performed my tasks well, I did well in the training courses, but I was accused of having a bad behavior because of my lewdness and my many illicit love affairs, and for this reason, I wasn't admitted in the Party early, even though I became a Labor Youth member in 1962. I should have been an official Party member at the end of 1964 during the training course for medics, but I was purged for six months because of my love affair with a female trainee.

Finally admitted to the party, he was "was purged again for illicit love affairs." But even here, in a case involving multiple punishments, it seems that the informant's career prospects remained favorable in spite of his "lewdness." If not for a serious wound incurred in 1966, one has a sense that he would have continued to rise within the Front. [31]

Women were granted less leeway. When Rand informants described scandals following on the policing of sexuality, their accounts were mainly about men. Some male cadres "flirted with," "courted," "seduced," and "slipped into the beds" of women, while others tried to expose and punish an immorality that damaged Front morale and undermined the reputation of its militants. When liaisons were uncovered, it was assumed that men were the aggressors and that their female partners had been passive objects of male desire. But even though they were seen primarily as victims, women were also held accountable and were subject to a condemnation more irredeemable than that imposed on males.

In many of the stories told by and about men, female partners are not mentioned at all, while in other accounts they are noted only in passing ("a villager's wife," "a villager's daughter," "a woman in the village"). A few are identified as spouses of absent males (soldiers in the PLAF, prisoners in GVN jails, Front cadres on assignment), and two were widows, while others appear as "mistresses," "concubines," or "second wives." In some interview accounts women fade into the background in a fashion that underscores their inferior status. When a guerrilla in Hung Thanh My was caught attempting rape, he was forced to apologize—to the victim's parents. In some instances, adulterous episodes appear as matters to be settled among men, with women serving as mere props. When asked how he responded on learning that a security cadre had "run off" with his spouse, an informant stated, "I did not chide my wife, I only threatened to shoot the security cadre." In response to his complaint, a meeting was called, with invitations to the security cadre, the chief of the village Military Affairs Committee, and the village party secretary, but not to the woman, whose preferences did not enter into discussion about how to resolve the matter.[32]

Whether coerced or consensual, sexual encounters with men who were not their husbands frightened and shamed women. Before assaulting his sister-in-law, the Thanh Hoa secretary "had indulged in such lewd acts several times with different girls of other families, but nobody had been able to do anything about him although all the victims had cried out for help." In Hoi Cu a people's court of two hundred villagers pronounced a death sentence on a man who "had raped two women in the hamlet—one of whom had a miscarriage after she was raped." The two victims "weren't present at the meeting because they were ashamed of what had happened to them." Speaking of a woman who had been assaulted by a cadre, an informant from Hau Thanh declared: "She is now living with the son she had gotten from this cadre. She worries about what might happen when her husband, gone three years with the Front, comes home." The chronicler of a scandal in Diem Hy related that a guerrilla "courted" and impregnated the wife of a villager who was being held in a GVN jail. In order "to soften the people's resentment," the guerrilla was expelled from the party. The transcript specifies that after being released from prison, the husband "abandoned his wife," but says nothing about the

· fate of the disgraced woman, now a single parent, though the informant did add, by way of an ominous postscript, that "everyone in the hamlet" knew what she had done.[33]

Most female cadres involved in scandals were identified sufficiently to show their connection to the movement, but were otherwise portrayed just as impersonally as the "villagers' wives" and other shadowy figures who elsewhere serve as foils in stories of male delinquency. Sometimes women caught in compromising situations were kicked upstairs or otherwise benefited from the indulgence extended to men, as when a female village cadre had "illicit relations" with another party member and "was transferred to the district," or when a district cadre "was pulled up to the province committee" because "she had been involved in a love affair." Another district cadre got involved with a married man working in the province Labor Youth group, became pregnant, and had an abortion. She was demoted but did not lose her party membership and was "on mission" when captured sometime later.[34]

Some women who continued to make controversial choices in their personal lives managed for a time to avoid sanction. A young woman in Hoa Dinh married a Viet Minh activist and had three children by him, and when her husband regrouped to the North, she lived with another man and gave birth to two more children. In spite of this liaison, she was able to join the Front in 1963 and gain promotion to leadership in the Women's Association. But then in April 1965 "she fled to My Tho, because she was afraid she would be criticized and purged for having lived with a village Troop [Proselytizing] cadre and for expecting a child from him." The grapevine reported that she had married a GVN soldier. Other women also paid a price for transgressions, as in the case of a female cadre who lived with a guerrilla in Xuan Dong village and became pregnant. "Because of this, she was purged from the Youths' Group and from the Women's League. Right now, she stays at home and takes care of her child."[35]

Liaisons sometimes destroyed reputations to the point where flight from the village was the only option. A leader of the Women's Association in Hoa Dinh "became pregnant as a result of all her illicit love affairs and fled to My Tho because she was afraid that this would become known to everyone." An affair, even if it did not result in a pregnancy, could lead to exile. A militant set up a hamlet Women's Association in Hoa Dinh, but it fell apart when she "slept with the guerrillas and the villagers found out about it. She was so ashamed that she fled to the city." When a "wanton love affair" with the party secretary of Quon Long was discovered, the head of the Women's Association "had to resign and left the village for Saigon to make a living up there." The contrast with her lover is telling. In one account he "was demoted and as-signed to a distant place," and in another he was relieved of his function and expelled from the party, then reinstated "after a year or so," albeit in a lesser position.[36]

These reports indicate that female militants entering into sexual relation-ships were more vulnerable than men and were more likely to be damaged by them. The affairs of women cadres were almost always with men in the Front who outranked them (whereas most of the scandals involving male cadres had to do with women who were not in the NLF), and in a number of cases they were forced to leave the movement for good. No female cadre in the DT series decided to rally and then succeeded in persuading a lover to accompany her to the GVN zone.[37]

THE STORMY CAREER OF THE MIDWIFE

The story told by interviewee no. 141 sheds further light on male-female dy-namics. In 1950, at age nineteen, she ran away from home to escape an ar-ranged marriage, went to Saigon, moved in with an uncle, and sought a job as a maid "for well-off people." Dissatisfied with her prospects, she returned to the village, then ran away again, this time to join the Resistance. She partici-pated in a medical training course organized by the Viet Minh and, after 1954, worked in a Hoa Hao maternity hospital, then set up her own midwife clinic. When a competitor denounced her as a Viet Cong, she was arrested, held for forty-five days, and "beaten a few times" until she "lost conscious-ness." After being released, she was forced to move into the Hau My agroville. Government authorities extended a loan to build a new house but, on the grounds that she did not have a license, would not allow her to practice. In debt and with no income, she was quick to join the movement, in April 1960, and was promoted to district, province, and region echelons before resigning in June 1964. She rallied in August 1966.[38]

This woman, whom I will call the Midwife, was one of the highest-ranking cadres in the Rand sample. Only two out of 285 informants had been pro-moted to region level, and the other was a prisoner rather than a defector. "I was not admitted to the party, because I belonged to the Petite Bourgeoisie—I had a house in the agroville," the Midwife asserted. But in a later passage she indicated that district cadres invited her to join the party, that the induction procedure was discontinued when she was promoted to province level, and, in turn, that a new invitation, from provincial cadres, could not be carried through because she moved up yet again, this time to the region. The NLF was reluctant to accept her resignation. "The Military Medical Branches where I had worked sent their men to see me, to console and ask me to resume working for the Front. They told me that I could choose the areas where I would like to work, and promised to send me to a training course for medical technicians. They said that if I didn't want to operate far from the village and if I was afraid of bombing and shelling, I could work in the village. But I'd seen how they exploited me, so I decided to rally instead." It seems clear that the Front was eager to have this disgruntled activist remain in its ranks.[39]

Though she presented herself as a convert to the government cause, the Midwife does not sound like a genuine rallier. She hazarded an anti-VC remark or two, couched in stereotypic terms ("I myself didn't like to have the state own everything"), and did not like what she had "heard about the class struggle," a lack of enthusiasm perhaps related to the way cadres had saddled her with an invidious "petty bourgeois" classification. At the same time, in her own words, she had served the Viet Minh with "enthusiasm and zealousness" and "wanted to see the country reunified." The interview contains graphic passages on the cruelty of the GVN and the violence of U.S.-GVN war making. Her appearance at the Chieu Hoi Center came over two years after she quit the Front, suggesting that there was no meaningful link between the two decisions.[40]

The Midwife was a brave and effective cadre who had repeatedly won promotion within the NLF, but she could not reconcile herself to the sexual politics of the movement. Several months after joining, she attended a training course for medics, then was appointed head of the Cai Be District Military Medical Section. It was a "guerrilla" dispensary, and when government troops swept through, the sick and wounded were covered with nylon sheets, put in sampans, and hidden in mangrove swamps. On the basis of her work under difficult conditions, the Midwife was then transferred to the Chau Thanh District Military Medical Section, in Hung Thanh My, where she was again responsible for program building and for running a dispensary.[41]

It quickly emerged that one of the nurses was five months pregnant as the result of a liaison with the previous head of the section. According to the Midwife, "the Party and Labor Youth members wanted to defend the former head of section who was a party member by keeping his illicit relations . . . secret." So he "was criticized privately by the other Party and Labor Youth members who had a heart to heart talk with him" and was then sent away to attend a training course. By contrast, the nurse was "purged." She "was very unhappy about what had happened to her, but she was afraid and didn't dare to protest." The Midwife had been brought in to replace the section head, but that did not deter her from pressing to reopen the case. "It didn't look right for a revolutionary to be an unwed mother," she explained, but "as a woman," she "wanted to defend the rights of another woman" by insisting that her predecessor receive a more severe punishment. Eventually the wrongdoer was summoned back to the district, criticized, and suspended from the party. At the same time, "the Party and Labor Youth members were mad at me and from then on we couldn't get along at all." She was accused of "trying to sabotage the Communist ranks," and as a non-party member, she "couldn't do anything but accept this criticism."[42]

Soon after, the Midwife was transferred to the province hospital at Hung Thanh My, where she helped run a midwife training course and where, again, she became embroiled in a sexual scandal. It began when trainees reported to her that one of the women in the unit "was having illicit relations" with the senior medical technician in the section, conduct they deemed "unbefitting a revolutionary." After waiting until the course had ended and the women who had complained were assigned elsewhere, the technician asked the Province Military Affairs Section to hold a criticism session to consider and rebut the accusations lodged against him. When the Midwife was invited to present her case, she could do no more than repeat what the trainees had said. The defendant comes off as a slippery character (delaying until the trainees were gone was a cunning move), and the Midwife may have been correct to assert that he "was hot tempered, arrogant and had a mandarin-like attitude toward his subordinates." But since there was no pregnancy and nothing but hearsay in the dossier, the organizers of the criticism session concluded that "they couldn't do anything to him." To make matters worse, the Midwife was again accused of "sabotaging the unity of the section."[43]

In the wake of this battle, the Midwife was promoted to a branch of the Region Military Medical Section. According to her account, "the province authorities chose me because they thought that I had the capability to bear the difficulties and hardships involved in setting up a new dispensary," a citation again suggesting that her work in the movement was both effective and respected by others. But within a matter of weeks "something happened which made me determined to leave the Front." When a nurse with a case of venereal disease asked for treatment, "I told her many times to stop sleeping with so many men, but since I wasn't a party member, she didn't listen to me. Instead she went around and told everyone in the section that I had been slandering her and that she wasn't a 'bad girl.'"[44]

This time armed only with information garnered while providing medical treatment, which perhaps should have remained confidential, the Midwife once again found herself before a criticism session. "I was told that I had been very virtuous during the whole time I was in the Front and that I had done my job well. But I was criticized for being hot tempered and bourgeois." Voices were raised as "the section members formed a clique and all took turns in saying that I had been slandering the people in the district and province military Medical sections where I had served." When her supervisor shouted that he wanted to "tie up" the Midwife, she responded: "You can go ahead and do that. As far as I'm concerned you have no authority over me and you are not genuine Communists." The supervisor shouted "that I dared to talk back to him and threatened to shoot me. I got mad and cursed them all. I said: 'if you don't shoot me I'll shoot you myself, and if you shoot me you're an s.o.b.'"[45]

After only three months in the section, the Midwife decided to resign from the NLF, then, twenty-six months later, rallied to the government side. "I'm like a child who has erred and after I finish my indoctrination I'll gladly do anything that the GVN wants me to," she said to the Rand interviewer. One would like to think that this independent and combative woman inwardly winced at the infantilizing rituals she seems to have thought were required by Chieu Hoi protocols.[46]

In the opinion of her critics, the Midwife was a "virtuous"—that is, an asexual—unmarried woman. As such, her only role when scandals erupted was to combat the double standard and impose austerity on males as well as females. Those efforts would have had more impact if she had been a party member, but no doubt Communist Party caucuses were also disrupted by quarrels when male comrades denied or minimized their transgressions. On such occasions outspoken women were certain to face the charge of damaging "unity within the section," a difficult allegation to refute in the context of total war, when solidarity alone offered hope for survival and victory. More than a few female militants must have despaired of finding a way out of that impasse.

The Midwife's "very virtuous" conduct won respect but no affection among men, who thought her choleric and divisive. She was also estranged from the female participants in love affairs. In the district controversy, a possible move would have been to ask why an "unwed mother" could not be a revolutionary, but the Midwife did not object to the purge of the nurse and instead concentrated on ensuring that the section chief was similarly punished. She adopted the same strategy in the province scandal and directed her fire at the medical technician, an approach implying that he was a predator and that the object of his lust was a victim. But the Midwife did nothing to help that woman, whose reputation was certain to be damaged by the public airing of the case.

Here again the assumption was that "illicit relations" were "unbefitting a revolutionary" and that punishment all around was the proper remedy. It was a flawed approach, likely to hurt women more than men and to block any move toward a more complex understanding of sexual desires and the responsibilities that went with them. It was also risky. After censuring a woman who was prepared to fight back against the imputation that she was a "bad girl," the Midwife was left in an exposed position, subject to criticism from every side.[47]

These stories call attention to the failure of the Liberation Front to go beyond a preliminary stage in its campaign against male privilege. Some men banded together in order to further erotic projects, while others combined in an effort to expose and punish them. It is not clear where women were supposed to fit into the resulting disputes. If the case of the Midwife is to be taken as typical, attempts to act as a kind of women's auxiliary in support of men who wished to enforce a gender-neutral policy of abstinence were not always welcomed. Meanwhile, nothing like a female caucus emerged. It seems inconceivable that activist women in trouble did not find other women to confide in and to ask for help, but when they became pregnant or otherwise drew condemnation, the impression emerging from the transcripts is that they were alone and unable to defend themselves. It was an outcome fully congruent with feudal backwardness and unworthy of a movement that had thrown down the gauntlet in opposition to so many other forms of oppression.

The popular movement was undermining the web of custom and ritual surrounding family life. When young women ran away from home to join the revolution, they disrupted household economies and flouted deeply ingrained notions of loyalty and obedience. The parents and siblings they left behind, often in material straits and with painful feelings of abandonment and betrayal, were asked to console themselves with the thought that the Front was fighting for a larger family, for the nation, and indeed for all of humanity, and that they—that everyone—would be better off after the triumph of the revolution. Still, the overturning of one moral code and its replacement with another was sudden and disorienting.

Women revolutionaries had stepped into an uncharted social space, and yet they were enjoined to remain "virtuous," a conception that took its meaning from the value system they had left behind. Criticism of polygamy and the double standard addressed some of the issues they faced but did not provide an adequate moral compass for the new situation. If "virtuous" women and "bad girls" had joined together, they would have been outnumbered and out-shouted within the NLF, but such an alliance might have saved some women from humiliation and ostracism and opened previously unimagined prospects for a humane sexuality. In the midst of an escalating war, this was a test that the modernism of the popular movement was not able to meet. It was the most significant unfinished business of the southern revolution.

ESCALATION AND THE END OF THE GOLDEN PERIOD

Escalation damaged many branches of the Front. Crisscrossing an increasingly militarized terrain, liaison agents were almost as much at risk as soldiers in main force units. Parents refused to send children to schools that were being bombed and shelled, and the same reasoning persuaded villagers to stop attending shows put on by entertainment troupes. Office work also grew more hazardous, as U.S.-GVN forces bombarded the northern tier of My Tho province, where NLF bases were located. As the Front switched from an all-volunteer army to mass conscription and ratcheted up its tax demands, Women's Association proselytizing efforts met stiff resistance. When a woman cadre could not persuade anyone to enlist in the PLAF, her superiors told her: "Comrade, you have failed to carry out the resolution of the Party. You haven't done your best to struggle for the cause. You are too shy and we are sure that you were afraid of the Youths and didn't dare to speak to them with eloquence." "I was hampered by the fact that I was a girl," she concluded; "I couldn't speak as eloquently as the men."[48]

Under such conditions, aspirations for self-development collapsed, and the women and men who remained active did so with the understanding that they would very likely be killed, wounded, or captured. Some of Rand's female informants chose this moment to quit the Front. A Labor Youth member was one of the last cadres to give up in Binh Duc, the target of a ferocious pacification campaign launched by the Americans in support of their Dong Tam military base. The Rand interviewer was charmed at first ("The subject was a young and pretty girl of about 20" who was "intelligent and articulate"), then noted: "She was friendly during the interview, but when she rejoined the other ralliers her attitude changed. She refused to acknowledge the interviewer's greetings when the latter passed by her. It seemed that by her hostile attitude she wanted to show to the other ralliers that she had been unfriendly and uncooperative during the interview and that she hadn't given the interviewer any information." Her loyalties do not seem to have changed, but it would have been unreasonable to expect an isolated twenty-year-old to hold out in a village crawling with enemy troops. While she recovered from a wound, a cadre implored her, "Don't you see that our fatherland is immersed in sufferings and that our people are shedding blood?" To such appeals she replied: "I'm poor and I have to work to earn my living. If you want to purge me, go ahead, I couldn't care less. I know that, while I'm living, I struggle for my own benefits and when I die, I will only be fertilizer for the grass on my grave (neu song thi chien dau cho ban than, neu chet lam phan cho cay co)." The Chieu Hoi option must have seemed the most logical, indeed the only, way out. But, one surmises, she was no rallier to the government side.[49]

A nineteen-year-old from Thanh Phu (CT) found herself in a similarly untenable position. A show put on by an NLF entertainment troupe inspired her to run away from home and join the Front in September 1965. After a year as a liaison agent she quit, went to Cai Lay to "make a living," got married, then returned to the village after her husband was drafted by the GVN. Adjoining Binh Duc village, Thanh Phu was a hot spot that was bound to test the staying power of a teenage girl who had been mobilized by the visit of a theatrical team. The interviewer's assessment ("She seems to like to have fun") may be patronizing, but it is true that anyone affiliating with the movement in 1965 in search of excitement and adventure was in for a rude awakening. It is also worth noting that she may have had a "heart condition." Here, too, the informant's rally, which came almost a year after she left the Front, does not seem to have been politically motivated.[50]

Other departures were prompted by economic considerations. The Feminist grew up in a family on the margins of subsistence. Her mother cultivated a domestic garden, while her father, a displaced tenant, ran a sampan on the Phnom Penh–Can Tho route transporting "oriental medicines for a Chinese medical store." In 1961 the mother died, and soon afterwards the father fell ill and "could only do slight jobs." In these circumstances, the daughter's labor became crucial. She had worked at home until 1960, then went to Cai Lay town and My Tho "to trade in fruit." In 1962 she was able "to buy a sewing machine and open a tailor's shop," but this source of income dried up when she joined the movement and no longer had time for customers' orders. Her days in the Front were punctuated by the pleading of a destitute father who needed help in order to survive.[51]

The Feminist saw her dilemma as part of a general trend. Since early 1966, she explained, "the people's lives have become more difficult. More people have been needed for production activities, to insure the families' livelihoods. Therefore, women have almost ceased taking part in NLF activities. At present, their days are entirely taken up with their trading or housework. They have no time to work for the NLF or to attend meetings." According to another informant, when husband, sons, and brothers got drafted, "the housewife and other female members of the family" were required to perform "all the jobs normally done by the men, such as planting, harvesting, and sometimes even soil digging." The same shift occurred in Hoi Cu, where "women have had to do hard work in the field because men were afraid of sweep operations and did not dare to go out into the field." Many informants noted the collapse of Women's Associations (as well as other mass organizations) after 1965. When urged to attend meetings, female villagers in My Hanh Dong demurred, saying they were too busy working "from dawn to dusk" in the rice paddies.[52]

But while escalation and family crises prompted some women to leave the Front, others were coming in. Straining to match U.S. escalation, the NLF called for a "reduction of administrative personnel" in its various branches, with the aim of shifting civilian cadres and rear service military personnel into combat units. Newly recruited females were then assigned to fill the vacated posts. According to one observer, almost two-thirds of the males in "the Front's various administrative sections" were replaced by females. In 1967, another noted, "the number of women recruits was larger than men recruits." "We never called on them to force them to go the way we did with the boys," a cadre remarked, and it seems that only a handful agreed to serve in the "Eastern Zone" (Tay Ninh). Nonetheless, stories about female soldiers in the PLAF circulated in the Rand milieu and in the villages.[53]

While these sightings seem tentative, encounters with Nguyen Thi Dinh, the legendary PLAF regional commander, left no room for doubt. According to a district cadre,

> she wore black pajamas, had a Colt hanging on her hip, and a large aluminum pot on her back. I took her for a woman laborer whose job was cooking for the troops. I asked Muoi Tien, the Village Party Committee Secretary: "Good heavens, why does a cook have to wear a gun!" He patted my shoulder and said: "Don't you raise your voice. She's Mrs. Ba Dinh, commander of the Region's Main Force." The cadres spoke about her with admiration. . . . They treated her as if she was the perfect leader in all fields especially in political, military, and troop [proselytizing]. She was also well known for her marksmanship with a Colt.

This informant told a story about the battle of My Phuoc in June 1962, a defeat for the PLAF caused when three battalion commanders disobeyed orders and embarked on a disastrous tangent of their own invention. "If we won," they reasoned, "the credit would be ours, and that Ba Dinh woman would be impressed by our talent." Summoned to explain himself, one appeared, "pale with fright," and received a merciless tongue-lashing. The next in line tried to beg off by saying he had a stomachache. Ba Dinh shouted: "May your ancestors be damned! Why didn't you choose to have a stomach ache during the battle? Then a lot of lives would've been spared."[54]

Perhaps the grapevine played on Ba Dinh's military prowess and volcanic temper in a way that exaggerated the female presence in the PLAF. But even an occasional encounter with women carrying guns was bound to unnerve onlookers, for sidearms were generally considered an emblem of command status and male potency. Thus a company officer in the PLAF was "very proud" of his Colt 45, "because the women went crazy about this Colt, which was dangling on his hips and which was the sign of a high position." When asked if he had ever come across NLF personnel using a "secret communication route," a member of an ammunition transport team responded: "Very often. I thought they were high-ranking cadres because they wore pistols. I also came across many women wearing pistols, and sometimes, the 267th and 514th Battalions during their moves." In this vignette, armed women appear in symbolically charged "secret" spaces, alongside "high-ranking" men with the power to kill.[55]

Similar redeployments occurred in the villages. In Tan Binh women substituted for men "in such works as standing guard in the street [and] acting as liaison agents." In Vinh Kim, after "two thirds of the young men in the village Party Chapter, as well as in the district administrative offices," were transferred into the PLAF, they "were replaced by women in all branches." According to a cadre, "whenever an ammunition transport team passed by my village, I had to motivate at least fifty villagers to participate in this team. Most of them were girls and women between 18 and 35 years of age." In Kim Son "there were about 25 women who volunteered to work in the porter team about one or two days a month. They transported the ammunition both by foot and by sampan." In Hoi Cu mixed teams of women and men worked in the "Civilian Labor sub section" and were expected "to have sampans and porters and stretchers to carry the wounded from the battlefield" and to work on hamlet fortifications.[56]

As the war dragged on, gender-linking in assignments receded. In 1967 there were six females among the nineteen members of a demolition training course, and the Ethnographer reported that "top Front authorities are now considering to recruit women to work as hamlet security cadres." These practices were bound to strip away the relative immunity women had previously enjoyed. An informant from Binh Duc thought that female militants were "high-spirited" because, "being women, they didn't have to flee as we, the men, did whenever a sweep-operation took place. They didn't run the risks of getting killed and, consequently, they aren't afraid." But by 1967 they could no longer count on that indulgence. A defector recounted that "after an hour of searching," he was able to help an ARVN detachment apprehend a female province-level cadre who operated "legally under the guise of a farmer's daughter. When she saw the troops—I was among them—coming she hastily pretended to be peeling cucumbers and bent her head to avoid our eyes." But the defector was able to penetrate a disguise that might have fooled the soldiers. Attempts to convert the prisoner were unavailing (she was "too imbued with communism"), so "the Captain had to order a helicopter to bring her to the proper authority to work on her."[57]

It was an ominous choice of words. After being captured, the eighty-six-year-old interviewee, who had served both the Viet Minh and the NLF as head of the "Soldiers' Mothers Association," was "mercilessly" beaten and could not sit up straight and cried incessantly during the interview. When ARVN commandos observed that the streets in Tan Ly Dong "were alight with torches and crowded with a great number of people busily moving around," they realized that a meeting had been called. The Ethnographer, who was chairing the session, could hear the troops "shouting and swearing while they made their advance toward the house. They said: 'You women, instead of staying home and being in bed, you attend meetings. You got what you asked for.'" In yet another manifestation of "modernization," allied forces accorded rural women a status equal to that of men. No quarter would be extended to either.[58]

Rand evidence suggests that women played a significant role in the popular movement. Quick to respond as the Liberation Front took control of the countryside, they worked in many sectors, perhaps most tellingly in the Women's Associations, where their success in arousing "the sensible instincts of the people" helped to make possible the advances of the golden period. Female contributions to the cultural revolution also deserve emphasis, as is evidenced in the generational struggles of the moment. Iconoclasts drew villagers into collective projects that achieved no resolution, not least with respect to gender, but did undermine prejudices and open minds and imaginations to previously dormant possibilities. Among the tragic consequences of escalation was the closing off of many-sided discussions about how to define and achieve the paradise on earth that many were longing to create.

As the war became more destructive, rural society was pushed to the brink with respect to the twin projects it had undertaken at the time of the concerted uprising. Under conditions of total war, the earlier balance between farm and movement work collapsed, and cadres had to choose between the two. Many women were then expected to produce the subsistence on which everyone depended in a war-ravaged and increasingly depopulated countryside. Those who plowed and harvested were performing an essential function, though one that carried them out of the Front and away from the positions of power the most ambitious among them had hoped to earn. The assignment was both a contribution and a setback, and in that sense was typical of their struggle to fulfill their responsibilities as daughters, wives, and mothers and also as activists in the movement.

Others joined or remained in the Front. Everywhere outnumbered but everywhere present, women continued to play a role after 1965, filling positions left vacant as men were transferred into combat units and sometimes themselves serving as fighters in the PLAF. "Ba Dinh" was not the only one to carry a gun. They and other intransigents kept the movement alive when escalation turned the countryside into an inferno.

CHAPTER SEVEN

ESCALATION AT GROUND LEVEL

The Soldier was a man of force and intelligence. Attracted by the Front's promise to "help the Poor Farmer class" and to provide education and a better life for young people like himself, he joined the movement in 1961, served as a village guerrilla, and in 1964 was invited to participate in a six-month course for medics, a coveted posting and a signal that he was held in high esteem. In March 1965 he asked for transfer to a combat unit and was seemingly headed for a distinguished career in the Front.[1]

Then in December 1966 came a shattering blow. During an ARVN sweep, "the underground tunnel in which I took cover collapsed. I was both wounded and suffocated. Blood flowed out of my ears, nose and mouth and I lost consciousness." He was evacuated to a dispensary for two months, then released—prematurely, he thought—and sent home to recuperate. "When I was strong and healthy," he declared, "I left my family to serve the Party day and night, but when I was wounded and no longer could fight, the Party didn't give me any money or any medical treatment, and sent me home to live as a parasite of my family. I was very hurt." His wife and parents "didn't even have enough to eat" and were forced "to pawn all their belongings to get the money to give me medical treatment. This awoke me from my dream, and I understood that I had sacrificed myself and worked for the Front uselessly. So I decided not to return to my unit, and not to do anything whatsoever for the Front." On hearing that a military escort was coming to get him, he defected to the GVN.

The Soldier was seeking a partial, one might say a gendered, liberation. He spent most of his adult life in the PLAF and volunteered for front-line duty in 1965, at a moment when more than a few cadres in villages and rear service positions were resisting the draft. Often punished for "lewdness" and seemingly among those combatants who, as he put it, were "entranced with fighting," he comes across in the interview as a tough and unsentimental man, not given to flowery language. And yet he recalled that life in the movement had been a "dream" and admitted being "very hurt" when the party set him aside.

The Soldier's choice of words was meant to explain his decision to rally, and indeed, in everyday speech people sometimes say that a remembered time was like a dream in order to emphasize the power of memory to inflate past happiness. But the image conveys another message, worth retaining. At first, popular consciousness did possess a dreamlike quality, as men and women left their families to serve the larger family of the revolution and came to believe that the usual constraints fixing limits on action and imagination had been overcome and that felicity was within reach. One might wonder how cadres and fighters who, unlike the Soldier, remained in the Front were able to survive and win the war. My purpose here is to pose a different kind of question, to ask what happened to the revolutionary dream when utopian hopes absorbed a devastating blow and when a shattered everyday life could no longer provide inspiration for the modernism of the popular movement.[2]

Villagers who spoke of the joyful mood of the golden period and of the horror and despair that followed often asserted that bombing and shelling were responsible for the change. In Diem Hy, "the best period lasted from 1962 to 1963. Life in the countryside was a lot of fun. Every village meeting was followed by a show given by the village entertainment team and the villagers were very eager to attend them. At night, the people stayed up late to drink or to chat. We didn't have to worry about shellings." In 1962 and 1963 "the morale of the fighters and cadres was high in spite of the fact that the troop strength of the battalion was low—only two companies—because the GVN didn't resort to bombings and shellings often." PLAF soldiers "had enough to eat and it was easy for us to ask the people to buy food for us. What's more, the people used to give us gifts, especially after an attack. Wherever the unit went, the troops saw the people joyfully going to the market, and they were warmly welcomed by the people as well." In Thanh Phu (CL), "the gayest years were in 1962 and 1963. It was the time everyone in my hamlet was happy. There weren't any shellings and bombings, and everyone could work on the fields without fear." But "from the beginning of 1965 on, life over there has been miserable. Shellings and bombings have occurred frequently and the villagers had to leave the hamlet for more secure areas. The hamlet, since then, has looked sadder and sadder."[3]

To Rand informants who did not understand why the government failed to respond in force before 1965, escalation seemed a logical, albeit belated, effort to seize the initiative. "After all," remarked a man from Hiep Duc, "we're at war." But within months, villagers realized that bombing and shelling were not primarily meant to answer guerrilla provocations and did not seem to be aimed at the PLAF. In hopes of isolating the Front, the government and its U.S. allies were trying to empty the countryside. In this new phase, the nature of the war and the possibilities available to the revolution were fundamentally transformed. This chapter examines the impact and especially the meaning of escalation from the point of view of people on the ground. It begins with the arsenal of modernization that U.S.-GVN forces deployed in an effort to empty the countryside. As costs multiplied and terror spread, villagers were caught in a holocaust that no one could explain or control. The rest of the chapter follows their efforts to account for the catastrophe descending on the countryside.[4]

ECOLOGICAL WARFARE

Rand informants who mention the use of herbicides by allied forces came from Hau My in western My Tho and Tan Phuoc in Go Cong province, located east of My Tho city, from NLF bastions and from areas of relative GVN strength, as in a Nhi Qui hamlet that "was in the government's hands most of the time." Thanh Phu (CT) had not been directly sprayed with "defoliation powder," noted a resident, but inhabitants "did notice that wind brought it over." It seems safe to assume that the spraying of chemicals from airplanes, whose pilots flew at high altitudes to avoid sniping, spread toxins throughout the province.[5]

Witnesses thought the purpose was to strip "leafy trees" and "thickly wooded and bushy places" that provided concealment for PLAF soldiers and to create sightlines, as in Phu Qui, where "GVN forces cut down a lot of trees and also sprayed chemicals on them," with the result that "from the Route, everything in the hamlet was visible." In Nhi My, "to prevent human beings from being hurt by the chemicals, the Front told the people to put lemon or garlic between two pieces of cloth and put the cloth over their noses and mouths when they were sprayed. Or the people could use ground reeds and coconut oil to put in their cloth mask." A witness from Phu Qui reported that at first, "villagers dared not even drink or use water which was judged to be contaminated," and that "they worried much about their crops," then later surmised that "defoliation chemicals did not kill the paddy and did not contaminate the water." A soldier also hoped for the best. "Our unit left the area where trees were dead," he declared, "but later when trees grew green again, we returned to the old place to camp." A more somber evaluation emerged in Thanh Phu (CT), where orchard production was "adversely affected by defoliation power and was noticeably reduced." A local observer reported that "fruit trees were not killed by this powder but their foliage turned yellow and their fruit rotted. Those orchards which were affected by this powder didn't yield anything."[6]

The Ethnographer conducted the most detailed survey. He began by affirming that defoliants "do not have any poisonous effects on human beings," then offered a more complex assessment of outcomes for plant life. Some bananas, coconuts, pineapple, sugarcane, and manioc ripened more quickly than usual and were "6 or 7 times bigger than their normal sizes," while others "will become dried up and die within three days," with bananas perhaps the most unpredictable and bizarre in their reaction to spraying. "Only banana trees and grass will sprout and grow again after a period of three or six months," while "coco trees, areca, pineapples and manioc are killed for good when sprayed." If "a great amount of chemicals are sprayed" on peach, orange, and tangerine trees, "they'd begin to dry up gradually from top to bottom," but if a small amount is sprayed, "all their leaves will also fall down, but after a period of six months, they will revive and grow up twice bigger than usual. Mango trees and bread fruit trees always die for good when sprayed." Turning his attention to yet another variable, he noted that "if chemicals are sprayed during the dry season, the trees can revive and grow again. But if they are sprayed in the rainy season, no trees can become alive again."[7]

As was his custom in all the work he did, the Ethnographer listened closely to what villagers had to say. Some reported that these chemicals "were like fertilizers" when dropped on rice paddies. "They only had to sacrifice one harvest and they would collect a double bumper crop in the following harvest. But orchard owners who live off their fruit crops strongly oppose this defoliation campaign. It usually takes them five to ten years for a tree to yield fruit, so if a fruit orchard is destroyed, the owner would go bankrupt." The Ethnographer was no botanist, but he was a curious man, fascinated by novelties, so it is not surprising that he devoted so much time to checking out the results of spraying. It was a scientific survey the Vietnamese did not have any choice about undertaking and one that was to bring consequences more sinister than even the most apprehensive of contemporary observers could have imagined.

Other forms of ecological warfare were more straightforward. According to an informant from My Phong, "there were cases in which armored personnel carriers came to a village, took all the rice and clothes, destroyed the ricefields so much that old women sometimes lay down on the road to prevent the tanks from destroying the harvest." In Diem Hy the Americans did not loot, rape, kill, or burn houses. "Quite the contrary, the soldiers even gave children candies, cookies, clothes, etc. They gave the old people cigarettes." Meanwhile, "out in the fields, amphibious vehicles have destroyed all the rice plants. Those amphibious vehicles moved by convoys of ten at a time, and they moved in horizontal lines. They moved forward and backward, and so there was not a single rice plant left standing. Each time those things were in the village, the villagers' sweat and toil all went down the drains." The intent was again clear in the story told by an informant from My Long. "In groups of ten, American amphibians ran through all the ricefields of Nhi Qui, My Long, and Phu Qui villages over and over again, until the rice plants were crushed, thus causing great loss to the population."[8]

Paddy fields were the main target: thirteen to fourteen hectares destroyed in Dang Hung Phuoc in 1965; one thousand bushels of rice lost in Nhi Binh (in a good year the yield of ten hectares of paddy fields) and two thousand bushels in a neighboring village in 1966. Another witness from Nhi Binh reported that "rice plants in the fields were crushed and fruit trees in the orchards were torn out of the earth by American amphibians and tanks." Other food sources also came under assault, as with "orchards and kitchen gardens" in Hiep Duc. In Tan Binh Thanh "fields and gardens were destroyed because amphibious vehicles tramped on them."[9]

In total, Rand informants noted crop destruction in sixteen villages, found in all four My Tho districts. This tactic, which had the effect of pillaging crops on which thousands of people depended, was employed in villages dominated by the Front, such as Cam Son and Nhi Binh, and in Thanh Phu (CT), which was plowed up "when the village was under VC control." But fields were also targeted in locales where the movement was relatively weak, such as My Long, My Phong, and Thanh Hoa. A plausible inference would be that crop destruction, among the most cold-blooded measures adopted by the Americans, was applied on a province-wide basis.[10]

THE SIN OF RUNNING

Again and again the transcripts portray villagers running for their lives. According to an observer from Duong Diem, "the people are afraid of operations, and run into hiding, gasping for breath. The cadres have to run even farther than the people, because they are afraid they might be captured." Evacuations were rendered even more chaotic when people took flight in different directions, as in My Phuoc Tay, where "those who had legal papers would run to the agroville," while others "would run toward the forest." In Binh Trung, when they heard that ARVN troops were approaching, the people "changed their clothes, wore white ones, rushed to the sampans and rowed towards the military posts while GVN soldiers walked on the canal bank and headed towards [the] village." Military deployment and civilian flight were orchestrated from above. "At each operation, there was always an aircraft circling over the villagers which directed the villagers to flee to the safest area." Among those refusing instructions were "youths who did not have legal papers" and who "fled and were resigned to accept the risk of being killed by the soldiers." Cadres sometimes joined crowds escaping toward designated zones. But more often they also ran and ran some more in search of a safe haven, as in Nhi Binh, where they "fled to Duong Diem or Binh Trung. If those two villages were not safe, again, they moved to Diem Hy."[11]

Air strikes were more difficult than troop sweeps to anticipate and were more likely to trigger a fatal panic. "Whenever an airplane flies by," stated a respondent from Tan Binh Thanh, "everyone stands still because if anyone runs out or into the house there will certainly be strafing. It is also because of this hanging threat that few people dare leave their children at home alone and go out to earn more money. Children aren't aware of the danger, when they see airplanes, and running here and there, thus bring much harm to the entire hamlet." Inhabitants in Hau My "got frightened and ran out to escape the fighting, but they were strafed by helicopters when they were in the ricefields, or orchards or when they were paddling their sampans to Hoa Khanh and Cai Be District Town." As a result, according to the Midwife, "over 30 people were killed."[12]

An informant from Hoi Cu explained that "if a person was detected by the helicopters it would be very difficult for him to run away and avoid the firing. Take the case of Ba Cay for example. He lived in My Hoa Hamlet. During an attack, he took cover in his orchard. But he was worried that his buffaloes might get killed and so he ran out to the fields to lead the buffaloes back to their shed. He was killed on the spot by the helicopters. This happened in May 1966. Cay was a civilian." In Nhi Binh in August 1967, during a sweep operation "about sixty people in the hamlet, including civilians and cadres, were strafed and killed by helicopters when they ran away in front of the troops to take refuge in the open fields." The informant in this case added that it was "the highest death toll the hamlet has ever suffered up to now." In the logic of counterinsurgency, running was a mortal sin.[13]

Helicopters were people-hunting machines. In describing a trip by sampan from Xuan Son to Cai Be Town an informant stated, "We were of course afraid of the helicopters with big lights." If they had attacked, "we would have jumped in the water; this was what the people usually did when the light hit them." Three people from that informant's village had been "killed at night by the helicopters." In Binh Duc helicopters hovered over the informant's settlement every night, "flashed the light on it and strafed it intensively. I came to the conclusion that if I continued to live in the hamlet, I would certainly be killed." The same tactic was employed in nearby Thanh Phu (CL), where helicopters "come over our village, shine lights on the ground and strafe." Even seasoned PLAF soldiers panicked when attacked. "They couldn't fire back at the helicopters because they were blinded by the powerful light, and also because they were frightened by the roar of the motors, the lights, and the bullets that were raining on them."[14]

Rural dwellers learned that individuals wearing "black pajamas" were coded as enemy combatants. A friend gave an informant from Phu Kiet "a set of white clothes" and a ride on his bicycle to Tan Hiep district. "I saw many ARVN soldiers," he recalled, "but they didn't stop to check me." Granting immunity to people dressed in white amounted to a declaration of class warfare, given that white was associated with affluence, while peasants wore black because field work soiled their clothes. Villagers were therefore obliged to participate in an incongruous charade. An informant from Quon Long noted that he and his neighbors "have been in a lot of difficult situations, but they seem so funny we cannot help laughing." For example, "farmers cannot expect to keep themselves clean while working in the field, but everybody has to carry along a set of white clothes and a white conical hat. We are ordered to do so by the [GVN] Village Office in order to avoid being shot at by aircraft. While working, if we see aircraft drop smoke grenades, everybody has to put on his white clothes at once and then walk slowly (no running) toward a nearby GVN outpost." The situation was laughable, but being forced on pain of death to dress up in one's best outfit and stroll with a stately gait was also humiliating. As more and more people in a risky situation put away their black pajamas, even the most obtuse counterinsurgency advisers must have realized that changes of clothing amounted to no more than a kind of "white flag," a guarantee that one would not fight back. That seems to have been the opinion of PLAF soldiers, who "were not supposed to be so cowardly as to don their white clothes to run away with the civilian population."[15]

THE BOMBING CAMPAIGN

Informants from several villages mention napalm bombs, which were dropped on a variety of targets: a school in Hoi Cu, a rice mill in Hung Thanh My, houses in Hau My. Hoa My hamlet in Binh Ninh was "completely destroyed" by napalm in 1965. According to a resident of Phu Kiet, "there were a lot of crops waiting to be harvested" in 1967. "Paddies were ripening then and all were burned by napalm. Since the beginning of this war, this was the first time the people living in my area had to endure such a calamity." In My Long a cadre's family, "including his pregnant wife, his two children and his mother-in-law, were killed by an incendiary bomb when they were taking shelter in a trench," and a similar blast was responsible for "four killed and twenty wounded" in Cam Son.[16]

B-52s carpet bombed a number of villages in the province. On the day of an attack on Hau My, the Midwife had a "premonition that something was going to happen" and decided to take refuge in her aunt's house. "I had just stepped into her house when the B-52s dropped bombs right near our house. I heard a deafening explosion and saw a big billow of smoke. We all ran to the trenches." Soon after, soldiers arrived on the scene but found no PLAF combatants. "I knew that the troops burned three houses near the Dap Ong Tai dike on that operation," she related, "because two of the women whose houses were burned down came to my aunt's house and wept. They complained that they had lost everything, that their houses had been burned down and their poultry had all been stolen." The bombs left craters "from 5 to 8 m wide." They had been "dropped in the ricefields and only the people who lived in the huts in the fields got killed."[17]

A raid near the Phat Da Pagoda left a deep impression on witnesses. According to a company officer, "after the bombing and strafing ended, the men went out to look at the destruction wrought by the B-52s and they were frightened even though the casualties had been light." The blasts resounded throughout the area. "The people were frightened to death, even though they were not hit." The informant in this instance was "seven or eight km from the bombed area—and yet all the houses were shaken to their foundations and I was awakened by the explosions. The people and troops were afraid." A Nhi My witness said, "My village has never been bombed by the B-52, but the people who have gone elsewhere to work came back and talked about B-52 bombing." Two bombs could "destroy 1 cong of ricefield, and B-52s are even worse." "If they drop bombs anywhere, the place is all cratered."[18]

THE CHOICE OF TARGETS

Rand informants thought that firepower was aimed at agglomerated settlements, as if the intent were to kill villagers and destroy their homes. A PLAF unit in Binh Ninh avoided casualties because "the artillery has often shelled inside of the hamlet whereas we lay along the edge of the hamlet, and therefore we very rarely got hurt." Another soldier remarked that for safety purposes his unit "was always stationed near the New Life Hamlets. These areas were sparsely populated. The aircraft usually flew deep into the liberated area where it was densely populated." In Hau My, the Midwife testified, "beginning in 1966, the village was heavily bombed and shelled. The villagers could no longer live clustered together." An informant from Cam Son noted that "the villagers do not dare to stay inside the village" and added, "I think that Cam Son was shelled so intensively because it was one of the first liberated villages."[19]

Clusters of people were bombed and shelled. In Thanh Hoa, "when a group of more than ten persons worked at any one place, they usually were good targets for airstrikes." Villagers in My Duc Dong "could not do anything on their ricefields during the day for fear of being strafed by aircraft," and in Tan Binh Thanh, "since 1966, the GVN has intensified its bombing and shelling, [so] people didn't dare to farm in groups." Weddings and funerals might also be hit. If villagers in My Tinh An did not secure permission from government authorities, "aircraft would take these parties for troop concentrations and would drop bombs on innocent people." It could be that pilots were unable to tell the difference between military units and players and spectators at a soccer game in Long An or a basketball game in Nhi My. Or perhaps the bombing of these crowds indicates that they thought of social life in the countryside as the enemy.[20]

Standing structures of all sorts were pulverized, and their community functions lapsed. In My Long "the only pagoda in the village was destroyed by a bomb," and in Tan Binh Thanh "a very big pagoda" was damaged, "and no repairs have been done." In Thanh Phu (CL) "both the Caodaist and the Catholic churches" were bombed in 1964, and a series of even more ecumenical raids hit the Buddhist pagoda and the Catholic and Cao Dai churches in Xuan Son. Schools and temples in My Phuoc were bombed and demolished, "all the schools" in Binh Trung were destroyed, four in Diem Hy were "completely destroyed," and one in Hoi Cu was "burnt down by napalm bombs." Even when buildings were spared, parents were afraid for their children, and in Hau My they made the "very painful" decision to keep them at home. In Cam Son, Hoa Dinh, Quon Long, Tan Binh Thanh, Tan Ly Dong, and Xuan Son, schools that were not demolished were closed when students stopped attending. In Vinh Kim parents kept their offspring at home because "the children had to dig foxholes near their school in order to have shelter when the village was shelled or strafed." In Phu Phong "two schools and one medical station" were leveled, as were a maternity clinic and a medical center in Quon Long.[21]

Many informants testified to the destruction of dwellings, which the Americans called "hooches" rather than homes, a usage suggesting that they saw them as small and flimsy places whose disappearance was only a trifle. An informant from Binh Ninh estimated that in summer 1965 "there were only 40 houses left from the 200 houses there were before November 1, 1963," and specified that "my house was burned by a shell in September 1964. My parents died in this shelling and all my papers were burned." Another, in spring 1966, declared that "about 95% of the dwellings are destroyed and Xuan Son looks very sad." In Tan Thuan Binh "all the houses" in one hamlet "are destroyed [and] therefore the people have all moved out into the fields to live." In Hoa Dinh bombing and shelling caused "a lot of damage to houses" and orchards, and in Huu Dao "many houses and trees were burnt." When areas near the Phat Da Pagoda were bombed, "one pregnant woman, one shopkeeper, and one child were killed," and in addition "about 100 houses were either completely burned down or partly destroyed." Eighty percent of the houses as well as orchards and "other properties" in Cam Son were "demolished," and an informant, hoping to buttress his credentials as a rallier, explained that "my service for the GVN was stated in a certificate which was given me at my discharge. All of them, however, were burned last March when my dwelling was hit by a bomb." Thanh Hoa was "devastated by bombings and shellings" and looked "very sad," and in a hamlet in Thanh Phu (CL), "all the houses were destroyed, and nobody lived there."[22]

A village guerrilla "felt quite discouraged at having seen so many bombings" and asked for leave to repair his house. His squad leader refused, saying, "Everyone's house has been destroyed or damaged and not only yours, so what do you have to complain about?" With churches, schools, clinics, and houses in ruins, it seemed as if no human effort could resist the U.S.-GVN campaign of destruction.[23]

THE HUMAN TOLL

The number of war casualties in My Tho is unknown, and it seems safe to assume that no precise estimate will ever be possible. But the Rand transcripts do at least suggest something about the pace and magnitude of the carnage. A few informants offered estimates for the pre-1965 period, indicating that in the years before escalation, artillery killed ten and wounded thirty in Cam Son and killed seventeen in Vinh Kim, and that thirty were killed "by acts of war" in Hoa Dinh. A witness from Long Trung stated that a 1963 bombing killed the wife of a policeman, while another, from Quon Long, remembered a bombing raid that year, which caused no casualties. The cost remained negligible in 1964 in Dong Hoa Hiep (a November shelling, no casualties) and Huu Dao, where a bombing raid killed one or maybe two, while elsewhere the tempo increased somewhat, as in Binh Ninh, with seven deaths, including the informant's parents; Binh Thanh Dong, where bombing killed five and wounded two; and especially Hoi Cu, where shelling killed nineteen, including two cadres and seventeen civilians, and wounded twelve. A war was going on and people were dying. But overall, these scattered reports seem consistent with the testimony cited earlier, which evoked the relative security of the golden period, at least in comparison to the bloodshed to follow.[24]

The death toll for 1965 emerges as a disturbing theme in the interviews. In Binh Ninh shelling killed six, and two bombing raids in February killed five and burned twenty. Shelling caused fifteen or sixteen casualties in Hau My, and a strafing incident killed three adults and five children. An April bombing sortie killed two guerrillas, two women, two children, and a man, and injured more than ten in My Hanh Trung, and another raid in February killed twenty in Xuan Son, while a second aimed at that village killed one guerrilla and "many women and children." Shelling in My Long caused "some deaths" and about fifteen wounded and in My Phuoc Tay killed and wounded twenty, while bombing killed a woman and her child.[25]

As firepower was increasingly deployed on a continuous basis, informants stopped focusing on individual incidents and instead tried to document the ongoing toll in more general terms, as in Phu An, where each attack left "usually one dead and one or two wounded," and Thanh Phu (CL), where each shelling killed one or two and wounded "many." Another informant from Thanh Phu noted that "in June, eight planes strafed and killed a lot of people." A witness from Trung An offered that shelling had killed many villagers and noted, "An entire family except for a baby died recently." Someone from Thanh Hoa had also stopped counting. "Bombings and shellings turn out to be incredibly terrible," he affirmed, "and people die like flies, but most of them are mere peasants because the cadres and the VC troops always manage to flee before the arrival of Government troops."[26]

Rand showed less interest in the topic in 1966–67, since everyone in its orbit already knew what was going on in the countryside and required no further intelligence on the matter. Besides, many villagers had evacuated, so in Hiep Duc there were no casualties because the people "had all moved elsewhere." (This informant did make an exception for two women killed during a B-52 attack.) Still, the evidence suggests that the death toll rose as the months passed. The Midwife noted that one strafing in Hau My killed thirty to forty and wounded a number of others, while another killed over thirty and wounded several more, and "a few" died as a result of a B-52 raid. She added, "Each time, two or three villagers were killed in the shelling." As for bombing, the best one could say was that "sometimes none of them were hit." Artillery killed "a lot" in Long Trung, and in Nhi My a family of seven were "crowded in their shelter when a shell hit it and killed them all." This informant specified that "only the children, women and old people (and not the guerrillas) got killed." Artillery salvos "caused a lot of casualties among the villagers" in Song Thuan, maybe four dozen, and "most of the dead were children," and in Tan Thuan Binh they killed about thirty. In Vinh Kim "random shelling killed many innocent people," and in Tan Binh Thanh, according to a resident, "the war has become more and more cruel, more and more people are being killed. In my village, sometimes shelling killed 5 or 6 persons in one night and 5 or 10 more were wounded."[27]

COLLAPSE OF MEANING

When asked, "Which reasons pushed you to rally?" an informant responded:

Life was getting more and more dangerous every day. The village was shelled day and night. Each day, we didn't dare to stick our necks out and go to work in the fields until 10:00 AM. At night, I didn't dare to sleep at home because I was afraid of shelling and of GVN commandos, so I had to wander from one place to another. Life was miserable and I couldn't stand it any longer. On top of all this, I still had to run for my life every time there was an operation. My wife was expecting a baby. I found that it was a sad, senseless thing for a married man like me to wander around every night and not to dare to sleep at home.

He evacuated in order "to rebuild my life and to do everything possible so that my wife can give birth to her baby safely." This speaker had left the Front in the summer of 1966 and had lived as a common citizen before rallying in July 1967. He quit the NLF and then, a year later, he "defected" from bombing and shelling.[28]

The reference to a "sad, senseless" life in this account suggests that physical danger only partially explains why villagers became refugees. Also responsible for spreading demoralization was the collapse of meaning, the senselessness of an existence at the mercy of U.S.-GVN firepower. The brute reality of a bomb or a shell falling from the sky and obliterating humans, farm animals, crops, and standing structures was so abrupt and devastating that it seemed an arbitrary stroke of fate rather than a human act. Seeking shelter from a menace that was difficult to explain or justify, the victims were gripped by a fear of death and by a fear that they were losing their minds. Fighting against panic, they tried to come up with an explanation for the destruction of their world.

At first they blamed the NLF. Those who had supported the initial revolt against the government were frightened and angry when escalation raised costs to unprecedented and unbearable levels. A guerrilla in Hoa Dinh declared:

> We often shot at the [ARVN] post because the Village Military Affairs Section ordered us to do so. The cadres said that we had to shoot at the post to shake up the soldiers and make them think about defecting from their ranks. The villagers knew that the shellings were the GVN retaliations towards our random pot-shots at the posts. Therefore they strongly hated the guerrillas. We reported this situation to the Village Military Affairs Section, but they argued that we were at war, and we had to shoot at the enemy. In 1961, the villagers were rather nice toward us but this year they changed their attitude. Before, they had often given us chickens to eat, but now, it was very hard to obtain anything from them.

In Vinh Kim the inhabitants were "angry at the guerrillas who shot at aircraft or at the sweep operation forces and made them retaliate by shellings. At those times, the villagers cursed the guerrillas to their face and accused them of being the cause of their hardships." In My Duc Dong "the villagers were most resentful of the guerrillas. They said among themselves, 'If the guerrillas did not shoot at the aircraft, the planes would not fire back!'"[29]

Some tried to negotiate local cease-fires. In My Luong district forces encircled a post in July 1965 and conducted a siege that wounded one and demoralized an ARVN platoon. In response, artillery demolished a shelter belonging to a trader, killing eleven members of his family. "The people protested against the encirclement and said: 'We are living in peace, why do you start shooting them and harassing them to make them return the fire and cause damage to the people?'" In Phu My a former hamlet cadre tried to mediate between the two sides. When guerrillas sniped at a post, he went to the marketplace and urged the GVN not to retaliate. The soldiers "told him to stop the guerrillas' harassment, otherwise, they would fire into the village and innocent people would be killed." On returning home, "he also requested the guerrillas to stop their firing into the GVN post so that the villagers could live in peace."[30]

These testimonies suggest that both peasants and guerrillas were caught in an impasse. Residents of My Luong and Phu My sought a way to "live in peace," to contract out of a war that allowed for no private truces. At the same time, continuing to fight when guerrillas seemed capable only of taking "pot-shots" at a heavily armed adversary seemed an exercise in futility. The Phu My mediator said, "If they wanted to attack the post, they could do so, but not just snipe at it." Villagers in Binh Thanh Dong declared, "We must say to the guerrillas that if they want to fight the GVN, they had better attack the post directly." Residents in Hoi Cu applauded the Main Force 263rd Battalion and contrasted its hammer blows with the feeble sallies of the local fighters. "It is better to carry out big attacks," they argued, "than to fight like the guerril-las," who "only cause the people to get killed and to suffer damage, while causing no harm to the GVN at all, because each time they fight against a GVN sweep operation and fire at aircraft the village is bombed and shelled." A hamlet in Hoi Cu "was shelled when the guerrillas withdrew through it after they had shot at Cau Ong Cu military post. That made the villagers angry and they said to the fleeing guerrillas: 'Why don't you stay here to enjoy the fight?'" In My Long, "whenever the villagers saw the guerrillas in their fight-ing positions they usually said: 'We all may be killed because of you! They're very strong, don't stand against them! You can't overcome them!'"[31]

At first, bombardment of the countryside made a kind of sense. Thus An Than Thuy was "bombed many times because of the presence of the VC," and Dao Thanh "was shelled only when the guerrillas shot at the post or when GVN officials got information about the presence of the Front's units within the hamlet." An informant from Binh Ninh declared, "My hamlet has never been shelled without apparent reason," and in Thanh Phu (CT) a hamlet "was shelled only when the guerrillas shot at the post." All of these observations date from 1965, when the larger intent of the bombing and shelling was not yet visible.[32]

Peasants who wanted to believe that there was some excuse for the fire-power aimed at their villages thought back to events in the hours and days before the attacks in hopes of pinpointing a cause. In Diem Hy, recalled one informant, "the guerrillas of my hamlet shot at an aircraft that came over to drop leaflets. Five hours later, the hamlet got shelled again. The villagers thought they were shelled because of the guerrillas' shooting at aircraft. Therefore, the guerrillas are strongly hated by the villagers." Perhaps there was a connection between the sniping and the artillery salvo, but the five-hour delay introduced a measure of uncertainty into the calculation. Doubt seemed even more in order when Front troops passed through Hoi Cu. "The village wasn't bombed until the afternoon of the following day, but by that time all the troops had moved away." Still, at least one observer surmised that the village was bombed "because Front troops had passed through it." The causal sequence was also murky in Phu Nhuan Dong, where, "on May 4, 1965, mortars sent in about seven or eight rounds at around three o'clock in the afternoon. An old man was killed and a boy, 13 years old, was wounded. The people blamed the guerrillas because the previous day the guerrillas had shot at a post."[33]

Gradually this way of interpreting U.S.-GVN warfare lost credibility. "Sometimes there were apparent reasons, sometimes we were shelled recklessly," stated an informant from My Hanh Trung. The qualifier "apparent," which is often employed in the transcripts with respect to reasons for attacks, hints at a growing doubt that bombs and shells were a response to guerrilla provocations. A man from Hiep Duc said, "If the village was bombed or shelled when there were liberation troops stationed near their houses or when the guerrillas shot at aircraft, the people couldn't blame the GVN." But they "resented the GVN when it shelled the village day and night even when there were no liberation troops in the village." Not surprisingly, the 514th Battalion's attack on a post in Hoa Dinh was followed by retaliatory bombing, but on another occasion two "skyraiders" bombed "without apparent reason, and that infuriated the villagers." A resident of My Long declared, "Sometimes we were shelled because of the presence of VC in my hamlet, but most of the time, they were only reckless shellings." In Long Trung, according to one informant, "when the hamlet was shelled or strafed because of the VC presence, the villagers were resentful of the VC. But if the shellings were reckless, they were resentful of the GVN." Another reported that "if the aircraft knew it was the people, they would not shoot. Sometimes, they could not make the distinction and shot blindly and killed 5 or 6 or even a dozen persons."[34]

As the months passed and the villagers tried to understand the violence deployed by the two sides, their anger increasingly turned against the government and the United States. According to an informant from Nhi My, "whenever the guerrillas shot at the post and provoked a shelling the people were very mad." But he also stated, "To tell the truth, the shellings only killed the innocent people. During the few months I was in the village following my desertion, I noticed that no VC got killed in the shellings, and that only the people did." At times, "the people were hit when they were walking in the village. Whenever they saw the guerrillas moving around in the village, they knew that something was going to happen so they gathered all their children and took cover in the shelters, [so] even if the village was shelled they didn't get hurt. But many times, they were on their way to the market when the village was shelled, [and] in this case there was no place where they could take cover." This informant might have been correct in claiming that the guerrillas were "hated," and he might have been correct again in saying that the Front was "winning the support of the people." His analysis suggests that villagers distinguished between the low-level provocations of the guerrillas and the massive firepower of the other side. He concluded, "The GVN is stronger in terms of weapons and equipment, but it doesn't have the support of the people."[35]

According to a witness from Binh Phan, guerrillas shot at a post, which responded with artillery shells and hit a wedding party. "The hostess was wounded and one woman had an arm broken," he recalled.

> I was told that the guerrillas shot at the post right at that time because this family had flown a National flag over its house. The villagers were most resentful of the guerrillas who caused casualties among the villagers by shooting at the post, but nobody dared to ask them to stop shooting. There were other injuries in other mortar shellings since 1964. At each shelling, my whole family rushed to the trench. I often heard my father complaining: "It is nonsensical to shoot at the post recklessly like that. If they want a fight they only have to attack the post once and for all. This reckless shooting only hurts innocent people."

The father's complaint had merit, but surely villagers noticed that, in responding, the government troops ignored the guerrillas and instead chose to assault people who had committed no offense. The business about the flag may have been an invention on the part of the informant, intended to curry favor with Rand by underscoring the malice of the Front. But even if the guerrillas shot at the post as a way of punishing those who displayed the GVN banner, there could be no justification for the artillery barrage, which punished supporters of the "national" cause for offenses committed by the NLF.[36]

This was not the only example of "friendly fire" in the transcripts. A hamlet in Diem Hy "has been shelled sometimes although it is controlled by the Government." When guerrillas harassed a strategic hamlet in My Long, "the Binh Duc artillery had often fired at the hamlet and wounded many people, when it was supposed to be firing at the VC troops in support of the defenders of the Strategic Hamlet." A similar lack of discrimination was evident when a strategic hamlet in An Thai Dong "was shelled about three to five times a month." Villagers in Binh Phuc Nhi complained, "The district chief does not have any compassion for us, he just ignores the fact that we are living within the New Life hamlet's boundaries and goes on shelling us callously." The same thing happened in Vinh Kim, where, according to a cadre, GVN soldiers "looked as dissatisfied as we did whenever Vinh Thoi [hamlet] was shelled without apparent reason. One of them was also killed by these reckless shellings because the shells hit square on their post." The government's readiness to strafe and bomb made clear that everyone in the countryside was seen as an enemy.[37]

In Cam Son villagers "accused the GVN of cruelty, and some of them cursed it." In Trung An they "accused the GVN of being too cruel" and "strongly cursed the GVN for these shellings." Even though the villagers were "extremely resentful of the GVN," they feared going on protest demonstrations because of the government's habit of arresting "many" demonstrators. Villagers in Song Thuan "were very resentful of the GVN. They cursed Thieu and Ky and the Americans violently. They accused the Americans of bringing mortars into Vietnam to kill the people." Perhaps I missed a reference here and there, but this is the only mention of Thieu and Ky in my notes on the transcripts, a neglect that makes manifest Rand's reluctance to explore the topic of peasant attitudes toward the Saigon government and its assault on the rural population.[38]

Villagers blamed the United States as well. An informant from My Long averred that the American troops "did not commit barbarous acts as had been rumored. They did not loot or rape anyone," then remarked: "Nevertheless, it should be pointed out that wherever they advanced, they were accompanied by bombing and shelling. Consequently five innocent people have been killed so far." Someone from My Duc Tay declared, "The American soldiers are friendly and outgoing, they like to help people, they talk in a cheerful manner with people, and they behave in a very friendly manner with everyone" and also that "the people who live in the Front-controlled areas hate the Americans a lot, because they live daily under the bombing and shelling of the Americans." Villagers in Binh Phuc Nhi complained that "the Americans shell us too much and cause casualties to the people, but they do not harm the VC!" and in Dang Hung Phuoc they "blame the Americans because they know that the Americans started this war and that the people are being killed by American weapons and bombs."[39]

Ambushes and sniping at ARVN posts brought retaliation, usually far in excess of the original provocation, and villagers had a right to ask if enemy counterattacks were raising costs to a point where the Front had to seek an alternative to guerrilla warfare. But the U.S.-GVN practice of responding at the expense of "innocent people," in the process killing far more children than soldiers, was politically counterproductive and morally odious. It also could not be justified in military terms, since PLAF combatants usually found ways to escape or to protect themselves, while civilians were likely to panic, thus increasing their chances of getting killed. Children and the elderly were often unable to flee in time, as in Tan Thoi, where VC and villagers took cover during an air attack, and "one old man was killed on the spot because he could not run."[40]

A CAMPAIGN TO DESTROY EVERYTHING

Perhaps hoping to embellish on his qualifications as a convert to the GVN cause, the Platoon Leader offered a plan to encourage defections. "Have the GVN take one or two villages from a district along a route of communications, and not fire on this place," he suggested. "Let the people concentrate there to trade. In order to avoid revealing the plan, the GVN should fire a few token rounds in the vicinity every once in a while to keep the Front from getting suspicious." The families of cadres would prefer to frequent a marketplace that appeared relatively safe, and when they did, the government would be advised to "help them with money," win their confidence, then encourage them to defect. Perhaps what is most notable about this scheme was the unintended humor in the suggestion that any pause in the bombing and shelling would arouse suspicion.[41]

Bombardments had become a fact of life, with a logic and momentum of their own. Even in 1965 an informant from Binh Ninh was saying: "We have been shelled as many as ten times a month. On some days, there were two or three shellings. In each shelling, there were about 50, 70 or 100 shells. There were no apparent reasons for these artillery shellings. I did not know why we were shelled. I tried to understand the motivation of these shellings, but I could not. I was very dissatisfied and angry because my parents were killed by the shells." At the end of 1966 a hamlet in Hau My had been abandoned by almost all its inhabitants. One resident recalled: "There were only six or seven men, a few old women, and women and children left, so the Hamlet Farmers Association Committee didn't have anything to do. The Front didn't have any other infra-structure organizations or cadres there. Even though the hamlet was deserted, we still had to live in hiding, because the hamlet was bombed heavily every day—it made no difference to the aircraft that the hamlet was deserted; they continued to bomb it all the same." When asked to speculate on the purpose of the shelling, a man from My Duc Dong said: "I did not know why. The GVN said it shelled to kill the Viet Cong or something. I really did not know." An informant from Nhi Qui was taciturn yet still spoke for many when asked, "Do you know why they shot these mortars?" His answer was "No."[42]

The truth resisted by everyone was that there was nothing villagers or cadres could do to prevent bombing and shelling. In My Long,

> the District Committee did contribute its opinions and sent down a plan of constructing several houses on orchard lands and camouflaging them in order to deceive aerial observation. Aircraft pilots might think that these were NLF bases and installations, and they might bomb or shell them. In this case, all the ricefields would be safe, and the populace would return to the liberated areas. However, this plan has proven unsuccessful. The ARVN airstrikes and artillery firing were all over the village, and no place was spared.

In Vinh Kim, villagers would say, "Each morning, when we wake up, we don't know whether we are living until we open our eyes." An informant noted that villagers in Thanh Phu (CT) "came down with colds most often, but recently, from late 1965 to late 1966, most of them were afflicted with heart disease because they were very scared of shelling." Someone from Thanh Hoa declared: "In the old days, life in rural areas was so quiet and peaceful, at present it is full of dangers and violent death. When you get out of your house, you must beware of booby-traps, grenades and land mines. Day and night, bombs and shells rain down on the village and people may be killed at any time. It is impossible to find a safe place to live in." In Phu Phong, "whether planes attack or whether bombs fall on their heads, the people are terrified." When asked if villagers discussed "current events," an informant responded: "No. They usually said: 'We are scared to death! The GVN is dropping too many bombs in the countryside.'"[43]

In Long Tien, "whenever a clash was over, we went home and saw only devastation and damage everywhere in the village. Houses were burned down, fruit trees were knocked over, and the mood of the villagers became most gloomy. Every villager looked depressed." In My Duc Dong people "could not do anything on their ricefields during the day for fear of being strafed by aircraft, and at night they had to cope with shellings. They often said, 'How miserable our life is! We fear aircraft, sweep operations and artillery shellings, and we cannot work for our living.'" In Phu Phong "in 1964, the people were still living in the hamlet. They constructed trenches, and built fences to make a combat village, but, lately, they don't have the spirit to do anything any more." "Demoralized" activists quit or rallied, as in Tan Ly Dong, and a soldier from Thanh Phu (CL) remarked, "Whenever I had to pass by my hamlet, I felt disheartened upon seeing that it was completely destroyed and realizing that all my property was lost." He added that the mood of despair was "shared by my comrades."[44]

Some in the Rand orbit were both troubled and excited to realize that the United States might finally have hit on a strategy to defeat the enemy. In the course of discussion with the Instigator, a staffer asked: "Now, if humanitarian considerations are to be put aside, do you think that shellings are helpful to the GVN to win over the Front? If yes, do you think the GVN would have to continue to shell villages in order to make the hostilities come to an end more quickly?" The Instigator was a skilled dialectician, a "master of polemic," as he was fond of saying, and he must have delighted in the opportunity to address this conundrum. "I think the shelling of Long Dinh is indispensable if humanitarian considerations are to be excluded from my judgment," he responded. "From experience, I realized that the Front is most strong in villages which haven't been shelled and that on the contrary, it weakens there where shellings frequently happened. To wage Front propaganda, to sow hatred against the GVN, Front cadres need quietude." It therefore followed that "if humanitarian considerations are to be discarded, I will say, as a pure military statement, that shellings really serve the final victory of the GVN."[45]

Another Rand staffer was pondering the same question. "In your opinion," he said to the interviewee, a former PLAF soldier, "the majority of fighters want to escape. What types of difficulties impede them from making their escape? What way can they be helped?" The subject was not as glib as the Instigator and did not bother pretending that the war could be won by "helping" Front personnel. "In my opinion," he declared, "there is one sure way to get all of them out here soon and that is to bombard them with F-105's and fighter-bombers." A witness from Quon Long was similarly blunt. "The GVN should fight more violently," he recommended, and "pour more bombs to push the people into rallying to it."[46]

U.S. war making was not designed to win friends, and local militants were on solid ground in claiming that "the United States and the GVN were murdering the people." The enemy "shelled into the orchards so that the people had to run out to the fields, then shelled into the paddy fields to make them move closer to the Strategic Hamlet, and finally some would move into the Strategic Hamlet out of fear of bombs and bullets." In Hoi Cu "the people resented the GVN a great deal," and in hopes of turning the villagers' anger to their advantage, cadres declared: "Even if you remain simple citizens and don't join the revolution, you'll also get killed because bombs and shells do not spare anyone. The American aircraft are not going to spare anyone." But political commitment was one thing, survival another. Inhabitants "understood that if they were attached to their property and stayed in the village to be with the revolution, they would have to run the risk of getting killed." The outcome of the war would depend on whether people of the Liberation Front would acquiesce and leave their homes.[47]

CHAPTER EIGHT

MAPPING THE EXODUS

In the years before escalation, rural dwellers were on the move. During the Resistance many rose to higher echelons of the Viet Minh, and the guerrilla army and the French both drafted young people away from their homes and assigned them to distant battlefields. After 1960 the Front promoted a number of village activists out of their native hamlets, and as war intensified, the armed forces of the two sides uprooted a new generation of soldiers. Destabilizing dynamics associated with the political and military history of the region were only part of the story, for even without war and revolution, modernizing trends were refashioning the social order of the countryside. Cultivators ventured out to markets in My Tho and Saigon, while others took to the road in search of work, often seasonally, but sometimes for extended periods. The popular movement of the 1960s was in part a response to the shifting of habits and relations already in progress. It aimed to satisfy the aspirations of country people whose horizons were widening, and at the same time its land reform and other policies heightened class consciousness among disaggregated peasants who were drawn back to their native places, where a village-based revolution offered prospects for a better life.

The policy of generating refugees should therefore not be characterized as an intrusion into a bucolic countryside. Escalation targeted communal groupings that shared a utopian hope and in the process jarred loose a population that had temporarily found a center of gravity within the Front. It revived and accelerated an earlier pattern of mobility, in the process scattering a beleaguered peasantry far and wide. The purpose of this chapter is to map the exodus set in motion by an escalating war and to reflect on its meaning for the peasants of the delta.

POPULATION SHIFTS

A sector-by-sector review indicates that the policy of generating refugees disaggregated agrarian society. Villages in the northern tier of the province bordering on the Plain of Reeds were subject to intensive bombardment.

More than 50 percent of residents had left Hau My by 1965, and later commentators estimated the refugee flow at 70 to 90 percent, leaving some areas completely deserted. A few people evacuated Thanh Phu (CL) in 1965, declared a resident, who added that the refugees were "not numerous." But by 1966 "many" had departed, and an observer in 1967 estimated that 90 percent of the people in his hamlet had moved to the GVN zone. According to an informant, Hung Thanh My was "almost empty" even in 1963. "At present, there are no houses left," noted a witness in 1965, "and Hung Thanh My is covered with mangrove plants." One informant thought that refugees had gone to nearby Phu My, but another, who was familiar with the situation there, suggested that in 1967 fewer than 10 percent of Phu My inhabitants remained, while still another noted that "almost all" had left for more secure areas in My Tho or had fled into Long An province.[1]

The three villages of Nhi Binh, Long Dinh, and Tam Hiep were situated in the center of My Tho province, adjoining Route 4, not far from the Plain of Reeds and within striking distance of the province capital to the south. Respondents familiar with Nhi Binh affirmed that a majority or "most" of the inhabitants had left the village, with one specifying that the decline was from eight hundred households to forty. Another witness thought that only 30 percent of the population remained in Ap Tay hamlet. Tellingly, he characterized this place, from which 70 percent of the residents had evacuated, as "relatively safe." Ap Bac was the site of a storied PLAF victory in 1963, but by 1967 the hamlet was "a deserted place," and in Am Nam hamlet "houses still remain, but there is not a soul there." By contrast, in another hamlet, close to Route 4 and therefore less likely to be bombed and shelled, there were 105 households in 1965 and 170 in 1967, because "several families have left insecure hamlets and resettled there." Rand learned less about the situation in Long Dinh, but one informant did offer that "the majority of the Village Youths have left and are now in Saigon or in the district or the province capitals." Often shaken by reverberations from nearby battles, Tam Hiep inhabitants repeatedly decamped. After being occupied by the ARVN Seventh Division, several of its hamlets were classified as "secure" places and received a flood of refugees from adjoining and still contested areas.[2]

Front supply routes from the coast through Ben Tre and on toward the Plain of Reeds passed through Cho Gao, at the eastern end of the province. Reporting in 1965, several observers noted that inhabitants of Binh Ninh were running for cover when battles took place nearby, with one specifying that only forty dwellings in his hamlet remained out of two hundred. A later commentator reported that the people had deserted their homes and were camping in the fields. A man from Hoa Dinh said that there used to be 4,800 residents in the village; that in 1964, 2,000 people lived in the liberated zone; and that in June 1965, a little more than 1,000 remained. An informant in 1967 estimated that two-thirds of the villagers had moved out.[3]

Establishment of the Dong Tam military base in Binh Duc, a few kilometers to the west of My Tho city, turned the area into a hot zone. Wide areas were paved over in preparation for the construction of the base, and mud spewed by dredges ruined paddy fields in adjoining Thanh Phu. Displaced peasants had to move into GVN-controlled Ap Cho hamlet to qualify for jobs with the Americans, while at the same time intensive patrolling rendered other areas uninhabitable. "My hamlet no longer counts," said one informant from Binh Duc; "there are no cadres and no people left." Another reported that his hamlet was "as deserted as a jungle." In Thanh Phu, where there used to be close to 1,000 families, in early 1967 only 115 remained. A former resident stated, "The village is now deserted." Meanwhile, as ARVN and U.S. troops secured Ap Cho as well as two other nearby hamlets, refugees from Thanh Phu "began to move there in great numbers."[4]

In the eastern sector of the Front's 20/7 heartland region lay nine villages, which U.S.-GVN strategists sought to secure. In Binh Trung calculations of the refugee flow ranged from two-thirds to seven-tenths to eight-tenths. "My village is now miserable," a resident stated. "No one stays in the village," declared a witness from Long Hung, while another remarked that "almost all" of the inhabitants had moved away and only twenty of four hundred families remained. "Most" residents of Phu Phong and four-fifths of the population of Ban Long were said to have evacuated. Half of the people had moved out of Song Thuan, while the stay-behinds "dug underground shelters and when darkness comes, their entire family gets into these shelters to spend the night." Judged by the Front a "weak" village, Vinh Kim was nonetheless heavily bombed. In Vinh Quy hamlet only twenty families were left of the 145 who had lived there before, and Vinh Phu hamlet was also "largely" depopulated. Meanwhile, after Vinh Thanh hamlet was pacified by the GVN and the Americans, five thousand of the village's eight thousand residents hastened to settle there, so many that people took to calling it "Vinh Kim town." "It is overcrowded because it is a gathering point not only for the Vinh Kim inhabitants but also for the villagers coming from the neighboring villages," an informant observed.[5]

Strategically located around a major intersection in the middle of the 20/7 zone, three villages in the Ba Dua sector absorbed the full brunt of the war, with Long Trung singled out for an especially heavy bombardment. A Rand interviewer was told that "all the people" in the village "had fled to Cai Lay because there were too many shellings and bombings." "Many" had also left Long Khanh in 1965, while "most" inhabitants deserted Long Tien, and after a series of battles in 1967, others "complained only about the destruction of their lodgings and the devastation of their orchards. They worried about leaving the village permanently, and their common opinion was that it was impossible to continue to stay in the village."[6]

Nine additional villages, including many Front strongholds, were located in the western sector of the 20/7 region. Hoi Son and Cam Son were the most heavily bombed in the area, and Rand interviewees from Cam Son offered grim accounts of a site laid waste by many "big clashes," with inhabitants fearful of "butterfly bombs" that the Front was unable to defuse. An observer reported that only 400 of the 5,600 residents remained in place, and several estimated that 90 percent or more of the residents had fled. My Long originally contained 700 households and 3,000 inhabitants, but "many" had departed by 1967. Speaking early in 1966, two witnesses said that only 142 people still lived in Xuan Son, and later reports suggest that the number had shrunk even further.[7]

GVN records indicate that by 1970, population levels in NLF bastions such as Ban Long, Cam Son, Hiep Duc, and Hoi Son had fallen below a thousand and in some instances below one hundred. But these are isolated cases, and population declines elsewhere do not seem as vertiginous as Rand informants claimed. The reason for this apparent disagreement is that, while an unknown but perhaps considerable number of refugees left the countryside for the towns, a lot of the movement was within the province, so that losses in one place were balanced by increases elsewhere. Government statistics call attention to an extraordinary volatility in residential patterns during the 1960s, with forty-two out of ninety villages in My Tho registering population losses of more than 10 percent, while thirty-eight others gained more than 10 percent. Even more significant was intra-village movement as people left areas thought by the government to be cleansed of subversion and therefore not so relentlessly attacked as were VC zones, a pattern we have seen in Nhi Binh, Tam Hiep, Binh Phu, and Vinh Kim.[8]

The village of Dong Hoa Hiep illustrates these tendencies. In 1960, according to government sources, its population of 14,063 was the largest in the province. Ten years later it had mushroomed to 27,197. According to one informant, An Nghia, one of the hamlets in the village, "has never been strafed or shelled to date, because it is close to the district town. Nevertheless, the An Nghia people were very afraid of being shelled and strafed. An Nghia hamlet has been considered a secure area, and the people coming from Hiep Duc, the next village over, poured into it to settle. An Nghia is now bigger than before." The near doubling in the size of Dong Hoa Hiep was the result of a desperate improvisation, as thousands of people from nearby villages ran for their lives. Fear also must have set people in motion from one part of the village to another, for after all, even the residents of a "secure area" such as An Nghia "were very afraid of being shelled and strafed."[9]

A second complicating factor when it comes to interpreting refugee flows has to do with the way informants defined terms such as "hamlet" and "village." Emphasis on southern individualism and on contrasts with the solidary villages in the North has created an erroneous impression of residential patterns and communal culture in the South. To be sure, hamlets in the Mekong Delta were often widely separated, so there was no one village residential area enclosed by hedges or bamboo ramparts as in the North. Speaking of Thanh Phu (CL), an informant observed that it "was crowded and was a big village strung out along many canals such as the Commercial Canal, the Bong Ray, Kinh Cha La and Kinh Muoi Canals." At the same time, houses were not "strung out" to the point where they could be characterized as dispersed individual dwellings. On the contrary, the village is pictured as a "crowded" place. With houses side by side and with orchards as a common point of reference, peasants in My Tho lived clustered together. When witnesses said that a "hamlet" or "village" was "deserted," they were referring to those agglomerated settlements.[10]

LOOKING FOR SAFE HAVENS WITHIN THE VILLAGE

Rand informants indicate that refugees fled to Cai Lay, Cai Be, Chau Thanh, and other district towns, to Tan Phong island in the Mekong River, to My Tho and Saigon, and to Long An, Kien Phong, Ben Tre, and Tay Ninh provinces. But most tried to stay within their home villages. They built huts in the fields, along roads or canals, or close to posts or marketplaces, which were less likely to be bombed and shelled than were settlements, or, for the same reason, into strategic or new life hamlets controlled by the government. The Midwife described a common adaptation when she observed that "beginning in 1966, the village was heavily bombed and shelled. The villagers could no longer live clustered together. They tore down their houses and built thatched huts in the paddy fields."[11]

Living in shacks here and there, rural dwellers gained a measure of security, but with no trees around, sun and heat were difficult to endure. Women "were used to life in the hamlet where their children had the run of the orchards," but now everyone had to spend the day in "narrow huts," where "guests didn't have a place to sit when they came to visit. This made life miserable for the people." As a man from Hoa Dinh declared, "farmers love to be with people from their own village." On their own, they were cut off from the grapevine and from Front informational meetings and could not keep track of what was going on in the war. Gone also was a sense of closeness to others who shared their problems and joined together to find solutions. "There are about 800 inhabitants remaining at present in my village," reported an informant from Nhi Binh. "But their houses are scattered out in ricefields, far from one another. They are not grouped together in one place and able to provide mutual support for each other." Cadres and guerrillas camped far away in the orchards, and so uninvited guests in the form of ARVN patrols felt free to "come by to check" for the presence of the Viet Cong. When an informant said, "Life became unbearable for me, and I felt isolated from society," he expressed a common loneliness.[12]

Field huts did possess one advantage in that they allowed residents to continue cultivation of the staple crop on which everyone depended. To be sure, the agrarian economy had to undergo a painful contraction. "Now that the people have had to move their houses to the middle of the paddy fields," explained an informant, "they needed more cash than before because they had to buy more food. Before they could raise poultry and pigs, but now there isn't any room for them in the middle of the paddy fields to breed these animals." Still, the ability to plant and harvest rice constituted a hedge against starvation and persuaded many not to risk a plunge into the urban labor market.[13]

In strategic or new life hamlets the government sometimes provided refugees with family and housing allowances, rice, wheat, sugar, milk, and cooking oil, blankets and mosquito nets, seedlings, and fertilizer, plus fish and pigs for breeding purposes. Cadres warned that "those who rallied would be helped by the GVN for the first six months only. Each day they would get six or seven piasters for food or something like that, but what would they do after six months?" One informant declared: "I was told that some months before, the refugees in Tan Phong were given assistance from the GVN, but that assistance has been stopped." As a result, "many of them are living in dire conditions." The Midwife noted that cash payments "were not enough," because even if the government distributed money to refugees, "it would do so for a few months only, and after that they would have to be on their own." Another commentator observed that funds intended for the assistance program were embezzled by officials, who also insisted on bribes before they would help with paperwork. "Many people who are not refugees were given financial assistance by the GVN," to the point where villagers exclaimed that government personnel "accepted so many bribes in the past, they deserve to be killed (*an hoi lo nhieu qua, bay gio chet cung dang*)."[14]

Even if it had been properly administered, government aid could not have secured the livelihood of the refugees. Land grants to cultivators who had abandoned their original holdings would have been a logical solution, but such an approach was not feasible, given that an alternate countryside, different from the one the GVN and its allies were bombarding, could not be conjured out of thin air. "There were people who submitted 5 to 7 letters to the administration to request some land," noted an informant in early 1967, "but all of them were turned down. The main reasons were that there is very little land available whereas the refugees have greatly increased. There is not enough land to satisfy every request." The presence of the Americans created jobs around Binh Duc, and the ARVN drafted as many of the young men as it could. But as the first trickle of migrants turned into an exodus of thousands, these measures did not come close to absorbing all of the refugees, who worried "about their everyday life because there are many people in the New Life Hamlets and very few jobs." The reality was that the GVN would help displaced populations "for a period of time only, and that once they were settled down, they would have to look for a job and be on their own."[15]

Located on the northeast border of Cho Gao district, Quon Long lay astride NLF communications routes and served as a campsite for the PLAF 261st and 514th battalions. In response, the government bombed and shelled, established two new life hamlets and two posts, and patrolled up and down the Kinh Cho Gao, a local canal. The Front tried to calm villagers, "but when they began to be harassed by bombs and bullets and the fear of death, nothing could deter them from leaving." Some built shelters in the fields, about 1,000 meters from their former dwellings, while others relocated along the canal, and still others "poured into" the new life hamlets. By 1967 the three hamlets used as campsites by the PLAF battalions had been "abandoned by their inhabitants."[16]

Quon Long refugees chose different destinations but did so in response to the same priorities. Those who wanted to continue planting and harvesting rice built huts in the fields, and the same consideration figured in the calculations of others who decided to settle near the canal rather than in the Long Thanh new life hamlet, which was "too far away to go back and forth to their fields to work." Meanwhile, villagers whose parcels adjoined a new life hamlet went there instead. According to one informant, all refugees from Quang

Ninh, the "strongest" of the Front hamlets, usually stayed there during the day "and returned to the New Life Hamlet at night." When the second of the GVN posts was built in late 1967, "the people who lived in the rear areas of the hamlet and who couldn't move out along the canal because of the lack of space built their shelters around the new post." As a result, "all the villagers in the hamlet lived along the banks of the canal and around the post. There was no one left in the rear areas." During the daytime these refugees "returned to their land to work and left for their homes in the evening." The Quon Long case was typical. Residents throughout the province had abandoned their hamlets but not their fields.[17]

REFUGEES WHO LEFT THE VILLAGES

Villagers were unnerved when neighbors moved away and were never seen again. Among the most respected residents of Binh Trung was a landlord who had "assisted many people in the hamlet." Coming from a family whose local history went back many generations, he was thought to be living in Saigon. "I only heard that," remarked an acquaintance; "I don't know for sure." Another man, an activist in Thanh Phu (CL), had served with the Viet Minh, worked as an underground cadre during the Diem era, and then rose to the NLF District Security Section. "At the end of 1966, he became dissatisfied over something and quit. He lived in the village for three months. He escaped death in shelling many times, so he became frightened and left the village to go no one knew where." In Thanh Hung "the case of the two guerrillas who had been sent to the district [local force] was often brought up among the villagers in private conversations, and everyone was puzzled about having not heard from them." More than any other sector of the rural population, thousands of soldiers who served in the armed forces of the two sides marched into oblivion.[18]

In the occasional references to people who left home, one sometimes catches sight of a workable adaptation or even a success story. Itinerants who had already lived in cities were in better shape than those who had no contacts or past experience in the GVN zone. Typical in this respect was the man from Binh Trung who in 1967 sought a "new life" by returning to the job as a Saigon pedicab driver that he had held seven years before. Some refugees drew on other assets in order to navigate the transition. "A number of families" from Hoa Dinh went to My Tho and Saigon and "used the money they had saved during the six peaceful years to enter business and become rich." Long Tien inhabitants "who had specialized jobs, such as tailors, merchants, alcohol makers," relocated and increased their capital "ten times."[19]

But these happy endings were not common. In towns and cities competition was fierce, and prospects were limited for newcomers with skills more suited to rural than to urban life. So it is not surprising that even among the people who moved out of their villages, one finds evidence of return to native places. Some trips home were no more than irregular foraging expeditions, as when refugees who had settled in Kien Phong province came back to Hau My "once a month or every two months in order to gather wood, fruit or catch fish." Elsewhere movement was more rigorously governed by the agrarian cycle. Refugees from Xuan Son settled on Tan Phong island and in Cai Be and Cai Lay towns. "About 100 of those who had left the village returned during the planting season to farm. They stayed from five to ten days each time to take care of their land, and then left again. Usually, they came back during the 7th, 8th, and 9th lunar months to sow and transplant rice and in the 12th and 1st lunar months to harvest rice." According to another report, "almost all the villagers" from Thoi Son who sought refuge in My Tho [city] and Kien Hoa province "returned to the village during harvesting times to gather their crops." Beginning in 1965, "about 1,000 people" left Hoi Cu for Tan Phong island and for new life hamlets in other villages. "Almost all of them still went back to the village once in a while to till their ricefields and gather the fruit from their orchards."[20]

To achieve a similar objective, refugee families originating in Hau Thanh, Hoa Dinh, Hoi Cu, Long Hung, and My Luong chose one or two family members to stay home and carry on farm work. Villagers in Binh Trung "all agreed that the best way was to move their family into New Life Hamlets while leaving behind only one member of the family. The group that went ahead would take care of building a new house in a New Life Hamlet and see to it that they could make a living doing something there, while the remainder would take care of the crop." In Thanh Hoa each family left "one strong member who was able to escape bombings and shellings, able to work in their fields, and to maintain their house." In Hau My departing families picked "one or two old persons to look after their crops." In Tan Ly Dong the husband stayed, and the wife and children moved out; in Thanh Phu (CT) men and children went to town while women and aged persons were assigned "to watch over their property." Even defectors adopted this strategy, as in the case of the man who wanted his family to remain in Phu Qui while he reported to the Chieu Hoi program. "If I had brought my family along," he reasoned, the Front "would confiscate my property."[21]

The policy of generating refugees was therefore only a partial success. It fell short in two respects. First, a band of holdouts remained entrenched in orchards and settlement areas, a place identified by many informants with the "hamlet," as in Long Binh Dien, Phu Nhuan Dong, and Thanh Hung. These depopulated areas were turned into fortresses. Tan Hoa hamlet in Tan Thuan Binh village was deserted "because it has been heavily shelled and strafed. But the fence of the hamlet is still standing and there are many spike pits and grenades which have been planted by the Front. All the houses of this hamlet are destroyed and therefore the people have all moved out into the fields to live. But it is still used by the guerrillas to lay ambushes and to shoot at the soldiers who come over in small groups." Villagers also got out of the way in Song Thuan. "They left the canal bank to the guerrillas and moved to the middle of the ricefields where they built their houses." At present, reported an informant, "the banks of the Rach Huong creek in My Nghia Hamlet are being used as a redoubt for the My Duc Tay guerrillas because there are no villagers left." So long as these holdouts remained in place, the government and the Americans could not win the war.[22]

From the U.S.-GVN point of view, stubborn attachment to the land constituted an equally ominous development. "The people were afraid of bombs and bullets if they stayed in an insecure area," testified an informant from Thanh Binh, "but they did not want to give up their land. What they really wanted was to move *temporarily* to the *nearest* GVN-controlled area," then return definitively when "security" was restored. A handful of entrenched militants would have been stranded if many others had not settled outside the hamlets but within village boundaries, or gone back and forth between more distant refuges and their fields and orchards. The revolution was a class more than an institutional phenomenon, and the actors determining its future were peasants who continued "to cling to their land in spite of the hardships and the risk of getting killed." So long as they stayed close to home, the popular movement was not dead.[23]

CADRES AND REFUGEES

At first cadres treated refugees as apostates. Guerrilla patrols tried to block escape routes, and the Front rebuked villagers who built huts in the fields. In Xuan Son, "to prevent the villagers from moving out of the village, the VC control system became stricter. There were unarmed guards on all the ways out." The lands of people who moved were confiscated, their stay-behind relatives were placed under house arrest, and if they returned to cultivate or to gather fruit or firewood, they were classified in the "bad category," kept under surveillance, or even made to understand that their lives were in danger. In Binh Phuc Nhat "cadres threatened to kill any youth who made an attempt to go to the GVN controlled area," and when some succeeded in escaping, their families were told "to call them back, otherwise they would lose all freedom of movement." In Dong Hoa the Front punished refugees "by confiscating their land and forbidding their kinsmen to visit them"; if caught, "they would be led back to the village and then criticized in meetings." In Hau Thanh "those who had to leave their hamlet for the town simply because of the shellings were accused by the Front of being reactionaries and their property was confiscated." An informant from Hoi Cu had the impression that "a great deal of land" was seized on this pretext in Hau My, My Thien, My Loi, and My Trung.[24]

As the war grew more destructive and greater numbers moved away, these policies became unenforceable. Even in 1965 truculent pronouncements were not always followed up, as in Hiep Duc, where refugees were forbidden to return and where "despite these statements the Front cadres, in fact, urged their relatives to call them back." As it became apparent that many of the departed families still hoped to plant and harvest, confiscation came to seem a self-defeating move, one that would sever the last remaining link between refugees and their hamlets. As one cadre put it: "We must try our best to induce evacuees to return to their native places to take care of their rice fields or gardens, or at least to let them visit their land freely so that we may have a good opportunity to apply the method of perseverance and whispering for inducing them to return to their old locality later." If families did not reappear during planting season, cadres followed a policy of "managing" or "looking after" abandoned land on a "temporary" basis, in the hope that the owners would retrace their steps. In My Thien "the VC wanted to keep the land of those who had left in order to use it as a bait to lure them to come back to their hamlet." In Nhi Binh "land given by the Front to people who have subsequently fled to the towns from fear of the war" was "still maintained and the Front has appealed to those people to return to the village to cultivate it." Common sense ruled out a punitive response. "If the Front confiscates these pieces of land, those people would leave the village for good."[25]

According to an informant from My Thien, land seizures continued "in some villages" where cadres did not agree with conciliatory recommendations from above and seized "the houses of those who had moved out to the GVN areas." A witness from Vinh Kim agreed that a number of village secretaries "did not comply with the Front's orders" and "eagerly confiscated the people's property." But with so many cultivators moving out, it was impossible for the stay-behinds to replace all of them when it came time to plant and harvest. "If everybody was gathered into the strategic hamlets, they could not confiscate anybody's land and then give it to others," explained an informant from Long Khanh. Surrounded by abandoned fields, those who remained stopped thinking of confiscation as a disciplinary measure and devoted all their energies to preventing the collapse of the agrarian system. In Hoa Dinh, when local cadres arranged for the working of fallow land, the primary motive was the fear that neglected terrain "would become nests for rats."[26]

In Hau My confiscations were carried out, according to an informant who was interviewed in June 1966, but an observer from the same village, speaking in October 1967, specified that in spite of warnings, "no one" in his hamlet had lost land to the Front. In Hoa Dinh "in 1965, since many villagers left the hamlet for the town, the Front took their land." A year later an order from above advised against confiscation. One resident of Hoi Cu noted that the land of those who had fled to strategic hamlets was seized, but according to a later witness, "if a family went back and forth to farm their land, then the Front didn't seize their land."[27]

Part of the impetus for these policy changes came from local militants who themselves were often stampeded by bombs and shells. When soldiers moved into Binh Duc, "the cadres and the guerrillas were busy fleeing, too, and there wasn't anyone left to hold the villagers back." In many villages the families of activists were among the departed. In Long Tien the possessions of refugees "weren't confiscated either, because there were cadres' relatives among them." In Tan Ly Dong "the village unit leader had his wife and children moved to the GVN controlled area and set up a house there," and "countless other cadres" did the same. In Thanh Hoa "cadres did not make things difficult for those who returned to the village, since their families have also been taking refuge in Cai Lay market." In Thanh Phu (CT) "the cadres were unable to stop the moves out of the village. They didn't want to forbid the people to get out either because their own relatives had to do the same."[28]

Cadres in Dong Hoa Hiep were told by higher echelons to inform the refugees that they had "to choose either to stay or to definitely leave the village." But "though it was an order, the Dong Hoa Hiep Village Chapter Committee did not carry it out because the rush to resettle in new life hamlets was too strong and we could not reproach the villagers who pretended they had only left their hamlets to avoid shellings." Militants in Vinh Kim were instructed to tell refugees "either to stay with the GVN and never come back or to come back and never to go to the GVN-controlled area again." The informant in this case did not follow orders, "because when I told them never to come back, they would stay over there for ever." No doubt he was influenced by the protests of returning refugees, who reacted to such stay-or-go ultimatums "by coming back in large groups" and saying "that if I were to kill them, I would have to kill the whole group."[29]

The Front posture evolved from exhortations ("The more bombing and shelling, the more trenches you will dig") to plaintive entreaties. "Please stay here to watch over your land and to till it," returning refugees were urged in Duong Diem. "If you move out there you might be caught in the fighting when our troops attack the enemy. You'll serve as a screen for the enemy and you'll get killed." In Phu My "the Front did try to persuade the people not to immigrate to the New Life Hamlets, stating that it is their duty to remain in their native village where their lands, their homes, and the tombs of their ancestors lie. However, the Front appeals remained unheeded because the people were too scared of bombs and death." In Thanh Hoa "once in awhile—once every month or every two months—the village cadres met with those who often returned to the village. They tried to motivate them, and requested them to bring their families back to the village in order to hold on to their fields and orchards." It was an exercise in futility, but "that's all they could do!"[30]

At first, families with members in the ARVN "were isolated by the local Front cadres and troops," but later "the cadres said that if they didn't treat these families nicely, they would become dissatisfied and leave the village." As for the youth who refused induction into the PLAF, when it became clear that insisting on enlistment would prompt them to flee, the Front suspended conscription and urged draft evaders at least to join the hamlet militia or village guerrillas and to participate in labor tasks. The fact that others had left increased the leverage of the recalcitrants, who could argue that they were demonstrating loyalty to the movement by remaining on the scene and could not equitably be made to serve when the cadres had no way of drafting those who had abandoned the village.[31]

In Vinh Kim militants begged the villagers, "Please come back to watch over your ricefields and orchards." Citing difficult material conditions in the GVN zone, they asked, "Why not make an effort to stay here to till your land to support your family and pay taxes to support the troops?" Returning refugees were no longer berated. "On the contrary, the cadres were very happy to have them come back. The more people there were in the hamlet, the happier life was for the cadres. Without the people, life was very dull and sad." Besides, if local militants hectored the returnees, "all the people would go away for good." It made more sense to strike a welcoming posture and take advantage of the fact that some families "left one of their members behind to watch over the houses and land."[32]

Under pressure from district-level superiors to halt the flight of villagers, cadres in Cam Son began with recriminations. "To the refugees coming back to their hamlets" they said:

> "You lied! You said that you are against the American imperialists and against the illegal government, but your statements were untrue. We know that when you reached the GVN-controlled areas, you received financial aid from the illegal government and, in doing so, you had to denounce the Communists. But denouncing the Communists means denouncing your children, your relatives, your family. That is why the Front forbids you to go to the GVN-controlled areas, and if you are not willing to stay here with your children, then you must leave your hamlet for good, once and for all."

Villagers were not intimidated. A typical riposte went like this: "So far, I have been a good citizen, I have never done anything harmful to the Front. If I had to move to the more secure places, it was only due to the shellings. We could not stay here and be shelled. Everybody wants to safeguard his life. Now, if the Front forbids me to come back to my hamlet, I must leave it all the same." The informant in this instance added, "The Front's threats made the villagers dissatisfied because they felt that forbidding them to leave their hamlets and forcing them to suffer the bombings and shellings amounted to letting them die." The exchange ended in a stalemate, demonstrating that "the villagers' security problem is, for the time being, an unsolved question for the Front."[33]

Cam Son cadres were left in a compromised and self-questioning posture. They themselves felt that instructions from above were "not only ineffective but incorrect as well because most of them had some relatives who had also taken refuge in the GVN-controlled areas." Abandoning their original insistence that residents stay in the hamlets and that a move into the rice paddies amounted to a betrayal of the movement, they asked refugees "to come back to set up thatched huts in the paddy fields to shelter themselves against the shelling." The same concession emerged in Long Thuan and Tam Hiep and also in Binh Trung, where cadres declared that building a field hut deserved approbation because it "showed one's determination to stay in the Front-controlled area." Unable to prevent the flight of refugees, militants had to accept the reality that people now lived scattered across the terrain.[34]

THE NEW SITUATION

Quon Long informants reported that relations between peasants and Front militants had become more troubled than during the golden period. Guerrillas and cadres and their relatives remained in the hamlets, while others settled in the fields or near the canal or one of the GVN posts or in new life hamlets. When they returned to pick fruit or gather firewood, the refugees would try to avoid Front personnel. "However, the cadres are not hard with them. Once in a while, the cadres try to talk with them for one or two hours, urging them to return to their native hamlet." Occasionally they would "send for the people who were living in the open field to fence the hamlet or to cut the road at night." Villagers felt safe along the canal banks, but the cadres were "afraid of calling on the villagers' houses, and the people have been left alone more often. But nevertheless, they couldn't avoid paying their taxes to the Front." Another informant enigmatically remarked that in the vicinity of the canal, "the Front cadres weren't active but secretly and often lived with the people." He went on to explain:

> Every two months, the cadres called all the villagers who returned to the hamlet to farm together to motivate them to fight against the Americans. The villagers listened to their lecture, then left without any comments. Usually, if they were asked to express their ideas, the villagers would say: "I have my family charge to look after. Life in the hamlet has been so dangerous that I'm scared and have to move along the canal to live, but I'm always with the revolution." The cadres had to be satisfied with this kind of explanation and couldn't blame these people for anything.

As a result of escalation, peasants were with, but not in, the revolution, at least not as they had been during the golden period. The political and military significance of this ambiguous posture remained to be tested.[35]

Among the most thoughtful meditations on the new situation was offered by a defector from Tan Ly Tay who had been an assistant squad leader in the PLAF. A poor peasant with no schooling who taught himself to read and write, chronically embroiled in disputes and possibly alcoholic, he was also an alert and sophisticated observer of people and events. His effort to capture the villagers' state of mind is worth examining in detail. "They more or less believe in the Front," he reported,

> but they no longer respond enthusiastically to its policies concerning taxes, economic production development and civilian labor policies which have all turned out to do harm to them or to their families. Besides the cadres' families, there are also those who have been living in the village since their childhood and are accustomed to the ways of life in rural areas. They think it is impossible to leave their homes behind and go

elsewhere to make a living. No matter if the Front or the Government wins the war, they will keep on living there, clinging to their ricefields and orchards. Whatever befalls them, happiness or misfortune, is predestined. In my opinion, those who are still living in the VC areas are all weary of the war. They can stand even great poverty, but to be constantly threatened by bombings and shellings day and night is beyond their endurance.

So, it might seem, peasants in their huts had been reduced to helplessness and were waiting for others to determine their future.[36]

As a teenager, the informant had gone to Saigon and "worked for a practitioner of oriental medicine," while his two younger brothers found jobs as masons. This itinerancy was common enough so that even "those who have been living in the village since their childhood" would have been exposed to the possibility of leaving home and going elsewhere to make a living. The putative fatalism among the stay-behinds also deserves scrutiny, given that they had lived through the golden period, when the idea that earthly destinies were determined solely by human beings acting on their own and without the assistance of supernatural powers had gained a wide currency and appeared to be confirmed by the rapid advance of the movement.[37]

But even if a belief in predestination was not carved in stone, the war was bound to heighten its appeal. The refugee option was inscribed within the history of a peasantry that was already living in flux. As modernization destabilized village cultures, local activists invested their hopes in the revolution. For them and for all country people it was a moment of anticipation and of danger, offering a promise of better days and also exposing everyone to the unknown. Escalation heightened this duality. When the flux gave way to a maelstrom and there was no longer solid ground on which to stand, no way to gain control over onrushing events, people who refused to give up on the revolution must have been tempted by the thought that fate rather than popular power would determine the outcome.

While the sense of agency among peasants in dire poverty and fearing for their lives had been drastically reduced, it had not altogether disappeared. "They more or less believe in the Front," the man from Tan Ly Tay explained, "but they no longer respond enthusiastically to its policies." This formulation plausibly suggests a widening gap between villagers and their leaders, while it also implies that the role of the movement was not yet played out. Further along he noted, with respect to the people in scattered huts, "No matter if the Front or the Government wins the war, they will keep on living there, clinging to their ricefields and orchards." Fronts and governments might come and go, but the peasants' demand for control over the countryside remained the central political reality of the moment. It might be true that "those who are still living in the VC areas are all weary of the war" and that continuing the war might be "beyond their endurance." But that breaking point had not yet been reached.

Peasant modernism had entered a period of extreme duress. Once drawing strength from a sense of agency throughout the countryside, it now seemed to be retreating into fatalism. Clinging to the land amounted to only a partial expression of the revolutionary dream, which earlier had led rural dwellers to imagine wider horizons and a richer array of possibilities for themselves than those offered by a parcel of land. But at least this refusal to let go of fields and orchards kept alive the hope that people's choices could make a difference. In the dwindling space where they exercised a measure of control, country people who were no longer sure they could make a revolution continued to insist on the right to determine what sort of progress was in store for Vietnam.

CHAPTER NINE

THE AMERICAN OTHER

During the golden period, internationalist perspectives inspired the Vietnamese to think that their revolutionary dream was more than a parochial fancy and gave them warrant to imagine the future in a global, a utopian, register. "As a rule," an informant recalled, before introducing new policies "the village secretary always spoke of the international and home political situation so as to make the villagers become more enthusiastic about paying taxes to help the Front to feed the soldiers and to buy armaments." Cadres assured them that "the 13 socialist states in the world all supported the liberation war in South Vietnam" and that they constituted "an evergrowing force while the imperialists have retreated everywhere." They told stories about the USSR, "its modern weapons circling the earth, and its satellites." Authors of a revolution and victorious in World War II, the Soviets had succeeded in building a modern society. Activists also saw the People's Republic of China as a redoubtable ally. "The Front propagandizes that China is a great nation, a strong nation with atomic weapons," and that the Chinese were capable of destroying "the strongest imperialist country which was the United States." Marching in step with a worldwide coalition, the Liberation Front was bound to win over a retreating enemy.[1]

In movement discourse the United States appeared as a hateful but also an oddly disembodied enemy. Cadres preached "that the Americans were blood-thirsty aggressors" and that Washington policymakers were "the ring leaders of all the imperialists in this world." While the French were "the old-style colonialists," the Americans were "the new-style colonialists. Even though these two types of colonialists are different in some respects, they are basically the same. The French had economic and political control, while the Americans only have economic control. But through their control over the economy the Americans control everything." Although the people haven't yet "witnessed the Americans doing anything wrong, and in reality, anti-American slogans weren't as appealing as anti-Diem slogans," remarked the Instigator, the Front "cleverly associated the Americans with Diem's misdeeds such as forced labor for the construction of Agrovilles, and arbitrary arrests of former resistance cadres." As a result, "even though they haven't come across any Americans yet," the villagers "have a preconceived opinion about them and regard the Americans as even more cruel than the French."[2]

In 1965 this shadowy adversary suddenly invaded Vietnam. News quickly spread that U.S. troops had arrived in central Vietnam and American planes were attacking the DRV, while in My Tho massive firepower was aimed against the liberated zones. As people talked among themselves and seized on scraps of information from newspapers and radio broadcasts and from the grapevine, their morale faltered. Company-level officers in the 261st Battalion, who "used to be so confident that no one could touch the North," now gathered over cups of tea and noted that the Americans "are bombing our granaries. If Russia and China don't do anything to stop the Americans, the North will be destroyed. When this happens, the only thing left for the liberation troops to do is to turn in their weapons to the puppet government and surrender." Company-level positions in the PLAF were not for the faint of heart, but even these battle-tested soldiers were frightened by U.S. escalation. The increasingly acrimonious Sino-Soviet split, which suggested that the USSR and China were more focused on denigrating each other than on countering the United States, only heightened a sense of isolation among local militants.[3]

This chapter focuses on the crisis in meaning that ensued. Before 1965 only a few people in My Tho had encountered U.S. personnel, but after that date foreign intervention came with a greatly added weight. Bombs and shells fell everywhere, tanks flattened orchards and plowed up rice fields, troops sacked houses and shot villagers. Rural dwellers were further disoriented by the realization that they were being forced to live in a different way, congruent with a "modernization" ideal of external origin. Fighting to adjust and to survive, the Vietnamese came face-to-face with the American Other.

FROM SPECIAL WAR TO TOTAL WAR

In retrospect the Vietnamese Communist Party characterized 1965 as a "hinge year," but in the moment local militants did not see things so clearly. For them the year was marked by a mix of hope and dread and by a growing sense that they were no longer able to grasp the logic of events. In 1964 it had seemed as if the Saigon government was about to collapse. "At that time," according to a defector, "the Front did not think that the Americans would intervene in the South." The GVN "was being torn by internal dissensions and more coup d'etats were expected," recalled one witness. According to another, "the documents that we studied also dealt with the changes in government in the South and said that the GVN would soon collapse, leaving the South without a government." Several interviewees reported hearing "that the general offensive and general insurrection would take place in 1965," as a result of which "the Front would win and the Americans would definitely leave the country."[4]

At the same time, bombing and shelling intensified, orders from above to draft soldiers and to fortify hamlets conveyed an ominous message, and news of air raids against the North indicated that war was engulfing the entire nation. "All the cadres tried to show the villagers that these bombings didn't have any effect on them," observed an informant, "but I knew that the majority of them were frightened. A member of the propaganda section whom I knew well told me one day while speaking of the bombings, 'I don't know where this will lead us.'" In May 1965 another activist heard "that the Party was 'turning the corner.'" But soon after, a district cadre "disclosed to me, one night when we had dinner together, that the United States was a very strong and rich country. He stressed that only one American capitalist could finance this war for a full year." Victory seemed so close, yet the enemy appeared even more determined to impose its will.[5]

The problem was that what happened next would be decided in the United States, and there was nothing anyone in Vietnam could do to change that reality. A June 1965 training session for district cadres put forward the following analysis:

> The U.S. is uncertain whether it should maintain its present special war policy or pass on to the phase of limited war. And taking advantage of this uncertainty from the U.S., we should strike hard in order to mark a new turn in the history of the South Vietnamese revolution. By striking hard, we should be able to know the U.S. reaction. For the U.S. has to definitely move, either forward or backward. By then, the NLFSVN [National Liberation Front of South Vietnam] would be able to determine its courses of action and its attitude towards the war. As things stand right now, it is impossible to tell whether the present war is special war or a limited war.

This analysis did not add up to a strategy. It amounted to saying that the direction of events was now for Washington to decide and that the best the Front could do was to prod U.S. policymakers into making up their minds.[6]

Never before had local activists been more in need of direction from above, but at this critical moment higher echelons could not clarify the situation. Commentators in a July 1965 training course predicted "a long-term struggle" and stated that "the war will last for a very, very long time." They then tried to reassure people by stating that "the war still remains a special war" and that U.S. defeats in Korea and Cuba and rising antiwar sentiment at home ("most American mothers refused to let their sons go to Vietnam to fight") would prevent President Lyndon Johnson from escalating. Their further recognition that "in the delta, it is very hard to establish secure bases" was puzzlingly followed by instructions to erase "all traces left by the former regime" from the countryside. A village cadre heard a similarly mixed message at an August 1965 briefing, when the instructor "asked us to keep in mind that the present phase of the war is the phase of hard and indecisive fighting (*Giai doan giang co ac liet*) which precedes the General Insurrection." Again, even though the war-ending offensive was being postponed, the speaker still asserted that the conflict remained "a special kind of war" and argued that, after their defeats in Korea and at the Bay of Pigs, "the Americans would not dare to wage a limited war in South Vietnam."[7]

These testimonies suggest that the movement feared a test of strength against the United States and shrank from recognizing that the fighting had entered a new phase. Even in March 1966, when there were more than 200,000 U.S. troops in Vietnam, instructors claimed that the war "was becoming, step by step, a limited war, and so, the war should be thought of as half a special, half a limited war." A district cadre who defected that same month thought that Front strategists were substituting wish for reality. "Before, we had a special war," he explained, "but now it has evolved into a limited war. The VC want to change this war back into a special war, because this is more to their advantage, and because it is easier for them to organize it. But I think that this war has evolved into a limited war already." In the fall of 1966 a province cadre declared: "A special war began in 1961 and has gradually become fiercer and fiercer until it took the form of total war in March 1965. At present, it is really a total war." To readers of military manuals, and from the U.S. perspective, the conflict in Vietnam might have seemed like a "limited war," but in My Tho, "total war" betters suits the calamity that was unleashed in 1965.[8]

Vietnamese observers at the time cannot be faulted for anticipating that U.S. leadership would respond with prudence to its reverses in Southeast Asia. The Front saw "the United States as the biggest capitalist nation in the world, as the hero or the big brother of all other capitalist countries," and maintained that the Americans had come to Vietnam "to take over this country [so as] to expand their commercial activities, to sell out their products." Perhaps dependency theory informed the assertion that the United States was seeking "a market for its economy," because it "is strong in industry and technology, but weak in the agricultural sphere." Another informant thought that "the Americans come here to do business and to help the GVN." But if capitalism and markets and "business" informed American thinking, and if the Saigon regime no longer seemed like a good investment, it made sense to anticipate that President Johnson would decide against escalation.[9]

When Rand posed the question "What are the Americans doing in Vietnam?" many subjects answered that they did not know. An informant who confessed, "It is beyond my comprehension, because I am not well educated," was perhaps masquerading as a simple peasant. But my impression is that most interviewees meant what they said. With access to evidence far beyond the materials at the disposal of instructors in NLF reorientation sessions, historians today are still quarreling about when and why President Johnson decided to escalate the war. Since these observers, drawing on a generation of scholarship, cannot agree among themselves, one should not be surprised that Vietnamese villagers in 1965 were also at a loss. Asked "What are the Americans doing in Vietnam?" a soldier responded: "It is beyond my comprehension. I do not know." The Rand staffer commented, "The subject was intelligent, but his comprehension was limited," with the implication that a better understanding could be found in other quarters. But if escalation made no sense, then puzzlement was appropriate to the situation. Though they surmised, as recent research has shown, that chances for success were slim, the president and his advisers opted to raise the stakes, and Vietnam was plunged into the madness of a total war.[10]

THE VIETNAMESE AND THE AMERICANS

Villagers met the intruders as soldiers and advisers, as employers and customers, and, after Rand arrived, as intelligence gatherers who sometimes masqueraded as journalists or "social science students doing research for their oncoming theses." Some had encountered U.S. personnel before the arrival of the Ninth Division. While working in Saigon, a defector "thought of the Americans as the carriers of the (western) civilization to Vietnam and that they were here to help the Vietnamese people. The proof was that they had built the Saigon–Bien Hoa highway and had brought to Vietnam modern construction equipment." Another informant stated, "I met some of them while I was serving the GVN as a draftee in 1958 and when I was captured by the 9th Division in Kien Phong." Although they behaved "very nicely," he also thought "that, more or less, they are aggressors. The fact that they are present in Vietnam is proof of that." During the six-year period of peace, recalled one informant, "I saw some Americans driving a car, but had no opportunity to talk with them. Moreover, as I could not speak English, how could I talk with them?" Later on, in September 1962, there had been a near meeting at Hung Thanh My when ARVN soldiers overran an NLF base camp and inflicted high casualties. "I saw some American servicemen following a GVN unit on a search-and-destroy operation," the speaker recalled. "They passed by the bushes where I was hiding, about 15 meters away." When a cadre from Dang Hung Phuoc was apprehended by ARVN soldiers, "there were two Americans who went along on that operation. They sat about 20 meters away when I was being tortured and probably had witnessed the scene."[11]

Rand employees were among the first to leave more than a passing impression in My Tho, and defectors and prisoners spoke of them in positive terms, especially when their new acquaintances were proficient in Vietnamese. "One of them talked to me and he was a very nice man," testified a former sapper. "He could speak Vietnamese very well, and he asked me about my family and so on." Another informant remarked, "I saw the Americans walking with other people and they even shook hands and talked to ralliers." Still another reported, "All the Americans, even the high ranking ones, treated me nicely and politely." Candy given to children and other offerings were seen as potent emblems of goodwill, as when a foreigner proffered a pack of cigarettes "with both hands, which is a very courteous gesture."[12]

These testimonies were meant to affirm that a measure of civility could overturn years of Front propaganda. "Although I didn't understand a bit of his language," said a rallier after a brief chat with an American, "I found he behaved towards me rather nicely. He shook hands with me and invited me to have a seat." As a result, "this hatred of mine had been completely overcome, because I found them very nice." It seems that Rand informants, especially the ralliers, were laboring to find something positive to say about their new friends. Or perhaps the testimonials were simple expressions of relief that some of the foreigners were not as brutal as the Front claimed.[13]

In everyday life, peoples of the two cultures were pressed into close, almost intimate, contact that was sometimes friendly, sometimes dangerous—and occasionally comical. One Rand informant described how, when U.S. soldiers at a checkpoint detained the village party secretary of Binh Trung, the only document he could produce was "a VC tax receipt," affixed with an NLF seal. Upon showing it to the Americans, "he was immediately released." As for a peasant who was stopped, "when the American soldiers checked his papers, he showed them a bicycle purchase receipt and he was freed."[14]

An out-of-uniform guerrilla in An Thai Dong recalled preparing lunch for GVN soldiers and their two American advisers, "one Negro and one white," who stopped at his house during a sweep operation. A platoon leader from Kim Son remembered the day U.S. troops landed in his village. "My wife knew a few words of English that she had picked up while she was living in Saigon," he explained. She poured tea for the guests, they chatted about the couple's infant child, and one of the soldiers passed around photos of his own offspring, a baby of ten months, and left coffee, cocoa, and cigarettes. "My wife said: 'Merci, Monsieur,' and they said: 'Merci beaucoup,' my wife thanked them, but they thanked her even more, and she was very pleased." In this instance, as elsewhere, even a modest surmounting of the language barrier appears to have facilitated a nonlethal encounter.[15]

Perhaps marketplace transactions were the easiest to negotiate. The Americans were not big tippers like the French, stated a man from Phu Phong. At least "this was what the taxi drivers and cyclo drivers working in Saigon said when they came back for a visit." Whenever people sold something to them, noted another informant, "they have to make signs to indicate the price of each item, or the Americans watch the Vietnamese customers and pay the same amount of money for the same article." According to women fruit sellers in Song Thuan, "the Americans are good buyers. If you are not pleased with the price they give you, you just shake your head. Then they raise the price. When you get the right price, you just nod. Then they pay you and take the things away." When it came to buying and selling, sign language seemed adequate to the task.[16]

Relations were more dangerous on other occasions, especially for women, as is apparent in the testimony from the Rebel. "In one village," she recalled,

> an American asked a woman "OK?" The American thought that she had agreed to sleep with him, so he took her in his arms. She became frightened, ran out and screamed. Then the interpreter came and asked what it was all about. He explained to her what the American wanted and said: "If you didn't want to sleep with him why did you say OK?" She said: "I didn't understand what he said. When he said OK, I okayed back." The American let her go and didn't do anything to her.

In another instance

> an American entered the house of a woman, who had six children. The American asked her how many men she could sleep with, and she thought that he asked her how many children she had, so she showed six fingers.

The American then ran out and brought back five others. Fortunately, the interpreter arrived and he explained to her what the Americans wanted. He said: "You're in trouble. He asked you how many men you could sleep with and you said six." She said that she only meant that she had six children.

Extending a license no Vietnamese would have offered to a compatriot, she hazarded: "I think that these Americans were either bachelors or married men who were separated from their wives. It was only natural, therefore, that they felt attracted toward women. After all they were virile young men."[17]

Another mix-up occurred when U.S. troops arrested ARVN soldiers in Nhi Binh. "The soldiers got mad and said: 'Hell, we fight against the VC and yet these guys tie us up. Where should we go now if our own side arrests us and ties us up?'" When the interpreter explained that these were GVN soldiers, "the Americans untied them. The soldiers didn't stay mad at the Americans because they knew that the Americans didn't know anything." American soldiers "never raped women," the Rebel next insisted. "However, if they asked and the women consented, then they slept with them; otherwise they never forced themselves on anyone." She then hurried on to yet a further case of bungled communication and ensuing mayhem:

> In another village, the Americans entered a house and asked the owner if there were any VC in the house. She didn't understand them, I don't know what she thought they meant, but she nodded and pointed to the house. They came in her house and started searching. They broke many of her things trying to look for the VC. She then asked the interpreter what the Americans were doing breaking her things, and the interpreter explained to her that the Americans were looking for VC because she had said that there were VC in her house. She became very angry and started cursing them. Afterward, the Americans repaired what damage they had done and left.

There was also the time when the foreigners apprehended a youth and took him away in a helicopter. "He cried like a baby because he was frightened. Finally, the misunderstanding was cleared up and he was sent back to his village." A moment later, striving to parry an accusation that refused to go away, the Rebel declared, "the VC said that the Americans raped women when they went on operations, but this only happened rarely and was due to the fact that they couldn't communicate with the women."[18]

In these anecdotes one observes Vietnamese in the Rand orbit, both interviewers and interviewees, working to fashion a comedy of manners, meant to represent the encounter between Vietnam and the United States.

The Americans were clumsy and dull-witted. Their notion of tracking the Viet Cong and their sexual habits were primitive and their mental powers slender (they "don't know anything"). Women and children sometimes got in trouble because they had not mastered the art of keeping the intruders at bay. The interpreter is the hero of the story. He enlightens the Americans, teases the Vietnamese, and arranges a happy ending, with innocents set free and no one getting raped. This, one imagines, was the master narrative that took form in the early days of U.S. escalation, when it seemed that lack of progress in the war was due to "misunderstandings" and that assigning more translators to work with the allies and to protect the Vietnamese from them would facilitate cooperation against the enemy.[19]

The Pentagon did not send U.S. soldiers to My Tho to exchange baby pictures with villagers or to dine with the Viet Cong. Their assignment was to find and kill the enemy, a reality that comes through only obliquely in the transcripts. Two conventions figure in this testimony. According to the first, positive references to U.S. soldiers function as critiques of ARVN behavior. "The Rebel testified that "the people like the Americans because they didn't steal the belongings of the villagers when they went on operation, unlike GVN soldiers who took anything of value in the people's houses." U.S. troops "didn't loot the people, nor did they beat anyone either," remarked a man from Binh Trung, in contrast to ARVN soldiers, who "liked to pick fruit to eat, to arrest people, and to beat suspects."[20]

Another common device involved the coupling of praise for American servicemen with reference, in the form of an afterthought, to violent acts. A guerrilla from Vinh Kim lauded U.S. personnel and quoted villagers exclaiming, "Heavens! I thought the Americans were like monsters but it turned out that they were very kind." He then added: "The only thing that the people complained about was that if a house was empty and there were sheets of paper scattered all over the ground or children's textbooks lying around, then the Americans mistook it for a VC office and they started rummaging around looking for documents. They even broke the locks of the chests to check. In so doing they messed up the whole house." Elsewhere in the interview it was reported that when a villager fled on the approach of the GIs, "they came in and burned down the house," a tactic that prompted the comment, "I don't understand Americans (Nguoi My minh khong hieu duoc)."[21]

Destruction of property was also noted by a witness from Thoi Son, who observed that "the American troops were very fond of burning houses. When they entered a house and saw a trench-type shelter, they used mines to destroy it. When they saw a water container, they broke it up. Particularly, they were fond of breaking the altars inside houses which are used to worship the owners' ancestors. From early 1967 to May, about 30 houses were burned down." This observer was struck by the fact the troops "never broke up a Christian altar." A resident of Thanh Phu (CT) asserted, "I have never witnessed any regrettable incidents between the American troops and the villagers to date," but "I was also told that the Americans liked to burn the people's houses." He added, "This inhumane measure of the American troops has made the villagers very angry."[22]

In Hau My it was reported that the foreigners gave the people medicines and materials and did not plunder or rape. "But they have often arrested innocent persons because they could not understand the Vietnamese language." In early 1967 "the American troops conducted an operation" in Thoi Son village. "Upon their arrival, they arrested all males 15 to 65 years old, whether they had their identity cards or not. From the beginning of this year to the present time, there were inhabitants who have been arrested by the American troops three or four times." People "said that they didn't see any evidence that the Americans were in the country to help the Vietnamese and that they only noticed that wherever the Americans went, innocent people were arrested." A defector from Song Thuan called attention to a sequence of arrests: five people at a Tet celebration, including two visitors from Saigon with connections to the GVN, plus a peasant minding a flock of ducks and another, an "absent-minded" man, working in the fields. Some of these detainees possessed proper ID and some did not; some were released promptly, while others remained incarcerated at the time of the interview.[23]

According to a witness from Long Hung, "the G.I.'s are very round and jovial. They greeted everyone and came across with smiles and waves of the hand." They took sick people to the hospital and gave candy to children. "There is one regrettable fact," she continued. "Nobody dared to go out of his house at night. This is due to the fact that the Americans were very quick to shoot at you at night, in case you didn't stop immediately when they called out to you to stop." A man from Long Tien said, "Most of the villagers do not hate the Americans because they did not loot or beat the people," but "they never failed to shoot at those who ran away. In my village, they killed a common villager who ran away out of panic." Following the same convention, an informant from Quon Long recalled that "the children liked the Americans very much. They used to greet the Americans and asked for candy and cakes"—this after having said, "American soldiers shoot at anyone who ran away without knowing who were innocent villagers and who were cadres."[24]

The U.S. Ninth Division was stationed in My Tho from January 1967 to the summer of 1969. With respect to the period after the Tet Offensive, David Elliott declares that the unit "directed an unprecedented level of violence at the villages, which resulted in the depopulation of large parts of the countryside and the further isolation of the revolutionary forces. Not surprisingly, this led to a catastrophically high level of civilian casualties during the year following Tet, and raises questions of moral accountability for U.S. commanders that, in some ways, go beyond the issues raised at My Lai."[25]

Rand staffers were in a position to observe the conduct of U.S. military personnel in My Tho and to broadcast widely and in detail what they had seen, and an obligation was shirked when they chose not to do so. A defector reported: "Cadres who fled from Thanh Phu told me that the American troops who came to Thanh Phu raped women and killed a lot of innocent people. They said that this was why whenever the people heard that the Americans were coming on operation, they became frightened and fled to the road"—to which the Rand interviewer responded: "Tell me about your life before you joined the Front." Sometimes, on reading that last line, I am struck by the faintheartedness of the questioner, who hastened to change the subject when ugly testimony surfaced. Still, the comment remained in the transcript, where, along with other reports, it calls attention, however fleetingly, to war-making methods that "go beyond" the horrors of My Lai.[26]

Rand bias compromised the inquiry, and in other settings expressions of antipathy toward the invaders, registered only occasionally in the interviews, would certainly have been voiced with greater emphasis. At the same time, I am also struck by the absence in the transcripts of xenophobic or racist references to the Americans. No doubt informants called attention to benign encounters in hopes of pleasing their interrogators, but perhaps also out of a sense that moments of human connection, however trifling—a greeting, a gift, a chat over cups of tea—deserved to be noted. The southern revolution had created a movement culture imbued with humanist and internationalist ideals. This consciousness made it possible for local militants to hate enemies who were guilty of many atrocities but also to recognize that they were human beings and to note their occasional kindnesses.

MODERNIZATION AT VILLAGE LEVEL

A female informant from Trung An grew up in a single-parent household, supported by the income from an orchard her mother rented from an owner in My Tho city. In 1952 the land was sold, "and all the sharecroppers who lived on it were chased out, except my mother, who refused to go away. The new owner of the land then dug up the sharecroppers' ancestor graves in order to replant fruit trees and to set up a coffin shop and a sawmill. The price of this land was only 60,000 VND, but by now it is rumored that the new owner is going to sell her land to the Americans for 3 or 4 million piasters. I was told that the Americans want to set up a military base for American troops over there."[27]

This passage indicates that construction of a military base in My Tho, an act of war, also belongs in the history of property relations and everyday life in the province. Before 1952 peasants were placing ancestral graves on holdings that legally belonged to others. This presumption might have been founded on a quasi-feudal custom that accorded tenants a claim on land they were renting, or, the more likely explanation, it was inspired by the Viet Minh revolution, which had routed landlords and eliminated rent exploitation. With the arrival of the Americans, a free market in land based on private property rights was taking shape. U.S. intervention came in the form of a potent killing machine, one that tore apart the cultural and ecological space inhabited by the Vietnamese and introduced them, in the words of another informant, to a "new kind of life."[28]

In June 1966 ARVN rangers and Seventh Division soldiers occupied Binh Duc, and a construction team began building the Dong Tam military base, which was intended to serve as headquarters for the U.S. Ninth Division. A witness from Thanh Phu, just to the north of Binh Duc, quoted the Front as saying that "the Americans are seizing the people's land and property to build up their own base, that they are ugly men because they dug up the people's ancestors' graves with their dredges and bulldozers, and that, for these reasons, everyone has to fight them." Later informants also mentioned dredges, which "blew mud all over the ricefields" in Thanh Phu, so that "the people couldn't till their ricefields." Local guerrillas were not strong enough to contend with an ARVN division, and when promised reinforcements did not materialize, they were reduced to low-level resistance. The road "was dug up so badly that they couldn't do any more damage to it," nighttime vandalism destroyed surveyors' equipment, and guerrillas sniped at the surveying team, wounding one, and staged an ambush that killed five soldiers.[29]

Still, construction went forward. Acting as if they were in a foreign country, ARVN soldiers "said that they were in a VC area and that if they didn't eat the fruit and take the poultry of the people, the people would give them to the VC." Troops "shot at the draft age youths who ran away when they came in. A few youths were shot by the soldiers or by the helicopters." Four militants in

Binh Duc and four or five guerrillas in Thanh Phu were killed, and over twenty Thanh Phu cadres and guerrillas died in a subsequent sweep. Surviving activists fled in the direction of Long Hung, and "many guerrillas and self-defense militiamen" defected. In October rumors spread that the Ninth Division was coming, and by January 1967 GIs were launching operations from the Dong Tam base.[30]

Americans tried to solve the problem of reconstruction on the basis of urban renewal guidelines that were prevalent in their home country, with compensation to villagers for their requisitioned land. A significant mass of property was at issue: some six hundred hectares in two Binh Duc hamlets, plus fields laid waste by dredging or other construction-related activities. Cadres did not think that the foreigners would make amends. "It is foolish to believe that the Americans are going to indemnify you," they insisted. "So why lose your time on this affair?" Still, many peasants filed claims. In Thanh Phu, three informants reported that compensation had not been received, and one observer thought "that some villagers who had moved into Ap Cho Hamlet to settle were given compensation." A witness from Binh Duc also indicated that the matter had been satisfactorily resolved. In that village people had hoped that the Front would protect their ancestors' graves, "but later on, the GVN indemnified them properly for their losses and the villagers turned out satisfied." By contrast, as in Thanh Phu, several Binh Duc observers called attention to a less satisfactory outcome. "The people had been told by the Village Council to list their land losses and to apply for compensation," noted an informant. "At present, many people are still processing papers to obtain compensation. The people wish to be compensated quickly, to have land to till and on which to build houses."[31]

The GVN could not be counted on to transmit aid to the victims of U.S. war making. A Binh Duc resident noted that people were being "asked to come to the Village Office all the time to supply additional information about the loss of their land," implying that the transaction was turning into a futile battle with bureaucratic red tape. Furthermore, since agreements between landlords and tenants often rested on verbal understandings rather than written contracts, many lacked documentation to back up their claims. "I haven't heard anything about anyone getting compensation," the Binh Duc informant specified. "The people are anxiously waiting for this to come about. Besides, there were many villagers who rented land from the landlords without making any contracts, and, for this reason, they won't be able to obtain any compensation." Of the twenty tenants in his hamlet, only five or six had contracts.[32]

Claimants in these instances found themselves in an awkward situation. As a result of land reform and, more generally, the power of intimidation wielded by a peasant-based movement, most landlords had fled, and those few who remained in the villages were not likely to protest on receiving only token payments, or if no rents at all were forthcoming. The two biggest landlords with holdings in Binh Duc were absentees, living in My Tho. Their former tenants had not been paying rent for several years and had become de facto owners of the parcels they worked. Insistence on written contracts in a context where many arrangements rested on custom and verbal agreement was bound to hurt tenants. But even if their claims had been honored, compensation would have been granted only for the income lost through cancellation of leases before the agreed-upon expiration date. The real injustice, from the point of view of the popular movement, was that the Americans were expropriating land from peasants that peasants had expropriated from landlords a few years before.[33]

The transcripts say that some landholders were compensated. Perhaps they were yeoman farmers with written leases, experience dealing with legal documents, and money to pay the bribes necessary to speed things along. Others accommodated to the new situation by moving into the Binh Duc agroville, obtaining GVN identification papers, and working for the foreigners. "Usually, new workers are hired by being introduced by old ones," noted an observer from Thanh Phu. "Only good poor persons are working for the Americans, and they were introduced by their relatives and friends." These employees dug canals, served as warehouse custodians, mixed cement, laid down pipeline, worked on construction crews or in repair shops, and laundered clothes. Wages were astoundingly high, with informants specifying payments of 20 to 30 piasters an hour and up to 300 piasters a day. In a countryside where the customary wage for a day's labor was 40 to 50 piasters, many were bound to be tempted by such largesse. "Those who work for the Americans have to leave their village permanently to settle in Binh Duc New Life Hamlet," observed a man from Thanh Phu. "Now, they couldn't care less about their fields or their orchards because the yield would never bring 10,000 piasters a month."[34]

While U.S. military efforts frightened, enraged, and demoralized the rural population, the American vision of modernization posed a political challenge to the Front. The intruders overrode customary arrangements and introduced a strict definition of individual property rights. They dismantled a village republic of smallholders and replaced it with a free labor market. They sought to diminish popular power and reinforce bureaucratic means of control. In the villages around the Dong Tam military base, their policies amounted to a rural variant on the "forced draft urbanization and modern-ization" of Vietnam celebrated by Samuel Huntington. Despite the geo-graphic limits of the event, which was confined to a cluster of villages around the Dong Tam base, Huntington was correct to speak of a "social revolution in the Vietnamese way of life."[35]

A change so abrupt and comprehensive was bound to prompt reserva-tions. Villagers "like having a job with the Americans very much," remarked an informant from Binh Duc. "Even the seven youths who are hiding in the hamlet to dodge the GVN draft are interested in working for the Ameri-cans. But they think that getting out to work for the Americans wouldn't do them any good because they will be drafted as soon as they go out." As for the older villagers, he added, "they also long to work for the Americans, but they decided to be on the safe side and continued to live on their own take." Said one thirty-eight-year-old villager, "I want to work at the American base, doing things like scooping dirt or mixing cement, because I'm not a strong man." With an itinerant history (he had served in the "French Com-mandos") and coming from a very poor family, he understood that wage-paying employment is never permanent. "I think that I can make more money working for the Americans," he speculated, "but the only thing is that the job might not last long." In the revolution, peasants had vowed to take control of the land "forever," and the competing lure of temporary work, even at wages up to ten times the norm, had to be weighed against that promise.[36]

The U.S. offer required a fundamental shift in consciousness. "My spe-cialty is farm work," the last speaker observed, thus transforming a social identity and way of being into a "specialty," one that could be exchanged for other employments "scooping dirt or mixing cement." Village revolutionar-ies who earlier had been striving to live in dignity were reduced to scrambling for menial jobs. "There are now in Thanh Phu village five families who have relatives working for the Americans as coolies," reported an informant. "They are living a comfortable life since they earn nearly 300 piasters a day." Such a sum was indeed a windfall, but one wonders about other costs for peasants who, not long before, had seen themselves as "masters of the coun-tryside" and who now earned their livelihood as "coolies."[37]

Modernization was not inscribed on a blank slate. An informant from Binh Trung declared that "from the political standpoint, whether the pres-ence of the American troops is beneficial or harmful to the nation is beyond my knowledge to say." But in practice it brought "a great advantage for the workers and laboring people" in the form of "easy money" to be made "working in construction sites, repair shops or laundries." He concluded by saying, "I hope that after being authorized to rejoin my family, I can go to Cholon to become a tricycle pedicab driver and build a new life."[38]

This was not the first moment in the interview when the informant spoke of his hopes for the future. An orphan, he had followed his older brother to Saigon in 1947, had become a pedicab driver in Cholon, then went back to Binh Trung village in 1960. "I was young," he stated. "I had no serious thoughts, I just wished I could live a better life." Binh Trung was a revolutionary bastion and not the kind of place a fence-sitter would have returned to in 1960, just at the time of the concerted uprising. The informant did hazard that when the NLF "came out of its underground activities and set up its infrastructure in the village, it paid special attention to and took special care of the poor peasants, who then gave strong support of it."[39]

These remarks suggest, first, that the interviewee worked as a pedicab driver in Cholon, then gave up that job and, in hopes of finding a "better life," returned to Binh Trung to join a movement that promised to take "special care" of poor peasants like himself. When the Front presence was menaced in 1967, he made a decision not to begin a "new life" but to return to an "old life," again working as a pedicab driver in Cholon, as he had done before 1960. For him, the U.S. "social revolution" was not so revolutionary after all. One might wonder if he experienced disappointment on returning to an earlier strategy for achieving happiness, one that had already been tried and found wanting.

The Americans were hard-pressed to compete with the modernism of the NLF, but their offer of a certain kind of mobility and freedom, more or less faintly heard beneath the din of battle, registered in the countryside. Before 1960 many a peasant who was later to become active in a village-based movement felt the urge to travel, to see "new and strange things," to start afresh, and the revolution had only begun to work out methods for satisfying that hunger. Even as the province went up in flames, there was "easy money" to be made and novelties to be found in the marketplace, some, such as mild cigarettes, that could be dismissed as frivolities, others, such as electric motors and transistor radios, whose utility even the most austere revolutionaries could not deny. If the Front had prevailed in 1965 and American personnel had gone home, U.S.-sponsored modernization, which was lodged in the global transformation of the era, would have remained a force. In that respect and in others, no matter who won the war, rural dwellers were going to be dealing with innovations that were sure to come, as they were coming and are coming to all peoples living in the flux of the modern world.

For the time being those issues receded to the margins as escalation imposed a hard lesson in cold war politics. Although it fit more or less into a view of the United States as an imperial power, the U.S. escalation came as a surprise, as did the temporizing of the Soviets and the Chinese and the Sino-Soviet split, so subversive of internationalist assumptions within the movement. Menaced by "the ring leaders" of world imperialism, and with allies seemingly content to watch from the sidelines, local militants were stricken with an awareness of their isolation and vulnerability.

Reflections on Vietnam's status as a small, poor, and weak nation were commonplace in the Saigon milieu, where few expected the government on its own to defeat the revolution. "Without the Americans, how can we be strong?" asked one defector. "We could not win over them!" After 1965, village revolutionaries, too, came to share this sense of frailty. According to a district cadre, "the instructor said that we are resisting against the worst and leading imperialist (*Mot ten de quoc dau so*), possessing air, sea and ground forces, with a great military potential, and it is a very great hardship." A militant acknowledged: "We are fighting against the Americans, the most powerful country in the world, and therefore it is difficult for us to achieve victory. The cadres recognized that the Americans are much stronger than the French before." A platoon leader confessed, "I am sure that everybody was putting on an appearance of being firm for fear of being criticized, but deep inside the Front soldiers were really afraid."[40]

The movement responded to this crisis by arguing that escalation was a sign of weakness rather than strength. In a reorientation course held in September 1965, instructors said that "although the Americans are fighting in the South and bombing the North, they are not strong. They bombed the North because they are bogged down in the South and therefore they do not have enough strength to go North." This conclusion was plausible, and indeed recent scholarship says the same thing about the gloom among sponsors of escalation. But it was hardly self-evident in My Tho, not when casualties soared and the Americans were arriving in force.[41]

Cadres and fighters tried to retain their composure. "Anyone who is accused of fear of the Americans always reacts strongly against it," reported the Instigator. "The usual reaction of the cadres, after they acknowledged being subdued by this fear, is to make greater and bolder efforts in order to prove they no longer fear the Americans." It was not just a movement trait, he added. "Within the Front-controlled area, anyone who is considered afraid of the Americans is regarded as an outcast, like a woman accused of illicit affairs." The party secretary of Vinh Kim admitted that his spouse was "very sad" about his decision to rally and that his eldest son wanted to commit suicide. "He complained that all his friends showed him great contempt because 'your father,' they said, 'had followed the American imperialist.'" Fear was stigmatized, while in the privacy of their thoughts villagers struggled to beat back a feeling of dread.[42]

These commentaries call attention to a fundamental shift in atmosphere within the popular movement. During the golden period, local activists debated questions across the whole range of village culture, but after 1965, issues that did not have a direct bearing on the war were tabled. The expansive spirit of the early days was at risk when militants strained to repress fear and panic, and when their vision narrowed to the steps required to survive and to keep on fighting. Modernist inspiration waned as the popular movement traded blow for blow with U.S. imperialism.

CHAPTER TEN

FATE OF THE LIBERATED ZONE

Speaking in October 1967, a poor peasant from Nhi Binh declared:

> Because of the war, the ways of life of the population have completely changed. Everybody is afraid of thinking of tomorrow and of the future. Trade and farming in the village have actually undergone a lot of changes to fit the new ways of life—a life in which everything seems to be just temporary and risky. Many families, having settled in their new houses along the highway, sold all their valuable objects to get a capital (amounting to about two or three thousand piasters) to start some kind of trade to live from hand to mouth. They usually buy fruit, chickens, and ducks and re-sell them at government-controlled market-towns making a daily profit of about 100 piasters, while other people try to earn some extra money by working as hired laborers to contribute to the daily expenses of a family of five or six people.

Themes of displacement and precipitancy impart to this account an unsettling aura. People have been obliged to move, the speaker affirms. They live in "new houses," and one is given the impression that these dwellings are temporary and may at any moment be abandoned as occupants scramble to a more advantageous perch. They are close to the highway and therefore to what is left of an infrastructure in the province, a network capable of moving commodities with dispatch. Speed is essential, given that "a lot of changes" are taking place, so that "everybody is afraid of thinking of tomorrow and of the future," "everything seems to be just temporary and risky," and people have to improvise in order to "live from hand to mouth." Peasants had been thrust into the "perfect market" so much anticipated by modernization theorists, a terrain without custom or law, inhabited by individuals who could draw on their capital and their labor and nothing else.[1]

According to David Harvey, the contemporary world is shaped by the pressure on corporations to reduce the turnover time for their capital and to move people, goods, and information at increasing speeds and over greater distances. Populations drawn into orbits governed by that imperative experience an acceleration in the rhythms of everyday life and are increasingly subject to decisions made by unseen, distant others, and as a result, consciousness in the maelstrom of modern life is infused with a mood of transience and doubt. Harvey calls this outcome a "time-space compression" and suggests that disruption in understandings of time and space are especially pronounced in phases when modernizing pressures are most intense.[2]

I see a link between Harvey's analysis and the work of James William Gibson, who calls attention to the "corporatization" of American military forces as Pentagon strategists sought to apply principles of "rationalized capitalist production" on the battlefield. In Vietnam, they reasoned, victory would come when soldiers generated overwhelming firepower at optimal speed, with rates monitored to assure efficiency and with prohibitively high costs for the enemy. Fighting against an army run according to time-and-motion principles, the Vietnamese were exposed to a militarized version of modernization logic and practice and to a variant of the time-space compression.[3]

After the failure of strategic hamlets and other devices to win hearts and minds in the villages, the Americans and their Saigon allies stopped trying to compete with the Front's projection of rural space and instead attempted to drive peasants from their homes. A military map of My Tho in David Hackworth's account of his tour of duty with the U.S. Ninth Division mostly features roads and firebases. Although the legend includes a symbol for "hamlet," only three out of the hundreds of hamlets in the province are pinpointed. Large sectors of the terrain appear as blank space, at the center of which is the notation "cultivated fields." But no cultivators are mentioned in the text. The map evokes the fantasy battlefield imagined by the Pentagon, a place where two "war making machines" were free to contend without any civilians getting in the way. It was an anticipation of the desired moment when all the villagers would have fled to the GVN zone.[4]

Bankrupt as a program of rural development, generating refugees proved effective in confounding the popular movement. Suddenly on the defensive, cadres were forced to de-center their portrayals of My Tho's role in the fighting. "There was no harm in the fact that the Front was not winning in the Delta," they insisted, "because, according to the Front policy, the Delta only played the role of immobilizing the enemy so that the Front troops in the mountainous region, especially in the center, would solve the war by modern warfare." Villagers in Binh Duc were not reassured by such assessments. "We don't know what is happening in other areas," they declared, "but in here, we have seen only death. Whenever a sweep operation takes place, about seven or eight people get killed." An informant from Ban Long reported that "a few" villagers "still believed that the Front would win in the end," but most took a more pessimistic view. "The war in my village has become very fierce, and the people believe that the situation in the entire country must be the same. This is why they've lost confidence in the Front."[5]

In a May 1967 reorientation session a cadre challenged the instructor: "You said that we defeated the enemy in the dry season, [so] why were we defeated by the enemy in Cam Son?" The answer was that "the battles we won were big and the battles in which we were defeated were small ones; therefore, we had to look for and understand so that we could distinguish the common affairs from the important ones." The questioner remained skeptical, for he had seen with his own eyes that "10 guerrillas and 5 civilians" were killed during the "sweeping operations." What looked like a "small" battle from a nationwide perspective, with only a handful of casualties, did not seem small to this resident, who added: "The village has been attacked by aircraft again and again. Many villagers were killed. The living conditions were poor. The villagers took refuge to secure areas. In my opinion, maybe the Front was winning the war in some other places, but not in my village."[6]

Conceptions of space and time, which were already marked by a degree of confusion before escalation, exploded after 1965, as peasants who before had imagined themselves as protagonists in the drama of their own liberation were forced back into a passive mode. U.S. troops, whose commander in chief was headquartered halfway around the world from Vietnam, drew on supply and communication lines that seemed shorter than those of guerrilla units fighting in their own backyards, and mass fervor, which had enabled the Front to outpace its Saigon rivals, could not match the lightning-fast deployments of an adversary drawing on an advanced technology. The challenge faced by the popular movement was not simply military in nature. Chapters 10 and 11 deal with the collapse of spatial and temporal constructions as a crisis in consciousness and understanding, showing once again how the war constitutes a phase in the social history of Vietnam.

SIGHTS AND SOUNDS

"The Front's maps are made by the Front, and are not like the maps out here," observed a defector. "They show every creek, trail and path going through the orchards. . . . 'In there' they pay a great deal of attention to maps, because many trails have spike traps, so that they need to know the area in great detail in order to avoid them." An informant from Thanh Hoa observed that

PLAF maps "are printed with colors somewhat like the maps used by the ARVN. But they bear no foreign words. Everything was written in Vietnamese. The place names were also those used by the people, and it was easier to spot the various locations on them." The phrase "in there" (trong do) evokes an enclosed, three-dimensional space, a realm unto itself. By conjuring up a frontier separating countryside from town, zones where the movement was in charge from zones controlled by the government, people who knew "every creek, trail and path" from people who did not, this language invites listeners to picture a Liberation Front secure its own dominion.[7]

The Thanh Hoa informant also reported that in 1962 "an imaginary demarcation line was fixed, and in the Front-controlled hamlets, the cadres began to operate openly." His words were meant to suggest that the popular movement had created an impregnable fortress. This notion of a liberated territory carried a potent emotional charge for revolutionaries who saw in it the embryo of a promised land so urgently imagined though not yet fully realized. Optimism was further reinforced by a sense of affiliation with an advancing socialist bloc and by the conviction that the United States was in retreat. The imperfect sovereignty of the liberated zone and the weak spots in the ramparts it had constructed seemed of little consequence, given the larger progress of liberation all over the globe.[8]

At the same time, the language of the Thanh Hoa informant indicated that lines between the movement and its adversaries were "imaginary" and that liberation had to be charted hamlet by hamlet and not on a province- or even village-wide basis. And indeed, government forts and the insurgents' own "spike traps" were scattered throughout My Tho, so that Front areas were not entirely secure. Rather than living in separate domains, GVN and NLF adherents shared the same space and lived so closely intertwined that they were generally able to see and hear each other.

In this crowded arena the two sides battled for control of the soundscape. The countryside had been quiet during the six years of peace, when, according to an informant from Hoi Cu, "the people were more demoralized than ever, and nobody dared to say anything because they were afraid that if the GVN overheard them they would die." Surviving militants were reduced to indirection and stealth. "They pretended to be drunk during banquets and said all sorts of things in front of the people, sometimes in the presence of GVN Village Council members." They "whispered things into the people's ears while they worked together with the people in the fields."[9]

Slogans shouted through megaphones at the beginning of the concerted uprising resounded so dramatically in part because they broke a constrained silence. One can understand why rebels banged on wooden fish with such vehemence and why the "diabolical concert" galvanized the movement and stunned local officials. Sounds traveled a long way in the countryside, and instigators with bullhorns addressed both villagers and GVN personnel stationed nearby. An informant reported: "At night, we waged propaganda through a megaphone at the edge of the 'liberated' zone. The quietness of the night in the countryside made our night propaganda audible in every hamlet for about four kilometers around us." The hovering authorities of old, alert for any sound of the Viet Cong, had now been turned into a captive audience for the broadcasts of an ascendant revolution.[10]

The Front went on to create its own sound system, so that beating on wooden fish came to be employed for a variety of purposes. At times it served as a psychological warfare tactic ("All the noise made the soldiers in the post worry because they didn't know what the Front was up to"). Elsewhere, continuous noisemaking for up to twenty minutes performed a celebratory function on Ho Chi Minh's birthday (May 19) or on "Labor Day" (May 1). Cadres beat on wooden fish to summon villagers to a meeting, and sentries did the same when government troops approached. "If the troops were still far away," said an informant, "they struck the wooden fish in a repeated series of six beats broken down into three groups of two: 2-2-2 // 2-2-2 // 2-2-2; or in a repeated series of nine beats broken down into three groups of three: 3-3-3 // 3-3-3 // 3-3-3."[11]

Militants who sometimes sought a wide audience for their pronouncements were on other occasions in danger of being overheard by eavesdropping enemies who were never far away. "Whenever we quarreled," a village guerrilla stated, the squad leader "used to calm us down, saying: 'You boys drink and talk too loudly. You can be heard by the enemy.'" In the same vein, the village secretary from Dang Hung Phuoc remembered that "the GVN had four watch towers separated from each other by a distance of 500 to 1,000 meters, and 75 soldiers positioned along the road. Therefore we could not dig up the road because the sound of digging might be heard from the GVN posts." By contrast, government forces were unable to suppress the commotion that accompanied their various maneuvers. The engines of ARVN vehicles announced their approach when they were still five kilometers away from My Hanh Trung, and in Binh Ninh the noise made by the outboard motors of GVN boat patrols touched off the alarm a half-hour before they arrived on the scene.[12]

In line with wartime requirements, the Front recoded ambient sounds. In Tan Binh Thanh the Buddhist bonze in the village pagoda who "prayed and beat on his gong night and day" threatened the monopoly on noisemaking that the revolution reserved for itself. In Thanh Phu (CL), "when the Front first arose and was still operating secretly, a few cadres acting on their own entered the pagoda and seized the bell and wooden fish, out of fear that the pagoda would use them to warn the GVN." Barking dogs posed the same sort of threat. Residents in Long Hung were warned not to let their dogs bark, and the same order was issued in Hoi Cu, where the barking "would 'give away' the presence of cadres on mission and would prompt the GVN to shell the village." In Cam Son, "because people feared the noise of the [rice threshing] machine would drown away that of the approaching planes, the machines were dismantled and moved away." In My Hanh Dong, villagers were enjoined not to "move around" in the early morning, and "the use of motor-sampans is strictly forbidden from 5 AM to 9:30 AM. This tight security is aimed at allowing the guards to detect easily the approach of the patrol boats and armored cars of the government troops."[13]

The two camps could observe as well as hear each other, with the revolutionaries at first possessing the better sightlines. According to one informant, "the Front built a wooden tower in a nearby hamlet to help the Phu Phong guerrillas to shoot at the post. This tower was hidden under the dense foliage of coconut trees and the GVN could not spot it. From this tower, the guerrillas could peer into the Phu Phong military post, and that enabled the guerrillas to shoot one soldier dead and to wound two others." Front units "often camped in Binh Trung at the junction of the three villages of Binh Trung, Huu Dao and Duong Diem," remarked a soldier. The site was favorable because of "many orchards laying at the edge of the villages with a dense vegetation of coconut trees and banana groves. When we camped in these orchards, we could clearly see all the vehicles passing by on Highway #4." Suspecting that the enemy might be close, the GVN took steps to eliminate the trees. An informant in Trung An said that government soldiers came "to clear the sides of the National Road by cutting down the trees in order to prevent the VC from sniping from behind them," and another informant from that village remembered how his mother's orchard was cut down in order to "clear the area along the highway."[14]

In the darkness, light traveled even farther and faster than sound, so when saboteurs in An Thai Dong used "their nail-level to dig up the road," they would "surround the spot with a canvas sheet to prevent the enemy from seeing sparks when the nail-lever hits the stones." A guerrilla reported that a neighbor sent signals to a GVN post that was only seventy-eighty meters from the hamlet. One day he was caught alerting the enemy "with his lighter when the Front troops came to make camp in my village."[15]

During the golden period, rural dwellers lived in a fragmented space in which every word and gesture had to be carefully calculated. But with the Front ascendant and the government in disarray, the closeness of the two sides helped the revolution spread its message. In 1965 the balance shifted. According to someone from Thanh Hoa, "we were shelled whenever the VC came there to broadcast their news through a megaphone. The GVN soldiers living in the Hoa Hung post, which was only five hundred meters away, could hear the broadcast distinctly and they shelled us." Escalation forced militants back into clandestinity and once again obliged them to whisper "into the people's ears," as in the dark days before the concerted uprising.[16]

THE OVERLAPPING MAPS OF EVERYDAY LIFE

The notion of a liberated territory also remained problematic because crowds traveled every day across the "demarcation line" between the two zones: to visit relatives, go to market, practice their religion, attend school, seek medical treatment, and take care of paperwork in government offices. These peregrinations indicate that solidarities created by the revolution did not exactly correspond to the larger network of social relations in the province. Dozens of the ralliers interviewed by Rand reported that they were able to call on relatives living in town to serve as guides and intermediaries when they decided to move from the NLF to the GVN zone. As has been demonstrated earlier, in the course of buying and selling and looking for work, many villagers had sojourned in My Tho city and the district capitals of the province or had ventured even farther afield, to Can Tho, Dalat, and Hue, and especially to Saigon.

Displacements associated with spiritual life also did not match up with the political map. Buddhists in Phu My "have to come to the GVN controlled area since all the temples are there," and Thanh Phu (CT) residents "worshipped the village spirit (Than Lang)" in a GVN-controlled hamlet. "This worship is considered a superstition which is strongly disapproved" by the NLF, but still, "even those who lived in the Front-controlled areas liked to escape from them to attend it." The same issue arose in Dong Hoa, where celebrants gathered to honor the village spirit, a practice the Front tried to block because it "was afraid that if the people from its area came to attend it, they would make contact with and pass the information to other villagers from the GVN-controlled zone." Meanwhile, "when there are big ceremonies," Dong Hoa Buddhists "usually go to My Tho to attend those ceremonies or meetings."[17]

While the NLF came to act like a state, conscripting soldiers, collecting taxes, and enforcing its own quasi-legal codes of conduct, it did not officially declare itself a government and therefore did not establish a civil register, issue its own currency, or develop other attributes associated with state power. Beginning with the confiscation of Saigon identity cards during the concerted uprising, cadres had tried to drive a wedge between villagers and the GVN bureaucracy. But as the war dragged on, this measure came to seem a mistake, so they had to look the other way when inhabitants took steps to replace the missing documents. "The Front couldn't meet all the people's needs," explained an informant from Duong Diem. "The people who lived in the liberated area still had to go out to the GVN area all the time to buy what they needed—food, motorized sampans, pumps, and other items that were necessary to their everyday life. Without "GVN papers they couldn't travel and trade."[18]

The Front effort to create an alternate school system in the countryside did not go beyond the elementary level, and what was achieved did not survive escalation. After ARVN soldiers burned down a school in Vinh Kim in 1962, cadres rebuilt it, but bombing and shelling persuaded parents to withdraw their children. "From then on, the villagers have become resigned to letting their children grow up illiterate," an informant reported, then added, "Only those who had their relatives living in the District town"—a category that, as noted earlier, may have included more than a few households—"were able to send their children over there to attend GVN schools." Even cadre families sent their offspring away to school.[19]

In the medical field as in education, the same process unfolded, with the Front at first striving for self-sufficiency, then retreating in response to wartime conditions. A report from an informant in Long Dinh indicates that it did not have the supplies, equipment, or personnel to take full responsibility for health care. "There were two nurses in my village, but no dispensary," he stated.

> There were some kinds of ordinary medicine such as anti-hemorrhagic pills, pills for headaches and stomach upsets. Those who were seriously ill were usually evacuated to the towns or to Saigon. The common diseases in my village were common cold, stomach ache and diarrhea. About ten people in the village had tuberculosis and were treated in the Saigon hospitals two of them have been cured and have returned to the village. They said that there was plenty of medicine in those hospitals. If they stayed in the village, they would have died. To which the VC cadres said that their diseases could be cured by the medicines made from local herbs, and that they did not need to go to Saigon. The people didn't believe the cadres however. Those who had diarrhea usually went to [a doctor] in My Tho.

The clientele of local healers were also scattered across political boundaries, as in the case of "a well-known practitioner of oriental medicine, an authority on Chinese studies, and a virtuous man" who resided in Duong Diem. "People from all the neighboring villages came to ask him for help" in choosing an auspicious day for a marriage or a funeral, and "sick people also came to him to get free examinations."[20]

In 1966–67, as traumatic war wounds multiplied, the Front developed a triage system that relied on government services. Cadres and soldiers were still treated in NLF "military dispensaries," and Front health workers continued to provide cholera and smallpox immunization, treatment for flu, fevers, and other common sicknesses, and first aid for minor injuries, especially to those without legal papers. Meanwhile, people with severe wounds or suffering grave illnesses or women about to give birth were advised to seek assistance in the My Tho hospital or elsewhere in the GVN zone. ARVN soldiers might be willing to call for an ambulance to transport the "seriously ill," but problems arose in other instances, leaving claimants and their families no choice but to bluff. Relatives of injured people "didn't worry about their lack of ID cards. They took the wounded into the district town and if they were checked, they simply replied: 'Because our relatives got seriously wounded, we were so concerned that we forgot to bring our ID cards along.'"[21]

Front practice itself undermined the notion of an integral liberated zone. While it attempted to regulate movement, the NLF was dispatching cadres on far-flung assignments, thereby taking advantage of and intensifying the restlessness of country people who longed to wander and explore. A desire for unfettered mobility led individuals toward the Communist Party, whose members were granted "much freedom, especially freedom of movement." And in spite of arduous material conditions and the fear of injury and death, some volunteered for service in the PLAF because, they reasoned, "all men want to go around and get to know more and learn more things."[22]

When one maps the pattern of social relations in the delta in these various ways, the imagined character of the liberated zone becomes apparent. It was not socially or economically self-sufficient and lacked the military capacity to seal its borders. It was a state of mind rather than a state.

THE MARKETPLACE

The discussion so far has sketched two kinds of spaces: rural communities, where the Front was well represented and the government hovered on the margins; and terrain judged by the authorities to be "secure." It has further emerged that movement back and forth between the two zones was an everyday reality for many peasants and indeed was a constitutive element in the delta society of the 1960s. This charting calls attention to the marketplaces, roads, and waterways that made possible networking among people who might be affiliated with the Front or the GVN, but who required a degree of interaction in order to survive. The Rand transcripts shed light on the distinctive social relations in these connecting spaces and underscore the impact of the war, always a factor but increasingly grim in its consequences after 1965.

Cover stories provided by defectors and deserters match up with the reasons that set all country people in motion. On running into a Front patrol, one informant recalled that he "came up to the guerrillas in a natural way" and told them that he was going to pay a visit to a relative. Counting on the fact that every household regularly frequented the marketplace, a rallier reported that, if stopped, he would have claimed to be "going to the market to sell things." Another hoped to blend in with the many villagers tramping in search of employment by identifying himself as "a working man." Since festive occasions drew people from all over, another planned to say that he was headed "to a wedding party." A defector told a boat captain that he "wanted to go to the city to cure my sickness and get some shots," and another, who was accompanied by his mother, asserted that "we had lost all our papers and had come to the district town to apply for new ones." Everyone understood that cadres were free to move around, which explains why a defector successfully "passed by many VC collection points." The guards "all knew me and asked me where I was going," he explained. "I told them that I was on mission."[23]

Marketplaces were centers of social life and links between town and countryside. Their varied roles are apparent in the comment of an informant who said that he and his friends "used to go to the market together, to have a drink or to do our shopping," while another went in order "to learn about the general situation and to see my friends." It also provided a setting for festive occasions, as in Thanh Phu (CT), where villagers gathered "at the market place to have a good time and the atmosphere was very lively." Peasants frequented village markets, but they also shopped and socialized in district capitals and in My Tho city and took advantage of these trips to sustain ties with relatives and friends living elsewhere. Letters and money transfers passed across the rural-urban divide with surprising rapidity. According to an informant from Hoi Cu, "communication between the village and Cai Be District town took only two or three days. If I could ask someone who went to the market to take a message to my relative today, then I would have an answer the following day." News also traveled through a grapevine that depended on multiple relay stations. Residents of Hoa Dinh "often went to the market. They got news in the town and related it to other villagers, for instance, the bombings of the North." Several Rand informants also reported buying newspapers in marketplaces.[24]

To fulfill their many functions, markets had to be open spaces, where revolutionaries, fence-sitters, and government personnel were all free to shop. According to one informant, "those who are still living in Binh Trung also had to go to the market in GVN-controlled areas to buy their food and to sell their crops, and most of them are cadres' relatives." The same convention applied when a marketplace was incorporated into the NLF zone. After the anti-Diem coup of November 1963, one market "fell into the VC-controlled area. The population from both sides came there to sell and buy things."[25]

A PLAF officer responsible for outfitting new recruits periodically asked a civilian sympathizer, a "Miss S.D.," to buy "over 100 mess plates, three or four rolls of khaki, and three or four rolls of nylon." Perhaps Miss S.D. divided up this shopping list among many purchasers in order to avoid drawing the attention of government agents. That, in any case, was the procedure followed by villagers responsible for feeding large military units. "Each time, they sent many women to the market—sometimes a few dozen—to buy food, because if only a few went they would each have to carry too much food back and this would arouse the suspicion of the GVN. Each woman bought a little food, and if anyone asked them they said that they were buying food to commemorate the death anniversary of their ancestors." In order to assemble mines and shells, Front munitions workshops mixed explosives from duds "with fire cracker powder they bought from the market," while other supply cadres "used to go to the market to buy fabrics to sew flags and banners." Medicine for NLF clinics "was purchased in Vinh Kim market or in My Tho." In calling attention to the absence of a boundary line between the co-belligerents, an informant remarked, "For the time being, there are no clear-cut areas, and the people fight, dig spike pits, and go to the market on the same day."[26]

So long as it held the initiative, openness worked to the advantage of the Front. "The VC will send the people to the market in large numbers to incite public opinion," reported one observer. "This usually makes the people react strongly." A cadre "knew what was happening in the district town through the villagers who came back from the market. Even if I did not ask them, they were always eager to inform me about any concentration of forces and about the number of military trucks and of APCs [armored personnel carriers], which had been gathered in the district town." But as militants increasingly worried about security, villagers on the road came under suspicion. "When a man went to the market and if a GVN operation occurred the next day, he would be suspected and watched. If he slipped a wrong word, he would be followed." The eldest brother of one informant "dared not go to the market too often to pay a visit to my second brother, because he feared being suspected by the Front."[27]

The GVN also kept an eye on men in public spaces, who would be in trouble if they were unable to produce a valid ID card. But with no other way of distinguishing "Viet Cong" from "simple peasants," they were at first ill-equipped to monitor and control foot traffic, a deficit that was at least partially made good with the arrival of defectors from NLF ranks. According to a cadre, "the women who came back from the town markets often said that they had come across many ralliers and that these ralliers were free to loiter around the market like everyone else." A female informant from Long Binh Dien used to shop for the Front. When the village party secretary rallied, she said, "my cover was blown."[28]

As the war became more total, it spread into previously exempted spaces. According to the Midwife, the large and prosperous Thien Ho market "stretched along the canal and it was very easy to go in and out to trade." But after the government took steps to secure it, "the market place was walled in for control purposes," and "the people didn't dare to go there to trade." On account of the high walls, she explained, "the place didn't look like a market place," suggesting that a fortified market struck rural dwellers as a contradiction in terms. After the Front seized control of the area, because of "constant shellings and bombings" and "the robbers who roamed there," the site was abandoned. "The market is now a desert," she concluded.[29]

The two sides could not permit the same outcome all over the province and so came to a tacit agreement that allowed women a greater freedom of movement than was accorded to men. The mother of a cadre who planned to defect was able to transfer family belongings to a new life hamlet because she "sold fruit at the Ba Dua market," and therefore "her frequent absences were not suspected by the guerrillas." On being asked if he went to market, an informant responded: "I dared not. If I went there, I would be suspected by the Front of secretly working for the GVN. Only women could go to the markets located in the district town." When a rallier in the marketplace bumped into the wife of a cadre, "she was scared and intended to slip away. I called her back and told her that I did not have any intention of arresting her." In explaining this forbearance, he said that the cadre "dared not behave harshly towards my wife because he also feared that I could get back at him." Since women needed to shop to keep their families alive, both the cadre and the rallier had an interest in preserving the neutrality of the marketplace. A similar complicity elsewhere allowed some markets to remain open. Often disrupted by war, they were not the most militarized of the public spaces in My Tho.[30]

HIGHWAYS AND WATERWAYS

The My Tho infrastructure ranged from the grand to the humble. The Mekong River and National Route 4, known among villagers as the "Indochina Road," were intensively patrolled by the government and were not safe places for cadres and guerrillas. The adversaries were more equally matched on secondary roads, canals, and lesser rivers. Also potentially explosive were the "intersections" where communications lines employed by the co-belligerents crisscrossed, such as those along Route 4, which separated the northern and southern regions of the province. At the other end of the spectrum, cadres and guerrillas felt most secure, though hardly safe, on the trails, creeks, and paths of the sort recorded on NLF, but not GVN, maps.

Rallier escape narratives convey a sense of the hazards involved in traveling on this network and suggest that the risks were shared by all itinerants. Many defectors chose to leave under cover of darkness, making their way through orchards or paddy fields in order "to avoid being arrested by the guerrillas who stood guard on the paths." While these fugitives hovered in the no-man's land between zones, the highway must have seemed like a safe haven. "Along with my mother," reported a man who had been a typist in a Front print shop, "I went to National Highway #4 and at the very last moment, the guerrillas heard of my rally and tried to catch me. I saw them pursuing me far behind and I ran to the road. I was saved because they dared not come there. We took a bus and reached Phu My." But the road itself presented a new set of dangers, especially at night. "I waded through ricefields and two small canals," recalled a deserter. "When I came near the highway, I did not dare go on walking to Cai Lay district town and had to hide myself in the fields, awaiting daylight." Other deserters were afraid to step onto the dark road "because we thought that we might be shot by the GVN soldiers."[31]

Once on the highway, travelers occasionally ran into a familiar face. "I was afraid of being beaten by the soldiers," a defector reported. "Fortunately, I met a cyclo driver friend who took me into My Tho." But for the most part this was a world of strangers, and people took a chance when seeking assistance, as when a deserter hitched a ride with a truck driver who turned out to be a helpful accomplice. "I pretended that I was his assistant," he explained, "in order to pass through the check points." Several conscripts on the run from the PLAF hid in an orchard near a post. "Early on that morning I saw a woman passing by on the road. I asked her to help us by telling the SDC [Self Defense Corps] men who camped in the post that we were willing to rally to the GVN. This woman agreed and a moment later, some SDC men came toward us." The tone was more adversarial in the narrative provided by another deserter, who recalled that "very early in the morning, I came to the highway. I had to hide in a bush because I was still wearing a Front soldier's uniform." When a student passed by, "I came out of the forest and asked him to give his clothes to me. Seeing that I was wearing a Front soldier's uniform, he got scared and quickly complied with my desire."[32]

Ralliers did not know if they could trust drivers of three-wheeled Lambrettas and other modest conveyances. A hamlet cadre escaping from Long Binh Dien took a chance and asked one to bring him to the My Tho Chieu Hoi Center, while a second fugitive trusted another to let him out at the nearest post. But then there was the driver who refused to pick up a group of deserters, then signaled their presence further along "to the GVN soldiers who sent out a squad to see whether or not there were VC laying in ambush." Buses seem to have been less likely than smaller vehicles to be stopped at government checkpoints; thus a soldier who went AWOL in Tay Ninh rode without incident to Saigon and then to My Tho. "I was not questioned because I traveled by bus," he explained. By contrast, fellow deserters who "traveled to Saigon by three-wheel 'Lambretta' cars [were] arrested when they tried to pass the Ben Cat headquarters." Perhaps because bus drivers conveyed many passengers and were expected to adhere to a fixed schedule, they seemed more likely to mind their own business. If the traveler could afford to ride, a bus was probably the fastest and safest option.[33]

The balance of forces appears to have been more favorable to the Front on canals and small rivers than on highways. "At night, on the canals, there were long caravans of sampans loaded full with ammunition cases and weapons" going through the province. Water transport became riskier as the war escalated, but even in April 1967, twelve-sampan fleets "covered with palm leaves" and "hidden under the bushes along the river side when airplanes were seen in the sky" brought ammunition from the Mekong River through Binh Trung village. Another informant reported convoys of six to eight sampans, each "loaded with 20 cases of ammunition weighing 25 kilograms," which were not "bombed or discovered by the GVN." Because the Front was not so much of a presence on major arteries, and because it did not have trucks to move heavy loads, highway shipments of this magnitude would have been inconceivable on the Indochina Road.[34]

Both sides patrolled the waterways. An informant from Phu Phong reported that "Front soldiers guarded the river at night" and would not have noticed a traveler who "left at noon," but in Long Trung "the guerrillas stood guard during the night as well as the day. They also inspected the sampans." In My Duc Tay cadres "stopped and searched the sampans going to the city. They let the women go, but sent back young men who were of draft age." Barges in the area around Thanh Phu (CT) were required to halt at Front checkpoints "all along the canals." As one deserter explained, he could have taken a motorized sampan, "but I didn't dare to do so, because I was afraid that the sampan would pass by VC check points and that I would be captured by the guerrillas." Instead he "took the bus to My Tho." For their part, government "River Assault groups" constantly circulated. In Tan Thoi "the GVN river craft stopped the boat for inspection and arrested all those who did not have regular papers."[35]

Sampan drivers often noticed travelers who seemed to have something to hide, and this factor, when combined with the patrolling of the two sides, created a volatile atmosphere among voyagers on water. Some trips were uneventful. "It was more than 25 kilometers from my place to My Thanh," noted an informant from Xuan Son. "I took a small sampan and rowed myself." Fortunately "nobody asked for my papers at all, neither the VC nor the GVN authorities." One deserter made his escape by wading across a creek, then got a ride from a woman on the way to the Cai Be market. "The lady on the boat asked me: 'Where are you going? Why are you so deep in the mud?' I told her I was going to Cai Be and asked her to tell whoever asked about us that I was accompanying her to the market. She said: 'I'll tell anybody who asks about us that you are my nephew and are going to the market with me.'" Another deserter was similarly assisted by a boat captain. The fugitive first pretended he wanted to go to My Tho for medical treatment, then added that he did not have identity papers and feared being arrested by the GVN. "He told me to come into the hold of the boat and stay near the engine. He would tell the authorities I was his workman in case the boat was searched." On arriving in town, the passenger confessed that he wished to defect. "The boat captain hired a pedicab and had me transported to the Chieu Hoi Center."[36]

When GVN soldiers accompanying her in a sampan questioned an eighteen-year-old female defector, she claimed to be headed for a visit with an aunt. "During the crossing, the GVN Lieutenant in charge asked me: 'Where are you going? I'm sure you are not going to visit any relatives. Tell me the truth.'" When informed that she wished to rally, soldiers helped her reach a Chieu Hoi Center. The anecdote indicates that voyagers sometimes had to be convincing liars and that even female travelers might arouse suspicion if their appearance and behavior seemed inconsistent with the assumption that they were going to market.[37]

Encounters with Front sympathizers could also be problematic, especially for young men. A deserter offered this report:

> I marched to the river bank with the intention of taking a motorized sampan to cross the river. But there were then many villagers who were going to the market and I dared not get into it. Another sampan passed by then and I called it over. An old man was rowing it and he agreed to take me to the other bank. When we were in the middle of the river, I asked him where the nearest military post was. My question made him suspicious and he tried to hit me with his paddle. Although I had a rifle in my hands, I did not have the heart to kill him. But he pushed me to the water and I wrestled with him. He shouted: "Help! Help me to capture a traitor! (Viet gian) Help! Guerrillas!" I saw then many motorized sampans moving toward us from the riverbank and I had to jump into the water and swim away. I had to dive under the water whenever a motorized sampan passed by.

A bit later, a GVN "River Assault group" picked up the informant and took him to My Tho. He estimated that "16 motorized sampan owners worked for the Front" in the Binh Ninh region.[38]

All villagers and not just defectors encountered an unpredictable environment on the roads and water routes of the province, whose traffic flows were subject at any moment to interventions by one or the other of the contending parties and where one was surrounded by strangers. In the hamlets, everyone knew everyone else. By contrast, social relations in the connecting links between town and countryside prefigured the anonymity that prevailed in an increasingly urbanized Vietnam.

MILITARIZATION OF THE TERRAIN

Travel was bound to be hazardous as the liberated zone disintegrated and the NLF and the GVN grappled from one end of the province to the other. After 1965 the entire terrain was inexorably militarized. In Dang Hung Phuoc a cadre was "killed by the guerrillas when he was on mission because he was approaching them from the wrong direction." In that village and elsewhere, people increasingly did not know which way to turn.[39]

During the golden period, Front efforts met with some success on secondary roads, such as Route 28 in the northeast corner of the province, where in

1963 "traffic was completely paralyzed, and in the daytime, guerrillas safely appeared," an observation that helpfully defines two kinds of "traffic," the motorized vehicles of the GVN, which were excluded, and the guerrillas on foot, who traveled freely. But even at the peak of its influence, the NLF was overmatched on major highways, where the enemy's superior firepower and transport capabilities could be effectively deployed. PLAF units moved all over the province, but on their own paths, and even in the best of times, they were careful about crossing Route 4 and would never have used the highway to get from one place to another. The optimal Front traffic on the Indochina Road would have been an individual cadre, preferably with legal papers, for example, a liaison agent pedaling a bicycle or traveling by bus.[40]

With escalation, government efforts to block the "intersections," thus severing NLF liaison routes and disaggregating rural space, were increasingly effective. "Armored cars are stationed all along the highway," a soldier reported, and ARVN units permanently occupied many sectors of Route 4 in Cai Lay and Long Dinh districts. "What the GVN did was to transport its troops in trucks along the road and then drop them off unexpectedly anywhere along the road to protect it." On secondary roads the NLF's earlier successes were rolled back, as on Route 24 in Cho Gao district, which the Front "knew it would never be able to destroy," and on Route 25, running along the Mekong River through Song Thuan and other villages, where "ARVN troops have constantly patrolled and set ambushes."[41]

As a result, an informant noted, "most of the dangers" for Front personnel occurred "while they were on the move and especially when they were going across roads and rivers." Forts at key points supported government spoiling efforts, as when Post 22 severed a supply link through Hoi Cu. "This post was set up in mid-1966 and, ever since, the Front has stopped using this route to carry its ammunition." Securing the highway also cut connections between cadres in the northern and southern regions of the province. In Nhi Binh, which was bisected by Route 4, the NLF divided its organization into two branches. "If the village remained as an integral territory," an informant explained, "the cadres who had to cross the National Route to carry out their duties would be either killed or wounded. In the past, four persons had been killed under this condition."[42]

Compelled to fight on unfavorable terrain, the Front was entangled in a maze of contradictions. Political and military capital had to be invested in order to mobilize teams of fifty to two hundred villagers to build dirt barriers or dig trenches on highways. Guerrilla units would have to seal off sections of the road and hold their positions for several hours so that the job could be completed. Difficult to organize and dangerous to carry out, such projects offered only a modest prospect for success. Roadblocks might temporarily impede traffic, with attendant benefit for a simultaneous military operation in the environs, but the overall result was no more than an interruption in enemy activity.[43]

The Front also tried to ambush or blow up "military cars" and "soldiers' trucks" and to assassinate GVN officials and their U.S. advisers. It was risky work in what one combatant characterized as a "front-line" sector and was made possible only if the various participating units could achieve a high level of coordination in the dangerous highway environment. In 1963 plans were made to assassinate a Saigon policeman. The idea was to put up barricades with the hope that the policeman would then arrive to supervise repairs and would walk into a platoon-strength ambush. But the barricades were finished two hours ahead of schedule, "so that a lot of buses and all sorts of vehicles had to wait along the roadside." As a result, "the VC Local Force Troops had to give up their plan of attack because it would do much harm to the vehicles and their passengers, and the militiamen could hide behind the busses to shoot at them."[44]

As this account suggests, mines and ambushes ran the risk of hitting non-military targets. "The Front never mined civilian buses deliberately," affirmed a sapper, but his account makes clear that accidents did happen when demolition teams were "inefficient" and hit buses instead of military vehicles, with the result that "only civilian people got killed." The hit-or-miss character of sabotage work, based on the notion that clothing helped to distinguish friends from enemies, is evident in this account from a platoon leader: "A military truck was then running ahead of the Americans' vehicle, and we intended to blow the truck up. But when it came nearer, we saw that it was carrying people wearing white clothes. We thought they were civilians and gave up. Then came the Americans' vehicle. We blew it up because we saw that the passengers were military men because they wore khaki uniforms. We then didn't know they were Americans." In 1967 another demolition team operating on Route 4 managed to damage a vehicle and kill two soldiers. But they also mistakenly demolished a fish sauce truck, an accident that cost the life of the driver. The responsible cell leader was "strongly criticized" within the Front and cursed by villagers, who "said that if the guerrillas wanted to attack the GVN military vehicles it was all right, but that it was wrong for them to attack civilian vehicles because then only innocent people got killed."[45]

Rural dwellers along the road paid a price for attempted ambushes. Speaking of a stretch of Route 4 in Hoi Cu, an informant reported that when district and province demolition teams blew up military vehicles, "GVN soldiers poured into the hamlets which lay alongside the highway" and that "these hamlets were mortared at night." As a result, life "was almost unbearable," and the inhabitants were relieved when Post 22 was established, since "the demolition teams didn't dare to come there to plant mines again." In such instances the asymmetry between the two sides is apparent, as one, with uneven success, tried to spare the civilian population, while the other as a matter of policy took vengeance on villagers for the sins of the Viet Cong.[46]

At hamlet level the Front often succeeded in wiping out roads and bridges. In Hau My "roads are completely obstructed since they have been destroyed and planted with booby-traps, spikes, and mines," and according to an informant from My Long, "None of the roads in my village can now be used for motor vehicles since all of them have been excavated." In Long Hung ten kilometers of road were destroyed and two bridges blown up. In My Hanh Dong, after sabotage of the road, villagers who wanted "to go from one hamlet to another" were obliged to walk "along the rice fields." In My Hanh Trung the villagers went to market "along the dikes of the rice field because the roads leading to the village were full of mines and booby traps," especially in "places covered with thick green grass." In Duong Diem "the people were allowed to use only one path; all the other paths were blocked by obstacles, rigged with grenades, mined and lined with spike pits by the Front."[47]

In a departure from their pledge to stand for progress and development, local militants were dismantling the rudiments of a modern infrastructure in the countryside. Even a small advance in the form of increased bicycle use had to be reversed. Before 1965 "almost every household" in Cam Son and "many people" in An Thai Dong owned bikes, and there were over one hundred bicycles in Long Dinh. But after escalation, in Cam Son "the bridges have been destroyed and grass has grown all over the roads, so the bicycles cannot be used." In Phu My "there are no bicycles since there is no road." The irony was noted by an informant from Vinh Kim, who recalled that "the Village Committee did urge the villagers to repair roads and bridges during the early years of the Revolution." But, he continued, in 1966 the committee "ordered the villagers to destroy every road and bridge and forced the people to use new paths." The "public works" of the golden period were thus tabled, as the movement sponsored a regression from "roads" to "paths."[48]

An informant from Nhi Qui claimed that "many villagers" were wounded by spikes but testified that he "did not see any GVN soldiers killed by that trick." Cadres insisted that people should be able to distinguish safe places from danger zones, but they also tried to frighten the enemy with fake warning signs along approach routes. Residents must have noticed when guerrillas fled "under the thick cover of bushes along the river or through dense gardens where special signs reading 'Tu Dia' (deadly place) are displayed." According to a cadre, "we informed the villagers about the new planting of spikes and grenades in the hamlet and asked them to take the routes we pointed out for their daily movements. Nevertheless, one man didn't follow our advice and stepped on a planted grenade." It turned out "that the old man had gotten killed because he thought our warnings were only propaganda," a predictable mistake in light of the acknowledgment from the informant that "we had given the same warnings many times before when no spikes or grenades were planted."[49]

A prisoner exaggerated in claiming that villagers "joyfully" mined roads and blew up bridges (the transcripts are full of complaints about this work), but it could be that the rural population saw some purpose in fortifying hamlets. "Compared to other assignments," remarked a cadre from Tam Hiep, "mobilizing the people to sharpen spikes was a relatively easy job. When we urged them to do so, we convinced them that spikes were only designed to protect their belongings. They agreed with us because, even nowadays some soldiers still loot the villagers." And yet these tactics offered no protection against bombs and shells, and while booby traps and pungee sticks might deter marching infantry, they could not halt enemy transport. "The amphibious tanks do not need the roads and can still come in the liberated areas," observed an informant from My Luong. "These tanks can go anywhere. This is why the VC have built 3m wide canals to stop these tanks. These canals can't stop the amphibious tanks completely, but at least they helped delay their advance." Local militants realized that the Front could not prevent the GVN and the Americans from invading the liberated zone. At best, obstacles were intended to delay their approach.[50]

Struggle for control of waterways followed the same pattern. As was the case on Route 4, the NLF could not prevent or even significantly trouble government transport of men and equipment on the Mekong River. A demolition specialist reported that it was impossible to plant mines because the river was too wide and too deep. Attempts to plumb the depths "went down to about 60 meters and still didn't get to the river bed," and boats that "ran in the middle part of the river" were beyond the range of recoilless rifles. But attacks could be mounted on the Ba Ria, Phu Phong, and Long Dinh rivers, and efforts were also made to interdict traffic on canals, as when "an earthen dam" was constructed in "Canal Three" in order to prevent "the GVN boats from coming into the liberated area and from shooting at the people."[51]

In My Phuoc the Front thought that tree trunks could be used "to obstruct the movement of ships" in a nearby canal, but in general they could not employ the tactics that were destroying roads and bridges to all the waterways of the province. To enforce an economic embargo against the Vinh Kim marketplace, saboteurs "strung wire in the canals to prevent the people from carrying their goods to the market," but "the villagers protested so much against the embargo that the Front had to give it up." Popular pressure and their own need for usable routes stayed the hand of Front demolition teams in other locales, for if cadres and other rural dwellers could not travel by road, then travel by water was the only alternative.[52]

One informant reported that "all the canals in the liberated areas were navigable, but all the roads leading to the liberated areas have been destroyed." According to an observer from Hau My, "the NLF has officially forbidden the use of roads in order to facilitate the construction of defensive emplacements to hold out against operations." With no other options, "the inhabitants travel by sampans or motorboats." In My Hanh Dong, a "mud road" was sabotaged, and so "the villagers mostly travel by motor-sampans along 'Governor Loc' canal." The same reasoning applied in My Long, where "the villagers traveled only by motor boats along Nhi Qui canal. The roads had been either destroyed or filled with booby traps and landmines to block the advance of Government troops." It is therefore not surprising that "most" villagers in Phu My, "almost all households" in Cam Son, and "a lot" in Long Dinh owned a sampan.[53]

DISSOLUTION OF THE LIBERATED ZONE

Escalation forced the movement to renounce strategic agency and fall back on tactical improvisation. In the words of Michel de Certeau, "a strategy assumes a place that can be circumscribed as *proper* and thus serve as the basis for generating relations with an exterior distinct from it." As war spread, the movement was without a place of its own and had to operate on "a terrain imposed on it and organized by the law of a foreign power." It did "not have the means to keep to itself, at a distance, in a position of withdrawal, foresight, and self-collection," and was therefore reduced to maneuvers of no more than a tactical import. It operated "in isolated actions, blow by blow." Options remained but did not go beyond "the chance offerings of the moment." Hoping just to survive, local militants no longer seemed capable of finding a way toward victory.[54]

Meanwhile, war was squeezing the life out of the peasantry. Troop sweeps, bombing and shelling, clouds of herbicides, and tanks rampaging through paddy fields were turning the countryside into a wasteland. Groping for ways to resist, the NLF planted mines, staged ambushes, and destroyed roads, thereby further degrading the environment in which the rural population was trying to live. Marketplaces remained open but had become danger zones, with little room for the everyday encounters that once held society together. On highways, three- and four-wheeled vehicles continued to carry passengers fearful of getting caught in the crossfire as the belligerents repeatedly clashed. Water travel imposed its own risks, as the adversaries battled for control over routes whose importance grew when other sectors of the rural infrastructure collapsed. Asphyxiation loomed as war cut off the movement of goods and people on which the agrarian system depended.

A sense of building a place of their own had once freed activists to move in imaginative flights as they anticipated the future and on the terrain as the Front zone expanded. When that sense of collective ownership evaporated, freedom of movement went with it, and surviving militants were forced to take refuge in trenches and bunkers. A countryside that had seemed "absolutely secure" was now a deathtrap. " 'In there,' life was miserable and dangerous," noted an informant from Tan My Chanh. "Life in there is extremely hard and one can hardly endure it," agreed a witness from Tan Binh. Memories of the liberated zone retained a potent charge. But activists were losing the base and framework that had given shape to their revolutionary dreams.[55]

CHAPTER ELEVEN

"LIVE HOUR, LIVE MINUTE"

In My Tho, the evolution of temporal as well as spatial categories was marked by abrupt and confusing shifts. The starting point was hardly tranquil, as revolutionary and government clock times diverged, the co-belligerents imposed time disciplines that were out of step with the agrarian cycle, and solar and lunar calendars uneasily coexisted. Just as it had done with space, U.S.-sponsored modernization "compressed" time. When it speeded up the pace of warfare, the Front was compelled to adopt slow-down tactics that frustrated the Americans but also impeded villagers in their daily rounds. The present chapter analyzes these instabilities in the measure and control of time.

TIME DISCIPLINES

During the war, clock time in the Republic of South Vietnam was one hour ahead of clock time in the Democratic Republic of Vietnam. The NLF followed the northern rather than the southern clock, so that the watch worn by a GVN official would have been set one hour ahead of the watch worn by a Front cadre. In some contexts this disjuncture seemed no more than an oddity, as when a soldier said, "One day, after I finished my training course for the day, at 4 PM (Hanoi time), I went down to the river to take a bath." But, then, consider this report, from a liaison agent: "Normally, I started for Long Hung at noon (Saigon time) on my working days because the period of time from 12:00 AM to 2:00 PM is the GVN soldiers' rest time. There were no patrols on the ricefields and no movement of troops." Benefiting from the lull, he said, "I crossed back over the open ricefields and arrived at my hamlet at about 2:00 PM. It was an easy job, with little risk or difficulty." Here and in other situations, completion of assignments and personal safety depended on a knack for switching back and forth between two clocks.[1]

The government and the Americans functioned within an urban environment where work was done in office time, and so, when defectors passed through the no-man's-land between NLF and GVN zones, they sometimes arrived in My Tho or a district capital in the evening or on a weekend, when Chieu Hoi Centers were closed. One rallier who showed up outside of business hours was warned, "If you wander around here tonight and run into some policemen you will be put in jail." An informant who had gotten a job as a salesgirl in Saigon recalled that work was confined to a fixed number of hours per day. When asked how the Americans treated Vietnamese employees, she replied: "I didn't hear much about working conditions. I only heard that the workers had a fixed time schedule."[2]

Some responded positively to this novelty. "Americans are behaving nicely and are paying the workers well," testified an informant. "Having to work only during office hours is also very much appreciated by the people." Others were nervous about work by the hour and about wage labor more generally, so different from the routines of smallholders who oscillated between periods of idleness and intense exertion and whose land provided for their subsistence. When itinerants returned to My Long and were asked about life in Saigon, they reported "living from hand to mouth. They would have nothing to eat if they didn't work daily." Looking at the problem from another perspective, the Rebel noted that "in the GVN schools, the teachers quit right after the end of the classes and they never stayed in the schools late to help the students who did poorly in the classes." It was, she thought, an inefficient practice. "Unlike the Front teachers, the GVN teachers didn't try to save time for the people by teaching whenever they were free." What must have seemed rational time management from the perspective of a school administrator resulted in time lost for others.[3]

In workshops, offices, and armed forces, the Front imposed its own regimen. Regroupees, who had gotten used to a "fixed time schedule for work and rest" in the DRV army, were sometimes "dissatisfied" after returning to the South, where "their life was no longer that good and well regulated." But for southern peasants, by-the-hour discipline in the PLAF was experienced as a break from village practice. Soldier-informants reported that everyone had to get up at a fixed time, with breakfast soon after. Two or three hours in the morning were given over to "military training," followed by two hours of "political" study in the afternoon. The second meal came at 4:00 PM, and kiem thao (criticism/self-criticism) at 6:00. Unless the unit was scheduled to march from one campsite to the next, sing-alongs or other entertainments followed before everyone retired at 9:00. Several free periods were spaced throughout the day when troops could mend or wash clothes, fish for their next meal, write letters, or take a nap. A soldier in a rear service company reported that his comrades liked one commander "because he wasn't status conscious. During working hours, we had to obey his orders, but outside working hours, he was egalitarian with all the men in the unit." Indeed, the drawing of a precise line between work time and the rest of the daily routine constituted one of the novelties of army life.[4]

Time discipline in some of the civilian branches of the NLF was even more exacting than in the PLAF. A man assigned to a munitions shop reported:

> We got up every day at 5:30 AM, got all our things ready in case there was an alert and we had to flee. At 6:00 AM, we had breakfast—each day we were each given one liter of rice and two piasters to buy food. From 6:30 to 7:30, we attended a supplementary cultural course. We worked without interruption in the workshop from 8:00 AM. We had dinner from 5:00 to 5:30 PM. We attended a *kiem thao* session from 6:00 to 7:00. We could rest or do what we wanted from 7:00 to 9:00 PM. We went to bed at 9:00 PM.

Some elements here (two meals, *kiem thao*) were comparable to those of the military schedule, but there was less free time, and the "cultural" segment had been reduced to half an hour. As for the work itself, references to "quotas" for production of grenades, mines, and cartridges suggest that the enterprise was run like a factory. "Conflict between the members and the leading cadres erupted very often, because the Managing Staff always set a quota that was too high," so "the members protested" and "didn't do their best." As a consequence, "the output of the workshop was always lower than the quota."[5]

Some activists responded positively to Front discipline. A medical officer in a printing house said that he and other workers got up at 6:00 and "took turns preparing our meals." Breakfast was at 7:00, followed by work from 7:30 to 11:30 and then, after a break, from 1:30 to 4:30. "In the evening, those who had a higher education degree helped the other people to learn." Everyone was in bed by 9:00. This informant affirmed that he and other workers willingly endured "hardships" and "even felt pleasure, for we thought that our work was helpful to our people and our country." By contrast, another employee complained that workers "were neither allowed to go home nor to visit the areas surrounding the printing shop. It was almost like being under house arrest." Conditions were so arduous that even the army seemed preferable, and "when the draft campaign was launched," workers "eagerly joined up in order to avoid having to go on leading a life of misery and solitude in the printing shop."[6]

The Rebel was assigned to the district committee headquarters, where the staff ate breakfast at 5:00, then worked from 7:00 to 11:00, from 1:00 to 3:00, and then again after dinner and a bath. "Every day I had to work for eight hours," she asserted, "and many times I had to work until 11 or 12 o'clock at night. I became sick because of this exhausting schedule and couldn't do any work." Another female informant, already in poor health, was assigned to a medic training program, with "learning" and "discussion" from 7:00 to 12:30 and "study" after dinner. In her weakened condition, afternoons devoted to "sweeping, cooking, gathering firewood, and digging trenches" proved taxing, and she eventually dropped out.[7]

Outside of workshops and military units, life was less regimented, but the Front still strove for to-the-minute exactitude. A tardy liaison agent might put lives in danger, as when news of a 1963 ARVN sweep did not arrive on time and five cadres were caught by surprise and killed. In Binh Duc a man overslept and missed the announcement that the village perimeter had been mined in anticipation of an enemy attack. When he got up and started to walk out of the hamlet, "the grenade that was rigged to the gate exploded and he was killed." In a 1966 battle the battalion command delayed giving a retreat order, and as a result, "all the wounded fighters were discovered and annihilated by planes at daybreak." "Logically," the informant in this instance declared, "the time to open fire would have been at least 2 hours earlier so as to allow the retreat in time." Even conscientious fulfillment of assignments could not be exactly calibrated. A liaison agent had to navigate three canals and keep an eye out for strafing and shelling in order to deliver letters to the edge of a mangrove swamp. Although her contact would be waiting in a sampan in an exposed position, the best that could be done was a meeting time fixed "at between noon and one o'clock."[8]

Communist Party discipline was not always strong enough to enforce punctuality. Every day, trainees at a 1965 reorientation course for Vinh Kim party members "were from twenty minutes to an hour late." In Thanh Phu (CT) self-criticism sessions "usually started at 9 or 10 AM and went till 3 PM. However, not all the participants arrived on time; some arrived there at 10 AM, some showed up at 12 noon." In a sign of their ambivalence, villagers, and especially the party members among them, were quick to criticize comrades with a "bourgeois" taste for items such as sandals, nylon shirts—and wristwatches. So long as many continued to look with "suspicion" on activists who "began to buy wrist watches," tardiness would remain a problem.[9]

LUNAR AND SOLAR CALENDARS

The clash between Front priorities and the agrarian cycle amounted to the most consequential fault line in the temporal economy of the movement.

Staffers in the NLF region office worked very hard, a typist asserted. By contrast, village cadres "had a rather easy job."

> If they had something to do they'd do it, otherwise they just stayed at home and farmed to support their families. If they had to go on a mission far away, they left the village for a few days, and then came home again. They went around drinking wine and getting good food with others. Their work was different from mine in the Region headquarters. There each person had a definite job to do and everybody had to follow a fixed schedule. But in the village, things were different. The work proceeded at a much slower pace. If the cadres couldn't finish something today, they just postponed it till the next day. They didn't try to save time and finish their work quickly. The organization of the Front in the village was much looser.

This twenty-two-year-old informant had gone to school and then worked in Saigon before being assigned a clerical role in the NLF. He was unfamiliar with the alternation of heavy labor and slack time in the agricultural sector and with the protocols of organizing at hamlet level, which tended to be integrated into patterns of local sociability, built around people eating and drinking together. His commentary reflects the gap between a time discipline adopted by some sectors of the Front and the customary rhythms of village life.[10]

The typist also did not grasp the need for an accommodation between farming and political work and between the lunar and solar calendars. In Rand interviews, mentions of the solar predominate, but the lunar is also noted, suggesting that villagers lived in two time systems (as do many Vietnamese today). Political and military events, such as the moment when one joined the Front or the Communist Party, were dated by the solar calendar, and indeed one could say that NLF time was solar time. An informant declared that liaison agents "travel on even days of a week, then on odd days of the following one. These days are counted according to the western calendar." It was the same with monthly meetings of village party chapters, as in Dong Hoa, where the members were convened on "the 30th day of the Gregorian Calendar."[11]

Evocations of the lunar calendar sometimes indicated that people were at odds with Front priorities. A young man who joined the movement in 1960 noted that "people tried to stop me because it was an inauspicious day, the fifth day of the fifth lunar month, but I refused to listen to them." Local militants condemned superstitious practices and therefore took exception when "village landowners" sponsored "a ceremony to worship the God of Agriculture (Than nong) on the 16th day of the first month of the lunar year." They were also ill-disposed toward rituals for "worshipping the village spirit," which informants invariably scheduled by the lunar calendar. Processions of Buddhist worshippers called attention to an inspiration and collective discipline outside the movement, an autonomy that, again, was underscored by lunar dating. Breakaway prophets followed a similar practice, as in the case of the blacksmith who founded the "Nui Nua" sect. "On the 15th day of every lunar month, his offerings on the altar were all vegetables and fruits. On the 16th day, however, the offerings were meat."[12]

Economic and social aspects of the agrarian system were measured in lunar time, beginning with the plowing, transplanting, and harvesting of rice and extending to the cultivation of other crops. Villagers "dug creeks behind their ricefields, and in the 3rd and 4th Lunar months they caught fish in the creeks to add to their daily diet." Market prices were recorded in the same way. "Each year the price of paddy was low at the beginning of the harvest season, in the 10th month of the lunar year, because there was much paddy available on the market at that time. But beginning from the end of the 1st lunar month or beginning in the 2nd lunar month to the 9th lunar month, the price of paddy got higher and higher, because the amount of paddy available had dwindled." Green onions were cheapest "in the 4th and 5th lunar months," and no doubt the value of other produce was similarly tracked. Household finances had to keep in step, as in the case of a very poor peasant from Long Hung. "Every year, beginning in the 10th lunar month, he had to go around borrowing paddy to feed his family. Every year he had to borrow 10 gia [bushels] of paddy which he didn't repay until the 1st lunar month."[13]

Seasonal and other climatic factors affecting farm work were inscribed on the lunar calendar. In Hoa Dinh, "every year the water turns salty during the 2nd, 3rd, and 4th Lunar months, and the water only becomes fresh again when the rains come." Taking a closer look, this informant added, "Usually, from the 20th to the 25th, and then from the 7th to the 10th days of the 2nd, 3rd and 4th lunar months, the water isn't salty and the people draw the water from the river to store in their water jars." A similar linkage of climate and calendar is apparent when "the old people in the village said there was a flood in Hoi Cu in all the years of the Dragon," and in Diem Hy, where people expected floodwaters to recede "at the end of the tenth Lunar month (in the first fortnight of December)." In Hau My, villagers did not like living in an agroville because "in the 8th Lunar month, the whole area was flooded and swarmed with leeches."[14]

These citations indicate that the lives of individuals who were militants and peasants unfolded in solar time when they were acting as militants and in lunar time when they acted as peasants and suggest that a balance was necessary between the two. Villagers making revolution were also making a living, and no matter how much the political struggle heated up, the allocation of a finite number of people-hours of work per day had to be distributed so that subsistence needs were met. While the solar calendar reigned supreme in movement discourse, the lunar calendar, attached as it was to an intractable material reality, did not go away.[15]

Success in the golden period depended on the integration of these two projects, as evidenced in the daily routine of the party secretary in Hoi Cu village. After breakfast he made the rounds with a plastic bag of documents over his shoulder and stopped to talk with cadres in charge of the hamlets, each session lasting about half an hour. "If he didn't see them, he left a message with their families making an appointment for the next time or telling the cadres that he wanted to see them in person." Usually these encounters took place in the paddy fields, where the hamlet activists were working. "When he came, they stopped and talked with him for a while. Then [the secretary] went on his way, and the cadres continued their work in the fields if they didn't have any important tasks to perform. If they had an important task to perform at once, they went home to take care of it." As for the secretary, once in a while "he had to plough his fields, or scoop water in his fields, or plant rice, or dig a fish pond." On such occasions he "took off for three or five days to take care of his family affairs," and while he was on leave, "the Deputy Secretary replaced him in his daily mission." For security reasons, the secretary slept in the orchard rather than at home, and in case of an ARVN sweep, he had to take cover in the Plain of Reeds. But still, a sense emerges of equilibrium in the lives of rural dwellers who were able to meet their obligations as both militants and cultivators.[16]

This harmony stabilized the Front and guaranteed its commitment to people's war. Peasant cadres remained anchored in their class and continued to share in its everyday life. "All the people in the hamlet liked him," a comrade said of the secretary. "His relatives lived near by his house and were his neighbors." It helped that the Front did not yet operate a systematic tax-collecting bureaucracy but "only collected contributions from the people," and that its demands on the population did not overburden local resources. In addition, the irregular rhythms of the agrarian cycle, with its alternation of more and less active phases, left free time for movement work.[17]

Compromise was possible because activists, especially younger activists, were able to fulfill their political responsibilities while working part-time for the Front. Whereas older cadres seemed "weary and slow," the young were "very zealous" and "never wasted any time." But the key enabling factor was mass participation, which, according to a witness from Hoi Cu, enabled the popular movement to flourish. "For example, before, whenever we had to complete a labor task, we could recruit many civilian laborers in a short time, and therefore we could obtain quick and good results." By contrast, the government, whose officials were the last to know and whose projects could be completed only through the coerced labor of foot-dragging peasants, seemed mired in torpor. With the help of two hundred civilian workers from several villages, the Front dismantled the Nhi Binh strategic hamlet four or five times, on each occasion completing the task in two or three hours. The GVN-sponsored work of rebuilding the emplacements took up to a week.[18]

Far away, in Hanoi and in COSVN, Communist Party leaders feared that the war would go on for a long time, and Ho Chi Minh proclaimed that the Vietnamese were prepared to fight for five, ten, or twenty years. But in the villages of My Tho, no one spoke of protracted war. "Why don't you join the Revolution?" a cadre asked the Midwife in 1960; "the country will be liberated in either 1961 or 1962." Villagers who enlisted in the following years were told that victory would come "soon." By 1963 war weariness was making itself felt in some quarters, but then, in the wake of the anti-Diem coup in Saigon, progress resumed. "I can recall the whole village was full of excitement," stated an informant from Phu An, with reference to the 1964 mobilization campaign, "and the new recruits seemed confident that glory and happiness were not far ahead. The cadres promised that the Front would win within one or two years and that the Front's victory would bring about welfare and happiness to everyone." As late as 1965 militants in Binh Duc "said that the time had come when the Front could re-unify the country and liberate the nation. When the people heard this, they were very happy. The cadres said that the country could be reunified at any moment."[19]

Instabilities and unresolved contradictions in the reckoning of time during the golden period reflect a larger pattern of turmoil in the everyday life of the delta. The GVN and the Americans on the one side and the DRV and NLF on the other did not agree on how to set the clock, and the bureaucratic practices on both sides broke from the rhythms of the agrarian system. But for the revolutionaries, these discrepancies seemed of only secondary importance as the Front rushed toward victory.

The rapidity of U.S. deployments after 1965 made a deep impression on rural dwellers in My Tho. "The GVN has talked of pacifying this village," cadres in Thanh Phu (CT) boasted, "but let's see how long it takes them." Then, seemingly overnight, the Americans constructed the Dong Tam military base in Binh Duc village, in the process decimating Front organizations there and in adjoining locales. Villagers said: "The Americans are extremely rich. They can pour their money out and finish all this in no time at all." According to the Rebel, "if it had been something gradual, the district could have devised plans to cope with the situation effectively. But here, suddenly, thousands of US troops were poured in the area, so what could the district have done?" Everybody feared air attacks, remarked an informant from Tan Binh, "especially those conducted by F-105 jets because they get there too fast, there is no time to run for cover." A sixty-one-year-old informant testified, "Whoever was seen fleeing was shot down by the copters." Air attacks "made our alarm system void, and the former 'hour precaution' set up by the Front to help us flee from sweeps was no longer effective." Young and healthy people could run away, he noted, "but a mature man like me simply has to resign himself to staying behind."[20]

Escalation brought about a demoralizing loss of momentum, as U.S.-GVN tactics forced on local militants an awareness of their material backwardness and the near paralysis it imposed. Guerrillas in Hoi Cu "said that the GVN fired their bullets as thick as rain drops, but they could only fire one shot at a time and still had to economize their ammunition." As sweeps, bombing, and shelling complicated travel arrangements, the circulation of reports and policy statements within the Front apparatus was delayed and sometimes interrupted altogether. In Vinh Kim, after liaison agents were killed, local guerrillas had to carry the mail. "This method of delivery took much more time than when we had a village liaison agent, because the village liaison agent always knew where the cadres were and could go straight to them, to deliver the letters." Guerrillas took "two or three days" to distribute instructions, so recipients fell behind in carrying out assignments. According to a hard-pressed hamlet cadre who complained to higher echelons about such difficulties, "I was told to do my best to catch up with my work."[21]

Beginning with study sessions during the concerted uprising, the movement had drawn strength from group discussion. Important in building solidarity, well-attended meetings also saved time and increased the tempo of political work. But after escalation, in the words of a cadre from Thanh Phu (CL), there was a "weakening process" owing to "the heavy bombing and shelling which occurred almost every day. The villagers no longer dare to attend meetings and indoctrination sessions." The Instigator reported that "villagers stayed home simply because they thought that a big congregation of people would make the GVN shell them and that was the surest way to get killed." The only remedy was to "split the cadres in smaller groups" and meet with "small groups of villagers at one time," a safer but also a slower procedure. Face-to-face organizing always "takes time," a cadre from Hoi Cu remarked. "We are not fighting [the enemy] with modern arms, and of course we can't have quick results."[22]

Without meetings, activists fell back on shortcuts. "They simply received the resolutions from above, discussed them summarily," then "executed them right away, leaving out entirely the studying part." The collective process that had once sharpened analysis and heightened morale was no longer possible. "Bombing, artillery attacks, and continuous GVN operations cause the cadres to be constantly on the move, and so they have no time for studies." The chain of command of the Party's vaunted organizational weapon could not keep up with the pace of total war. With no time for "the studying part," confidence and cohesion drained away, and those who presumed to lead were reduced to rote formulas and perfunctory gestures.[23]

Militants believed that evolution from small-scale harassment to big-unit assaults would pave the way toward a general insurrection. But after 1965 the PLAF was going in the opposite direction. "It is employing small and weak units to stand against forces that outnumber its own a hundred times," declared a cadre in My Long. "Therefore, how could the NLF be able to be victorious?" Front strategists seemed to be anticipating a war that would drag on "for 5, 10 or 20 years," to the point where "the populace will become destitute and miserable." Another informant said: "In a small nation, we have to progress from guerrilla warfare to modern warfare in order to achieve victory. If the NLF has done the contrary, it will never win this war." Success had seemed so close. Now, "all cadres are very well aware that if they return to guerrilla warfare, they will never be able to win even if they have to fight for one hundred years."[24]

Retreat was also apparent at ground level as cadres fell back on tactics that made survival the primary and often the only objective. Villagers in Ban Long "were told that the first thing we should do was to reinforce the combat village, by planting more spikes and mines in the village." The measure "was somewhat effective, because without these obstacles, the troops on operation could move very fast in the village." With hazards in their path, attacking forces "were delayed and this gave the Front members enough time to go into hiding and to move their equipment and documents elsewhere." The informant in this case added, "So far, no GVN or American troops have been injured by the combat village fences." Given the logic of the situation, slowing down enemy soldiers was more important than killing them. In My Duc Tay "the women and old people" were instructed to tell advancing troops about the mines and spike pits that lay ahead, in order "to delay the troops and give the Front cadres enough time to hide." A strategy that required combatants to avoid inflicting casualties on the adversary amounted to a recipe for endless combat.[25]

Escalation brought about a shift in perspective as expectations for a quick victory ceded to fears of protracted war. The result was a jolt to the morale of PLAF fighters, cadres in the civilian branches of the Front, and peasants throughout the countryside. "The Front has promised that the war will end in [the] very near future and that the Revolution will be victorious," noted a deserter. "Yet since 1960, not only the war hasn't been ended, but it has become more terrible and savage every day." When informed that the war might last for "ten, twenty or forty years," local militants "were discouraged. We were all anxiously waiting for the war to come to an end so we could enjoy the fruits of our struggle. We were all disappointed because we didn't know when our hardships would end." As for the villagers, "they don't have enough food to feed their relatives. They have to sleep in trenches at night, and during the day time, they have to flee from sweeps. Life is very miserable." By way of conclusion this commentator declared, "Since it's very difficult for the people to bear the situation now, how can they willingly stand it for twenty more years?"[26]

As the Americans tried to speed up the war, the Front was trying to slow it down. For villagers, "each movement took a lot of time," in the words of a defector whose hamlet bristled with "grenades, anti-personnel mines, and spikes planted in every path." Villagers had been attracted to the revolution because of its commitment to progress and the collective euphoria they experienced in the work of building a new kind of society. Now they were trapped in a slow-motion nightmare with no end in sight.[27]

COLLAPSE OF THE SOLAR-LUNAR COMPROMISE

While the Feminist threw herself into the movement "day and night," she also had to take care of her elderly father. After working for the Front, she returned home at midnight to tend the family garden until 4:00 or 5:00 AM, then did the cooking for the next day. Most "people who make the revolution," her father pointed out, "attend meetings sporadically, and they also spend their time doing their home chores. You, however, are always away, and I have to cook your meals, although I have been sick and am old." Perhaps thinking back to the equilibrium of the golden period, he wished for a compromise according to which cadres would serve the Front "sporadically," so that there was time left over for "home chores." But with more at stake and more to do, part-time militants could not meet all of their obligations. They had to choose between the revolution and their families.[28]

Escalation destroyed the balance between political activism and the agrarian cycle and in the process called both projects into question. Bombing and shelling killed many cultivators and damaged the infrastructure that made possible the sale of farm goods and the purchase of inputs necessary for survival. Those who remained attached to the land were reduced to penury and no longer participated so readily in movement activities. At the same time, cadres were wounded or killed or grew discouraged and quit or rallied to the other side, so the remaining activists had to cumulate functions. Without mass participation, they were required to do more ditch digging, spike planting, and ammunition carrying without assistance from others. As in the case of the Feminist, whose daily routine left no time for sleep, many were placed in an impossible situation. The more they concentrated on Front assignments, the less able they were to meet the needs of their families.

According to an informant from Hoi Cu, the people "didn't like to go to meetings, especially since 1966, when the bombings and shellings have become intense. Besides, meetings took much time from work." When cadres insisted on compliance with their demands, protests were not slow in coming. "While I was working for other people," reported a day laborer from Binh Duc, "the cadres sent for me and said that I should go on mission at once for them." He responded: "I'm poor and I have to work for my living. You don't give me any time to work and earn some money; how do you expect me to survive?" The problem was that "time is very precious to the farmers because they had to spend all the time they could spare on their fields and orchards, and they don't like it when you force them to spend their time doing something else." Even the most politicized villagers had to set limits on their participation. They would say: "We are ready to serve the Front in doing necessary labor, in paying taxes and in attending village or hamlet meetings, but that is enough for us. We don't have any more time left to do other things if we don't want our families to starve."[29]

Some cadres were inclined to treat these objections as an administrative problem. From the point of view of a military recruiter or a tax collector, time was a sequence of days and weeks and months, conceived as homogenous and uniform units, subject primarily to fiscal and military necessity. Responsibility for keeping track of crops in the fields or price fluctuations in the marketplace belonged to others, whose routines clashed with the imperatives of waging war. A bureaucratic mindset was superseding the ethos of militants whose links to the agrarian cycle and to their neighbors had remained intact during the golden period.

To be sure, dialogue between the two regimes, each with its own time scheme, was unavoidable, and even the most exigent tax collectors understood that their work would be easier if scheduled right after the harvest. At first glance it might have seemed that there was also room for compromise with village guerrillas, who, in principle, were supposed to function on a full-time basis, but who could request leave to help with farm tasks. In Hoi Cu, if a combatant did not show up at the prescribed time, others went "to his house to help him so that he could return to the unit quickly." In Nhi Binh, guerrilla units were accorded "a paramilitary status," giving members the option "to do their own chores to help their families." But what was gained on one side of the ledger was lost on the other. In Vinh Kim "it was difficult to contact all the guerrillas who were staying at home because they lived scattered all over the village. It took time to contact them all. For example, if there was a mission to be carried out in the afternoon, the guerrillas on home leave had to be contacted in the morning. Sometimes those who were on home leave were halfway through their farm work when they were contacted, and in this case they didn't bother to show up in the afternoon to accept their mission." The attempt to allocate work time to the fields inevitably slowed operations on the military side.[30]

Zero-sum calculations were impossible to avoid when recruits were assigned to district and main forces, which pulled them farther away from home. Cadres told draftees that the Front would help their families with farm work while they were gone, but as the army grew larger and militants were swamped with assignments, such guarantees could not be honored. Some high level cadres argued that the pledges were a mistake. "This is your fault," one recruiter was told by his supervisor. "It's because of your wrong promise! The job of the Party is to best the Americans, and soil tilling is the business of the farmers." As the "job" of besting the Americans and the "business" of tilling the soil competed for control over a shrinking labor force, militants were tempted to turn their backs on economic realities. In March 1966 a cadre was ordered to gather one platoon of new recruits at any cost. "I was in a very difficult position," he noted, "because February and March were harvest months and people were busy with their work; therefore I could only recruit six youths." The agrarian calendar was not accepted as a valid excuse, and he was criticized for failing "to meet the request of the Party."[31]

Activists were no better off than villagers. "We ourselves have to be self-sufficient and we don't have any money to help you," they explained to neighbors. "Please try to go through this difficult period." The informant in this instance concluded his report by noting, "The cadres weren't paid for their work and had to work for their own living, so how could they help anyone?" The Communist Party exhorted its members to set a good example by paying taxes on time and in full, "bad crop or good crop," and to respond promptly when given an assignment. It was a discipline imposed at the expense of their families. An informant from Thanh Phu (CT) remembered that at first, when there were spike pits to be dug and fences to be built, "the villagers participated in these works in great numbers. Now, every time they are called up for this labor, only four or five or them turn up. That's why the village cadres and guerrillas had to replace the missing people and work on these exhausting jobs." As a result, they noted, "there isn't any time left for us to take care of our fields and to raise our families."[32]

Misery eroded political commitment. "Most of the cadres and Party members in my village have begun to think more of making their living than working for the Party," said an activist from An Thai Dong. "If they don't have enough to eat and wear, how are they going to survive?" An informant in Xuan Son reported: "The Party members did not have enough to eat. They were only worried about earning 'enough rice' to feed their families and thought more about making a living than attending meetings. Also, if they had meetings, this would just mean more tasks for them and they wouldn't have any time left to earn their living." Cadres and party members "couldn't implement the tasks allocated to them, because they had to think of their farm work," he concluded. "This was why they did everything superficially, just for form's sake." Others chose to drop out, as when demolition fighters asked for leave to help with farm work. When the request was denied, "they just quit and went home."[33]

During the golden period, a female cadre reported, "neither my family nor I was given land because I wanted to care for the people first." But after escalation, this ideal of self-denial began to seem like a snare. "Those who didn't work for the Front were better off than those who did, because they could spend all their time tilling their land," complained a guerrilla from Hoi Cu. "The revolutionaries just got poorer and poorer, and their families didn't enjoy any benefits at all," he noted. "The majority of my friends were discouraged, and they all said that they would be better off being simple farmers."

According to a hamlet cadre, the Front said that "revolution was a glorious path leading to future happiness. Indeed, I have not seen any glory or happiness. There's only a fact that while I worked for the revolution, I had to neglect my family. I wasted a lot of time which I could spend to earn my living. My family has consequently been living in poverty. On the other hand, those who didn't join the revolution have been living in plenty." Bitter disappointment was perhaps responsible for this informant's allowing himself the implausible claim that others were "living in plenty." Once experienced as a sacred mission, the revolution had come to seem like a "waste of time."[34]

HOURS OF THE DAY

People liked to head for the marketplace early in the morning, at around "the 'tan chim' hour, that is to say the hour when the birds scatter to look for food." During the war it was renamed the "hour of precaution," because GVN forces were in the habit of conducting sweeps at that time. At dawn, while people could not yet "see clearly in the ricefields," they looked and listened for warning signals. Later on, tension eased. A platoon leader observed that "ten AM was called the 'end of danger' hour, and from this moment on, we needed no longer fear [an] attack." In Quon Long people waited until 9:00 or 10:00 before heading for market "because they wanted to make sure that no operation would be conducted during the day."[35]

Equally complex timing regulated the twilight hours, as cadres, ammunition trains, and PLAF units prepared to move from one locale to another. Liaison agents checked out the scene at 5:00 or 6:00 PM, then "led guests or carried supplies across the roads" at sunset. Dusk was the preferred moment, when "there was still light, and they could reconnoiter the roads, and at the same time it was dark enough so that no one could detect them when they crossed the roads." They would not try to cross later, at 9:00 or 10:00 PM, "because then it is too dark for them and they can't see anything and they can't be on the alert against unpleasant surprises." Some informants seem to suggest that road traffic thinned out after 10:00 PM, thus creating an opening for small-scale Front crossings or sabotage missions. Cars stopped passing by at that hour, and buses did not run again until 4:00 the next morning.[36]

By contrast, later stages of the war were not fought according to fixed timetables. A cadre remarked that in 1967 "ARVN soldiers had changed their operating procedures and had started carrying out sweeps at any time of the day. Sometimes they came at noon, or even in the afternoon, and the Front's cadres were often caught by surprise." The situation had "changed completely," according to an informant from Thanh Phu (CL). "Before, the cadres were never afraid that they might be captured, even when the GVN troops conducted operations in the village, because they had enough time to go into hiding." But now, he continued, "the people and cadres in the village are most afraid of the commandoes, because these soldiers can appear suddenly in the village at any time, be it day or night, like ghosts." U.S. deployments were also impossible to anticipate. "Before," remarked a cadre from Ban Long, "if the GVN troops conducted an operation in the village, they came only in the morning. But now the American troops enter the village at any time [of] the day."[37]

During the concerted uprising, darkness had provided a cover for activists and peasants, and after escalation, the night seemed briefly to offer a similar refuge. Inhabitants of Phu My "have to gather 'ban' reeds for their living. But this job has become more difficult. In the daytime they are afraid of air strikes, so they have to work at night." Fear of the dark and of unseen enemies who might erupt out of the shadows weighed on people's minds. Some responded by forming teams, which could "work at night when there was moonlight to make up for lost time. Since there were many of them in the group, they were not afraid." The living patterns of the inhabitants of her village had been "completely changed," reported the Feminist. "Daytime activities have been changed for those of the night and vice-versa. Farming work starts at 7:00 or 8:00 PM and lasts until 1:00 or 2:00 AM or until 3:00 or 4:00 AM if there is moonlight."[38]

Increasingly this nocturnal labor also became hazardous. Villagers had "to spend the whole day taking cover," reported an informant from Nhi My. "Before the people could work at night to save time, but now they don't dare to, because if the soldiers see lights in the fields they will open fire." Flares that "illuminate[d] the village from 10 PM to 4 or 5 AM" obliterated the distinction between daylight and darkness, while helicopter gunships equipped with powerful searchlights lit the terrain. In Duong Diem, "from 10:00 PM till the morning comes, helicopters light up the whole area—it's so bright that you can even see a needle on the ground." Front tactics contributed to the militarization of the night, as when cadres in My Hanh Dong set "booby-traps, spikes, land mines, and grenades" on roads leading to the village at sunset and imposed a 7:00 PM to 7:00 AM curfew on the inhabitants. "The villagers were extremely discontented with such a measure," an informant reported. "As they couldn't do anything by day because of mortar shellings, they hoped to take advantage of the night to work, and now they were forbidden to do so. How could they manage to get enough to eat under such conditions?"[39]

By 1967 all schedules, all routines, all hope of a lull had disappeared. In Vinh Kim "the hamlet was frequently shelled at night and no one could sleep well. During the day the farmers were afraid to go out to the fields and work. Every day, they didn't start working until 9 or 10 AM and sometimes they hadn't started doing anything when bombing and shelling drove them back to their shelters." In My Thien "no one could sleep a wink because helicopters lit up the whole area with their powerful lamps, and then, in the morning, no one could catch up on his sleep because of the jet aircraft strafing."[40]

In Tan Binh Thanh field work had been wrenched out of the agrarian cycle. "No one could farm his land on time and according to the seasons," reported a man from the village. "Instead he had to wait for the time when there was no bombing, no shelling, and no operations being conducted. There were times when we just got through ploughing and planting when amphibious vehicles destroyed all our efforts. Night or day, it didn't matter any longer, as long as there was no harassment, we worked on our land. It has been a year now that farming has become a thousand times more difficult because the war has escalated, operations were conducted continuously, bombing and shelling rained on us night and day." In Xuan Son, a guerrilla reported, people were "on the lookout all the time. We didn't have time to farm our land or take a rest. Even when there was no operation or shelling, we couldn't enjoy our rest thoroughly or work diligently on our fields, because we kept on wondering with anxiety when the next operation or mortar attack would take place. And in the long run this life turned out to be unbearable."[41]

Rural society was headed toward a breaking point when people were so busy running and hiding that they no longer had time to maintain the most elementary routines. Already frayed before the revolution, then strained by military recruitment and the refugee exodus, family ties were further tested as people scrambled for safe havens. "Members of the same family do not necessarily eat in the same place or at the same time, as in the past," observed the Feminist. "Each person now eats his meal at his own convenience." While household groupings splintered, festive time was "compressed." In hopes of securing a protected status for such occasions, villagers asked permission for marriages and funerals "from both sides, the Viet Cong as well as the government authorities." But no guarantees could be fully trusted amidst the dangers and hatreds of war. And so people "cut down the length of time devoted to religious ceremonies, funerals or marriages. That is, instead of spending two or three days eating and drinking as before, they now perform all the traditional rites as fast as possible." Villagers were running out of time even for honoring and burying the dead.[42]

Under conditions of total war, people came to think they had no future. Guerrillas "didn't know what their struggle was leading to, and all they knew was that the war was getting bloodier and bloodier and more and more frightening. They used to tell each other that they could count the minutes and the hours they still had till their deaths (*Song gio song phut*)." The literal meaning of the Vietnamese term is "live hour live minute." It became the credo of the moment. Some militants, said an interviewee, "still keep their faith in the Front's ultimate victory." But they could not "foresee when this victory will turn up, or how much longer they might have to sustain hardships and dangers. So, when they look toward the future, they find very little light or hope ahead." One confessed: "I did not think of my future or that of my children, because we are engaged in a war. Our lives are not certain, and I don't know when my end will come."[43]

According to an informant from Hau My, "those who were still living in the hamlet—from the cadres to the people—thought only of living from day to day and taking shelter to avoid being detected by airplanes." The lives of cadres "were counted by hours and days in the NLF," declared a witness from Thanh Phu (CT). "They were very miserable. At night, they had to endure the cold weather, wind and rain, and exhausting movements. As daylight came, they waited with impatience and anxiety for the GVN troops who could attack them at any time." For their part, Thanh Phu villagers "worked half heartedly since they were not sure whether they could enjoy the fruits of their labor. Their lives were counted by hours and days." In contrast to "the happiest years," from 1960 to 1963, "air-strikes, artillery and continuous operations" now made agriculture seem like an exercise in futility, so "they worked just to get enough rice to live from hand to mouth." In the past there were "very few cases of burglary and robbery in the village," remarked a man from Thanh Phu (CL). "But starting in 1966, there have been many cases of drinking, gambling, and brawling, because the people are tired of the war and because they don't know when they're going to die—this is why whenever they have a chance they drink and gamble to their hearts' content."[44]

The popular movement had come up against the limit of the spatial and temporal economy afforded under conditions of total war. Without food and shelter, militants could not live, and without a belief in a future, which is the beating heart of all revolutions, they would no longer be able to think and act as revolutionaries. U.S. war making had disarticulated the agrarian system and shattered NLF organizational structures. The librated zone had collapsed, and earlier notions about how and when the war might be won were discredited. Social life in the countryside was disintegrating, and those who remained on the scene were losing their grip on reality.

The shift in consciousness among "young people of both sexes" was especially striking. According to a man from Nhi Binh, "the youths of today seem to be careless about their future. Because they may die at any moment, they never think of putting aside some money. They spend all their money on food and clothing. If they don't enjoy life when they can, what a pity it would be if they die tomorrow. So, in my opinion, they only think of trying their best to avoid being killed in an air raid or a mortar shelling, in order to enjoy life as much as possible." According to another observer, young people were "obsessed by the atrocities created by the war, obsessed by the uncertainty of life and death," and feared that they might "die before enjoying all the charms of life." Hard-earned money was spent on "nylon clothes, watches, fountain pens and what not, to keep pace with fashionable people. Their oft-repeated motto is 'let's enjoy life so that we regret nothing if we die tomorrow.'"[45]

These passages echo earlier reports on spending habits during the six years of peace. The initial experimentation with novel clothes and hairstyles and identities came with an edge, in the form of the rebellious posturing of "cowboys" and "modern girls," but was generally expressed in a playful register: "just for kicks," as one witness put it. Issuing out of a frantic, an "obsessive," state of mind, the hedonism of 1967 was the work of young people who saw corpses all around and who really believed that they might "die at any moment." The "uncertainty of life and death" haunting the countryside had created a highly volatile collective mood, one verging on nihilism. Observers could be excused for thinking that it signaled a desire for peace at any price. But an insistence on the end of time is not an act of surrender. People who had lived in the revolution and who had not forgotten its prophecy sensed that an Armageddon was near, when redressers of wrongs would rise up in majesty and crush their enemies.[46]

CHAPTER TWELVE

THE TET OFFENSIVE

By 1967 the armed forces of the two sides had arrived at a stalemate on the battlefield, and the same might be said of the competition between the modernization of the Americans and the modernism of the popular movement. As warfare made a shambles of the countryside, many fled from their homes. Some of the refugees settled in urban areas and never came back, but people who doubted that they could survive in town or who were attached to native places or who wished to stay "with the revolution" did not fully embrace a new life in the GVN zone. Instead they designated a family member to remain in the village or themselves periodically returned to their orchards and fields. The more numerous displaced persons who took refuge in field huts or along roads or canals or in new life hamlets were even more likely to continue working within the agrarian system. Forced-draft urbanization had not succeeded in emptying the countryside.

The revolutionary modernism issuing out of the concerted uprising had also reached an impasse. War exposed the Vietnamese to what David Harvey characterizes as "the deep chaos of modern life and its intractability before rational thought." It tore apart spatial and temporal constructions that had achieved equilibrium during the golden period and provided a framework allowing both household economies and political projects to flourish. The liberated zones lay in ruins, and villagers walked in fear across a terrain littered with booby traps and unexploded munitions. Tracked by artillery batteries and helicopter gunships, a scattered population was hard-pressed to maintain the rudiments of social life and the solidarity on which the popular movement depended. The departure of refugees created labor shortages for the agrarian system and the Front, and both sectors foundered as they made competing demands on the peasantry. In a situation where danger might erupt at any minute and distinctions between morning and afternoon and between day and night had ceased to matter, clock time lost its purchase on reality, and people searched in vain for a moment to eat, work, or sleep. Once full of confidence that they could create their own route to modernity, rural dwellers now thought first about saving their lives and their sanity.[1]

THE MEANING OF TET

Festive occasions helped villagers resist despair and periodically reintegrated the shattered fragments of their world. Since an acquaintance today might be a rallier tomorrow, "relations between neighbors are no longer sincere," asserted a witness from Nhi Binh. "They are afraid of each other. For his own sake, nobody dares speak his mind." But, he added, "everybody tries to live on friendly terms with others to avoid arousing animosities which might lead to revengeful acts. From time to time, especially on festival days or on the anniversaries of their dead, they ask each other to come to their houses to eat and drink alcohol." In this account one observes a movement away from fear and constraint to customary socializing, as villagers found ways to maintain ties with others.[2]

People were particularly stubborn in their unwillingness to let go of Tet Lunar New Year celebrations. "Those who lived in New Life Hamlets enjoyed Tet a great deal," remarked a witness from Hoi Cu:

> They set off a lot of firecrackers and wore new clothes. On the contrary, in my hamlet, as well as in the neighboring hamlets, there wasn't any excitement. People just slept as if they wanted to catch up on their sleep. So, life was dull and the contrast between the two areas was so obvious that the villagers liked to say: "They (those who lived in New Life Hamlets) are from the same country, but they are much happier than we. We didn't have any Tet festivities to enjoy. We have only death" (*an chet chu khong phai an Tet*).

The tone was hardly cheerful: "We eat death and don't eat Tet" would be closer to a literal translation of the Vietnamese. But by way of qualification the informant added: "Nevertheless, they were very pleased to have a truce. Most of them said: 'If this could keep going on, how much happier we would be!'" The speaker seemed reluctant to give up the prospect of a happiness to come. New Year's Day was the one occasion in the year when it made sense to think of each moment as a beginning as well as an end. It reclaimed the future that war-induced time compression had blotted out; it was a collective manifestation against the specter of death tyrannizing the countryside.[3]

Tet made possible a mending of spatial as well as temporal fractures. "The people have been yearning for peace and a cease fire since the beginning of 1966, when the war became extremely bloody, but none of them dared express his thoughts," remarked a man from Hau My.

On the occasion of Tet, when both sides stopped fighting temporarily, all the villagers—from the cadres to the people, old and young, and from the fanatic Front followers to the fence sitters, and the bad elements—were extremely happy. They were very cheerful and paid visits to each other. Those who lived far from the village returned to look at their orchards and ricefields and to visit their relatives. On these occasions, wherever one went, one heard the people openly express hope that the war would come to an end. They said that they could rebuild their material life and that their families could be reunited only if the war ended.

Tet brought about a *rassemblement*, a coming together of cadres and villagers, old and young, fanatics and fence-sitters, good and bad elements. Celebrants who at first did not dare to "express their thoughts" now felt free to voice "hope that the war would come to an end." Gloom gave way to "cheerful" socializing, and people once more imagined that they might be able to "rebuild" their lives. I cannot help thinking that these meanings, more or less consciously felt, had something to do with the decision to stage an offensive on the eve of Tet.[4]

DUAL PARENTAGE OF THE TET OFFENSIVE

Two threads came together in the making of the Tet Offensive. The first went back to early 1967, when Communist Party leaders began thinking about ways to break the stalemate on the battlefield. Their order for a campaign against the cities went out from Hanoi in September and reached COSVN and the delta in October or November. Planners on the Central Committee thought that an offensive might force the Americans to negotiate a rapid withdrawal from Vietnam. Success on some fronts was also possible, they surmised, with the United States continuing to fight while gradually giving up hope for military victory. A third conceivable result was U.S. escalation, with combat spreading into Laos, Cambodia, and North Vietnam. Making the best of a murky prospect, Tet planners told themselves that no matter what transpired, the movement would be able to cope.[5]

Reflecting uncertainty at the top, the plan was broadcast haltingly. It was "finalized" in December and "promulgated" in January, with a "final decision" taken on January 18, only a few days before the offensive was to begin. David Elliott emphasizes "the incremental, contested, and improvisational nature of the Tet decision" and suggests that in late September province cadres in My Tho did not know what was coming. The Region 2 winter-spring operations order, which arrived on November 22, still said nothing about attacking the cities. Battalion commanders believed up to the last minute that they were supposed to observe the holiday cease-fire, and soldiers and villagers in the province did not realize that other targets were also being attacked until they heard radio news of battles elsewhere in South Vietnam.[6]

With bombs and shells falling everywhere and U.S.-GVN forces blocking access routes, the PLAF somehow managed to recruit and concentrate eight battalions in the environs of My Tho city. But once the offensive was launched, the attackers got lost on urban streets and were unable to converge on their targets, then were forced to retreat by U.S. firepower, which destroyed five thousand residences and left one-quarter of the inhabitants homeless. Main force units involved in the offensive and its sequels suffered casualty rates of 60 to 70 percent, and losses among cadres, many of whom sacrificed legal cover in order to lend support to combat elements, must also have been extensive. In 1969 the Ninth Division pulled out of My Tho (it was the first big American unit to leave Vietnam), but for rural dwellers "the most significant immediate impact of the Tet Offensive was the virtual abandonment of the already inadequate restraints on the use of massive firepower in populated areas." The policy of generating refugees, imposed with an even greater ferocity than in 1966–67, "led to a catastrophically high level of civilian casualties." ARVN forces vastly outnumbered what was left of the PLAF, which subsequently had to rely on replacements from the DRV, and government posts and watchtowers multiplied everywhere. There were close to a thousand in 1971, when, according to David Elliott, "the revolution reached its lowest ebb."[7]

The significance of the Tet Offensive remains in dispute. The campaign can plausibly be interpreted as a turning point in the Vietnam War because it set in motion a chain of events leading to U.S. withdrawal, thus isolating a Saigon government unable to survive on its own. Although the design was confused and preparations belated and haphazard, the Communist Party deserves credit for this decision, the riskiest and most consequential of the war. No one but the Central Committee could have initiated a nationwide offensive, and without an effort of that scope, fighting might have dragged on even beyond 1975. Trends in 1966–67 appeared to point toward an endless war, and leaders in Hanoi were not unreasonable in thinking that they had to create a more favorable dynamic. At the same time, no policymakers in any of the relevant capitals could have achieved conceptual mastery over all the variables that would determine the course of events in 1968 and after, and when a DRV official spoke of "a decisive step in a process" tending toward victory, his cautious wording drew attention to the uncertainty hanging over the enterprise. By launching an offensive, the party was opting for a leap into the unknown, and the ghastly sequels cannot be left out of any attempt to draw up a balance sheet for the undertaking.[8]

By itself, the order to attack the cities—and, in the end, the Hanoi contribution did not go beyond a few general guidelines—would have proved of little consequence. To be effective, it had to be transmitted through the chain of command and carried out by village and hamlet cadres, who, in spite of horrendous conditions, had decided to stay with the Front. Most of all, the plan required mass participation to give it life and force. The response of the popular movement constitutes the second thread in the history of the Tet Offensive.

Throughout many years of puzzling over the Rand materials, I have searched for words to characterize the militants whose steadfastness prevented the Americans and their Saigon allies from winning the war. One Rand informant, a defector from Hau My, addressed the problem in these terms: "There are a very small number of cadres who are still remaining in the village or in higher headquarters to carry out their activities. Perhaps it is [that] they are high-ranking cadres and they have such absolute confidence in the NLF that they have become fanatics with high morale and an everlasting endurance of hardships. They are very aggressive to carry out NLF activities, awaiting a final victory." "Fanatic" is generally considered an unkind word, and indeed there is something frightening about people who refuse to bend when engulfed in destruction and suffering far beyond what others could bear. But the speaker also appears ready to concede a degree of nobility to intransigents with "an everlasting endurance of hardships" and an unshakable confidence in final victory.[9]

In the second half of his commentary, the informant from Hau My sought to undo what he had just said:

> But, in my hamlet, I strongly believe [that] the cadres who remain there do not have such high morale or firm confidence which stimulates them to fight vehemently. There are other causes which compel them to remain. Some of them were criminals and were imprisoned in GVN-controlled areas. Some were draft-dodgers, such as the five guerrillas still in my hamlet. Some have never lived outside the hamlet and don't know how to make their living if they leave the hamlet. So all these can do nothing but remain in the hamlet.

In this passage the stay-behinds are portrayed as victims rather than heroes. But since other militants, including the speaker, had resigned or defected, and since those who stayed in the hamlets knew that they could do the same, the passage rings false. References to "criminals," "draft-dodgers," and peasants unable to cope with conditions outside of their villages amount to another way of saying that fanatics were ordinary people who refused to give up.

Other sightings indicate that while the Front had been damaged, its framework remained intact. A forty-four-year-old resistance veteran who was captured in 1967 warned that militants who remained in hamlet redoubts "harbored their hatred towards the United States" and took comfort from the fact that "they get the support of the masses. They consider that an honor and [source of] pride. They work zealously because of their honor and pride and not for their individual benefit," and whereas others despaired of the future, they anticipated that the Front would win. "I also believe in this view," he stated. Another witness explained that the village party chapter had withdrawn from Dong Hoa and now operated "from another village, occasionally coming over to work (the vot can cau: like a fisherman on the bank, casting out into the river)." Meanwhile, "armed Party members," the ones with "a high fighting spirit," barricaded themselves in otherwise deserted hamlets and maintained underground passages, recruited "liaison agents working under legal cover," and kept in contact with "leading cadres" hiding elsewhere.[10]

A poor nineteen-year-old from Phuoc Thanh became a fanatic. After her mother died in childbirth and her father took off for Saigon, she was raised by grandparents, then made a living as a seamstress. She was outraged when ARVN soldiers burned houses, murdered villagers, and "seized everything they could bring away, paddy, writing pens, clothes, stuff of my customers and even fruit we had put on our ancestral altar." As for cadres, they "worked without pay, without any advantages whatsoever. Many of their families didn't even have enough rice to eat, but still they agreed to continue to work for the villagers in the hamlet. They are willing to accept any sacrifices required of themselves and of their relatives for the country." They were "living embodiments of heroes of our legends," exemplars who stood up "to fight the evil in order to protect the people."[11]

In spite of her grandparents' objections, this young woman joined the Front. "I felt a little homesick while we were marching away," she confessed. "It was the first time I left my relatives behind to start a new life of my own." Her escort "seemed to be aware of my feelings and we talked abundantly, trying, I suppose, to alleviate my pain and to build up my morale. She said: 'You are a true daughter of the Revolution.'" Initially employed as a liaison agent, she was obliged by ill health to transfer into a nurse training program, then later was switched into a demolitions course. In April 1967 she was captured and tortured.[12]

The seamstress from Phuoc Thanh was the most redoubtable informant in the Rand sample. After repeated beatings, she fought back, punching her interrogator in the face ("His spectacles were broken and his eyes were wounded"). Unable to endure further abuse, she made an unsuccessful attempt to commit suicide. But when asked what would happen if she were released, she responded: "As far as soldiers, exploitation, oppression would plague the countryside, I would continue to fight the GVN. If I am freed now, I will return to my grandparents to take care of them until their death. After that, I'll join the Revolution again." Accustomed to dealing with informants who were deferential and sometimes groveling, the interviewer did not know what to make of this subject, still only a teenager and not a party member, and sought to explain her dedication by suggesting that "she was a special case."[13]

This assessment was both wrong and right. Many country people left home with a mix of excitement and apprehension at the thought that they were beginning a "new life," and their decisions help to explain the triumphs of the golden period. But by 1967, after some had been killed and others had taken their distance from the movement, the cadres with "high fighting spirit" who remained active were people of abnormal fortitude. Lying in a pool of her own blood on the floor of a dark prison cell, for a moment the seamstress despaired and tried to kill herself. But that was not the end of the story, and when she announced, "I'll join the Revolution again," it was a signal that the war was not over. These were the people who maintained the rudiments of an NLF infrastructure and who received and disseminated news of the Tet Offensive.

A decision to launch an attach on the cities had been made in Hanoi and widely circulated, but to understand what happened next, one must go beyond the "special cases" and examine how the general population responded to this summons. A clue emerges out of a commentary from Thanh Phu (CT) indicating that the first village secretary was killed in 1964. The second was called up to the district, then resigned, then was killed in a sweep. The third was also promoted to the district level, but was killed when he came back to the village "to attend the anniversary of his mother's death." The fourth was killed in February 1967. A similar impression emerges from Xuan Son, where there were twenty-two party members in 1965. Two were assigned to the 514th Battalion, then deserted, returned home, quit the Front, and were living in the village as "simple farmers." Four were purged, including one "for opposing the Party" who later went over to the GVN Civil Guards, while the other three were dismissed for "neglecting their work," then were killed during a search and destroy operation in 1966. Of five others who were expelled for dereliction of duty, two left the village. Another cadre quit the Front and was killed during a sweep in 1967.[14]

These accounts indicate that there was no sharp line dividing cadres from "simple villagers." Some quit or were cashiered, while other testimonies suggest that the NLF often asked dropouts and suspended cadres to rejoin the ranks. The Ethnographer's account provides examples of both sorts of departures and returns, and others have emerged in the course of this study. But the main point to note is that individuals who stood with the Front and individuals who left the Front both measured their lives in hours and minutes. Even migration to the towns did not guarantee safety, and a cadre from Tam Hiep was certainly not the only one who went to Saigon and was then conscripted by the GVN. With no way out of the war, people could not avoid choosing sides.[15]

Born in 1906 and a Resistance veteran, a security cadre in My Thanh was captured and "savagely" beaten, and his wife was "mistreated" by ARVN soldiers. His description of "local circumstances," which, in the opinion of the Rand interviewer, he understood "very well," is worth summarizing in detail. In 1967, he reported, government troops had swept through My Thanh four or five times, and "many youths were killed while attempting to flee. Last August, thirty of them were killed during a single sweep." When the interviewer asked why the victims had tried to run away, the answer was: "They had no choice. They had to flee, because if ARVN soldiers happened to lay their hands on them, it meant arrest, jail, beatings, and finally draft into the GVN." Survivors "were furious at these calamities, and most of them finally volunteered to join the Front's armed forces," over one hundred in My Thanh, plus others from surrounding villages.[16]

The mobilization caught cadres by surprise, given that the draft they had instituted in 1963 had achieved little ("at most, about ten volunteers every year"), and "in 1966, despite tremendous mobilizing efforts, none of the youths agreed to join." But "this year, while the Front has stopped waging propaganda in favor of its conscription policy, the youths took the initiative on their own to volunteer." My Thanh cadres earned no special praise from higher echelons because they had done nothing to prompt the mobilization and because "the enlistment movement of the youths was blooming all over the area." Parents who earlier opposed conscription had changed their minds. To their children they said: "Whether you stay home or you enlist, you will have to die. It would be better for you to join the Front, because that will enable you to shoot back at those who want to kill you." Volunteers refused assignment to guerrilla units, which were "too weak" to punish the ARVN, and insisted on joining "Main Force battalions in order to be able to fight against GVN soldiers."

"The girls seemed to adopt the same attitude as that of the youths," it was further noted, "and also joined the Front in great numbers. Rumors spread that young girls would be arrested also by GVN soldiers, and that's why a lot of them agreed to join the Front. In my village, about thirty girls have left their families for the Front, so far." The Rand staffer interrupted to ask: "If the girls also wanted to join the Front, why was the village Women's Association disbanded, as you told me before?" It turned out that the association had fallen apart when its leader was killed "during a strafing" and her assistant had to step down after she "had just been delivered of a child. Since no one was taking care of the association, it hasn't been rebuilt." This and other passages indicate that "the recent enlistment movement of the youths" could not be attributed to the NLF or the Communist Party, given that in 1967 the Front had "stopped waging propaganda in favor of its conscription policy" and that its administrative machinery was in disarray. It was what the party would label a "spontaneous" phenomenon, or, in the language I prefer, a sign that peasants of the delta were still capable of seizing a leadership role.[17]

One of the last subjects interviewed by Rand indicated that in August 1967, "everywhere in the countryside, the village cadres were mobilizing the people." In their appeals they announced that the Front "was going to definitely win over the GVN and that they were heading towards very special circumstances which would help the Front to be victorious." They said: "We are heading towards a very propitious situation, a situation which only takes place once during a thousand years, and which will help the Front to seize power and to end the war. Eventually, everybody will have to go all out in their assignments to seize the opportunity to defeat the enemy and to bring about peace." Guidelines for the Tet Offensive had not arrived in My Tho in August, when cadres were already "mobilizing the people," or perhaps one should say when people were already mobilizing recruiters with their demands for places in main force units.[18]

Meanwhile, the grapevine spread rumors "that something big was about to happen," and villagers rallied to the prospect of a "once-and-for-all" (dut dien) showdown. In preparation for the coming effort, province cadres collected and stockpiled fifty thousand tons of rice, and tax payments in Phu Phong village were running three times over the amount paid in the previous year. In My Tho the offensive took the form of "a rural uprising," carried forward by combatants who were "enthusiastic," "fired up," "really into it," and certain that the war was about to be won. With hesitations at the top, apocalyptic rumors overriding muddled guidelines, and people in the grip of a frenzied enthusiasm, the Tet Offensive recalled the concerted uprising. It was another of the peasant revolts marking the history of My Tho in the era of the Vietnam wars.[19]

Whereas the first thread in the history of the offensive can be traced to Hanoi, the second went back to discussions in trenches and bunkers, field huts and new life hamlets. Communist Party leaders did not share a common reading of the strategic situation, but most seem to have thought that the offensive would set off a chain reaction leading toward a triumph that would take months or more likely years to achieve. By contrast, the anonymous men and women who concluded that there was no alternative to fighting the war to the finish and who surprised cadres by volunteering for the PLAF did not envision the campaign as a "step in a process." They looked forward to a showdown that with one mighty stroke would put an end to their suffering. Without them, instructions from afar would have eventuated in a campaign of modest impact. The rice donations and taxes paid in advance, and, most of all, the peasants rising up with a millenarian fervor, are what gave the Tet Offensive its stupendous force. Those who survived must have been heartbroken when it did not bring victory and peace.[20]

LEGACY OF THE LIBERATION FRONT

The time-space compression brought on by the Vietnam War burned through generations of revolutionaries with a cruel rapidity. Some of the people who were caught up in the passions of the golden period were killed or disabled before escalation, and many more, a great many more, fell after 1965, while others quit the Front or fled from the countryside or rallied to the GVN. A new wave of young people, who had been children at the time of the concerted uprising, responded to jubilant watchwords on the eve of Tet and affiliated with the movement, and that cohort must have been chewed up at an even more rapid rate in the dreadful battles of 1968 and in the charnel house that followed. To those who participated in "the great spring victory" of 1975, the golden period must have seemed like ancient history.

The formative contexts for these generational groupings differed profoundly. Attitudes and expectations of the 1960 militants took shape during the Diem era, a time of political repression and destabilizations associated with the social transformation. And yet the phase could also be characterized as "the six years of peace," which in part explains why those who were politicized in the concerted uprising imagined that they could fight a war and still have time and space to revolutionize village culture. The first years of armed struggle, when a still small PLAF seemed to be winning over the GVN, did nothing to shake that confidence. As everyday life and political activism found ways to coexist and a democratized public sphere created opportunities for collective explorations of many issues, the southern revolution inspired militants to anticipate an idealized future.

The 1965–1967 escalation shaped the awareness of many who participated in the Tet Offensive. As conditions deteriorated in the countryside, people set aside imaginative flights and tried to find the strength within themselves to outlast a fearsome adversary. Pauses for festive occasions, and especially for Tet, briefly allowed villagers to reflect on their situation, and if the Rand materials are to be trusted, conversation during these celebrations was focused to the exclusion of all other concerns on hopes for peace. Social and cultural issues that dominated movement discourse in the early days of the Liberation Front were then forced to the margins.

The revolutionary modernism of the Front was thus a singular phenomenon, the product of complex and multiple forces, not easily conjured up and not destined to last indefinitely. The debates that it stimulated were interrupted, and one will never know what might have emerged if the United States had withdrawn in 1961 or 1965 and if cultural revolution had gone forward in more auspicious circumstances. Those who came later had new problems to solve and inevitably thought about them in different ways. In his study of the war in My Tho, David Elliott suggests that the Communist Party and the people of the province played a significant role in campaigns that led to victory in 1975. But it is less clear how much survived of the earlier revolutionary agenda.[21]

Projects undertaken in one context, then suspended, cannot be resuscitated intact and continued in another, but an unnecessary price is paid when they disappear entirely from collective memory. In the recent literature on society and culture in Vietnam, scholars and their Vietnamese informants, who are separated from the concerted uprising by a nightmare of death and suffering, have forgotten the southern revolution. It is as if no zealots dreamed of a paradise on earth where people would be "free to work and free to enjoy"; no village iconoclast refused to "bow to the sky"; no young people, animated by a heartfelt internationalism, gathered over cups of tea to discuss "the world situation, socialism, Russia and China"; no dutiful daughters surprised friends and neighbors by announcing that they were going "to liberate themselves from the oppression of the men."[22]

Two of Rand's female informants had made a living as seamstresses before affiliating with the Front. Both worked at home for customers who purchased the fabrics and specified what sort of apparel they wanted. A generation later a researcher's inquiry into the garment industry uncovered a very different situation. Thousands of women were employed in textile factories owned by Nike or other foreign corporations or continued to sew at home, working off templates passed on by middlemen, with finished products disappearing into the circuits of international trade. Some resided in Vietnam, while others had emigrated after 1975 and were living and working in Australia and American Samoa. "The increasing pace of fashion turnover" put both managers and workers "under enormous pressure to complete orders on time," so that the women had to work through the night to complete their assignments. The DRV and the NLF won the war, but the time-space compression of the 1960s has been radically intensified, with clock disciplines far more stringent than any imposed in the 1960s and diasporas that have carried women to distant locales, including some outside of Vietnam. The result is a situation far more complicated than those faced by female militants of the Liberation Front.[23]

This evidence—and examples could easily be multiplied—demonstrates that, no matter who won or who lost the war, once the social transformation came to Vietnam, the Vietnamese were going to be living in the maelstrom. Front campaigns against hierarchies of every kind and in favor of a full realization of human potential could therefore not have achieved closure. At best one might imagine outcomes that satisfied their authors and then were questioned and revised in the following years by people who lived in different circumstances and needed to find their own solutions. Stalwarts of the Liberation Front understood that "everything in this world never stood at one place" and did not pause to draw up blueprints for the future. Popular sovereignty is what mattered most to them. Later generations have something to learn from ancestors who refused to submit to others, who set out to change themselves and the world. The drama, the grandeur, lay in their refusal to give up hope that, when human will is tested to the limit, "the deep chaos of modern life" can be mastered.

APPENDIX: THE USES OF A SOURCE

As one might expect in a project that depended on U.S. and GVN funding and logistical support, Rand Corporation interviews in My Tho often took the form of an intelligence-gathering operation. Rand staffers probed for information on the routines, campsites, and leadership structures of guerrilla units; tried to learn more about NLF reaction to different weapons, battlefield tactics, and pacification campaigns; and kept track of the names, whereabouts, and activities of local Front militants. In hopes of encouraging defections, they sought information on what the rural population thought of propaganda leaflets, how they reacted to loudspeaker broadcasts from helicopters, whether they listened to Saigon radio, and what considerations were most likely to prompt a "rally" to the government side.[1]

Rand also made a critical choice at the beginning of the motivation and morale project, one that launched it in a promising direction. At a time when others in the U.S.-GVN orbit showed no interest in the opinions and experiences of the Vietnamese peasantry, DT series interviewers gave the floor to country people and questioned them at length about their backgrounds, experiences, and opinions in the midst of revolution and war. In their turn these previously unheard subjects tried to steer the interviews in directions of their own choosing. In hopes of protecting themselves in an inhospitable environment, they sometimes responded with lies and evasions, flattery, and expressions of contrition verging on the abject. But most were manifestly fighting to hold on to their dignity, and in the end, their voices come through with a startling force.

A POWER-LADEN CONTEXT

The forty-two prisoners questioned by Rand could not be counted on to speak truthfully. Some provided misleading answers in order to protect still active comrades, while others were primarily concerned to deny or minimize their participation in the revolution. According to one interviewer, a number of POWs "gave false information to the interrogators to prevent the GVN from exploiting them effectively for information and to reduce their jail term." Rand staffer Phillips Davison notes that "many prisoners had been mishandled or even tortured during earlier interrogation sessions." Prisoner-informants must have hesitated to speak of such incidents to Rand staffers allied with the people who had mistreated them, but even so, eleven of the forty-two reported that they had been tortured. Interviewee no. 144 was questioned by Rand "in a small room with ARVN interrogators milling around and listening in on the interview, so that the subject had to be guarded about what he said." Interviewee no. 57 was "sometimes frank and sometimes reserved depending on the presence or absence of police officers in the interview room." Interviewee no. 81 "was not sincere in his answers, perhaps because he still suspected and was afraid that his answers would influence his forthcoming trial by the Military Court."[2]

Prisoner narratives feature implausible accidents and more than a little special pleading. Several informants claimed to have quit or been purged from the Front or to have deserted from the PLAF weeks or months before being apprehended and insisted that they should be treated as simple citizens and not enemy combatants. Others professed to welcome capture because they were disillusioned with the movement. Still others were familiar with GVN catechisms. A man who had been incarcerated under the Diem regime offered the following report:

> I found that the study sessions in the prison had nothing interesting, therefore I later resumed my work for the NLF. In the study sessions in prison, I was taught of the differences between nationalism and communism. When we discussed our subject matter in order to be able to understand the reasons for this, the instructors did not allow us to freely express our ideas. Anyone who said something to defend his ideas would be considered as having been influenced by Communism. Consequently, he could be handcuffed or put into a cell. Therefore, the inmates only studied for the sake of study. They unanimously agreed to the ideas of the instructors so that they could be released early.

This prisoner and others could be pardoned for anticipating that the same sort of dynamic would apply in the Rand interviews. With no reason to assume the good faith of their "instructors," and hoping to be "released early," they must have been tempted to say what they thought researchers wanted to hear.[3]

Although their situation was not as bleak as that of the prisoners, the 243 defectors interviewed by Rand nonetheless found themselves in an uncomfortable and sometimes dangerous predicament as they tried to explain—or explain away—their service within the revolution. Many complained about being detained in Chieu Hoi Centers. Rumor had it that ralliers were held for two or three months "and would be in the situation of 'a fish on a chopping board.'" One informant noted that defectors "must stay at the Chieu Hoi

Center a whole month or even 2 or 3 months," whereas "in the Front area, deserters from the GVN side were released to go back to their villages after 3 or 4 days." Even the French, according to another informant, were quicker to process ralliers. "All the above work was completed within a week, and the people who surrendered didn't have to wait two or three months as they do now at the Chieu-Hoi center."[4]

A number of ralliers were, in Davison's words, "treated roughly, or at least without respect." After defecting, interviewee no. 187 was assaulted by militiamen, one of whom had been a rival for the affections of a young woman. His interviewer went to some lengths to figure out what had happened and seemed reassured when the informant said, "This whole incident was only due to personal hatred and had nothing to do with the policy of the government." But it also emerged that GVN interrogators in an earlier session had yelled at the subject and threatened to hit him when answers did not come quickly enough. "At first," another interviewee recalled, "when I was at the District, I was very scared and forgot everything because whenever I was slow in speaking, the interrogator would drum the table furiously and sent me to jail for two days."[5]

After coming over to the GVN, interviewee no. 91 was sent to Saigon for vocational training, but then was arrested. "Someone from Hoa Dinh Village, his area of operation, filed a suit against him for the assassination of a villager committed while he was operating for the VC in the village." A man who rallied after murdering a cadre ran into another defector who had joined a U.S. commando team and "who questioned him harshly" about the assassination. The informant fled and agreed to return only after the interviewer promised to guarantee his safety. A villager who worked for the Front in Binh Trung reported, "I made a few people angry at me by forcing them to do things for the Hamlet Civil Affairs Section." After some of these disgruntled neighbors rallied, "they happened to come across my wife many times on her way to the market, and they threatened her saying that they would retaliate against me. This made me afraid and hesitant about rallying since I feared that I would have to encounter them out here." Some Rand informants worried that there were NLF spies in the Chieu Hoi Centers. "Who knows," said the Platoon Leader to his interlocutor, "you might be a plant."[6]

According to David Elliott, defectors could not speak freely, not when they hoped to "mollify" and "feared antagonizing their interviewers" and sought to "ingratiate themselves with the new authorities who controlled their destiny." A staffer reported, "His hands were trembling, he looked frightened, and talked hesitantly," after questioning interviewee no. 50, who in turn remarked: "Although I have been well treated, my fear is not yet eliminated. I will stop being apprehensive only when I am released." Interviewee no. 241 was so nervous that he could not sleep the night before the session or eat anything when the interviewer invited him to lunch.[7]

It must have been painful for Rand personnel to be associated with brutal militiamen and interrogators and painful as well to note how interviewees persisted in suspecting that they themselves were working for the government. Interviewee no. 208 "mistook the interviewer for a GVN official, even though the interviewer had done his best to explain the purpose of the interview to him." Some dealt with the problem by claiming "that they were reporters," while "others posed as social science students doing research for their oncoming theses." Perhaps subjects believed these stories, and it could be that some Rand staffers did succeed in putting subjects at their ease. But transparency was impossible in the power-laden context of the project.[8]

Davison states that the political opinions of Rand's Vietnamese employees were "highly diverse," but his further affirmation that all were "non-Communists" can be read as an acknowledgment that none were close to the southern revolution. In the transcripts, interviewees present themselves as supporters of the regime and the Americans. Some appear to have seized the opportunity to trade polemical blows with unseen adversaries, as if Chieu Hoi Centers served as a battlefield equivalent to the village forums where communists worked their wiles. At the end of interview no. 171 the staffer commented: "In the early days of his rally, the interviewee was very skeptical and suspicious. However, as time went by, he became less skeptical and more confident (in our cause)." Also seeking to win converts, interviewer no. 15 "tried to summarily explain . . . the American aims in Vietnam and drew a map of Southeast Asia to help [his subject] to understand."[9]

Some interrogators come across as crude and naïve. The staffer responsible for interview no. 45 remarked that the interviewee "seemed sincere when he talked about his realization of the Front's unreasonableness and imbecility." The person who conducted interview no. 161 opined that the subject "has been deeply indoctrinated with atheist materialism. However, he still loves his family." Testimony from interviewee no. 230 promoted this comment: "Subject was deeply indoctrinated, and he was not sincere or cooperative with the interviewer. If the subject were released now, he would join the VC to fight against us. That was what he had in mind, unless we could change it by giving him a good brain-wash in prison." The same remedy was prescribed for another prisoner: "He is not a fanatic Communist. Even though he has been well indoctrinated, we could still re-indoctrinate him if we apply the right methods and use the right dose of indoctrination."[10]

Rand interviewers took notes during and after sessions, which were then translated and typed, and as a result, they exercised a near total control over the transcript and were free to edit the testimony they were hearing. These men and women seem to have viewed the United States as the leader of the free world and, as far as one can tell, liked and admired the Rand staffers who supervised the project. No doubt they were reluctant to credit stories that reflected badly on their new friends and were tempted to suppress evidence of allied misdeeds. They also knew that potential readers in the Saigon police and intelligence branches, and perhaps among the Americans, would notice comments that appeared to echo the Communist Party line and would regard with suspicion anyone who appeared to be passing along enemy propaganda. Davison's suggestion that interviewers were placed under surveillance "by agents of the Saigon government" may have been an attempt on his part to disarm antiwar critics who portrayed Rand employees as lackeys of U.S. imperialism. But it also calls attention to the apprehension felt by many working under a regime that dealt summarily with real or imagined dissidence. Given all these considerations, the prudent course was to leave out unwelcome testimony, and as a result, the DT series offers only a partial account of U.S.-GVN conduct during the war.[11]

SUBJECTS PUSH BACK

Rand staffers misrepresented themselves to subjects, edited the transcripts, and vainly labored to understand a popular movement whose ethos surpassed the limits of their imagining. But they could not entirely control the people sitting on the other side of the table. When "pushed" for military-related information and for confirmation of cold war dogma, subjects "pushed back" with reports organized around their own interpretations of everyday realities in the countryside. The result was a kind of stalemate and even a grudging complicity, as interviewers reminded themselves that they had a job to do and tried to maintain the integrity of the record, even in the presence of testimony that clashed with their core assumptions. The result was a dialogue characterized by manipulation and evasions, by hints not noticed and not followed up, but sometimes by common efforts to bring painful truths to light.[12]

Rand experts came out of an academic culture in which peasants were thought to be empty-minded rustics, and the Vietnamese interviewers they hired, who were drawn from the ranks of the urban bourgeoisie, tended toward the same view. To some the peasant was a biological other. "His features show that he comes from the very poor farmer class," declared interviewer no. 247 of his subject, while interviewer no. 67 remarked of another, "His appearance is also that of a very poor farmer." Borrowing an idea from Orientalist travel literature, in which the Vietnamese were said to get along with a vocabulary of only a few hundred words, interviewer no. 18 commented that his subject "spoke with difficulty [and] understood only the most common words." These "simple peasants," to use an expression often encountered in the transcripts, were seen as passive creatures, easily gulled by enemy propaganda.[13]

A number of interviewees played on the "simple peasant" stereotype as a way of getting around awkward details in their own personal histories: their revolutionary commitments, first of all, and also the sometimes less than edifying circumstances—the crimes, peculations, or illicit love affairs—that had forced them to leave the countryside. Rand would have been well advised to heed the words of the informant who noted, "The villagers never revealed their secret feelings to strangers." When asked about government changes in Saigon, another witness responded: "Some people understood the matter but did not speak out. They said in this time of great troubles, one should not show off one's knowledge, and one should not be too stupid, but one should be informed and yet keep silent. There is a saying that: 'to know too much is fatal, to be stupid is fatal, but to know just enough will permit survival (khon chet, dai chet, biet thi song).' " By way of reinforcing these habits, the Front instructed peasants "to tell the GVN soldiers on sweep operations that they 'didn't hear, see or know anything.' When a stranger asked about any cadres, the people answered that they didn't know anything."[14]

When questioned by Rand interviewers, a number of informants employed the same strategy. "I was only a peasant and I had to comply with orders," was the humble plea of interviewee no. 14. Interviewee no. 17 declared, "I just did not think anything," and with an equally farfetched modesty, interviewee no. 34 insisted, "I did not know what I liked or what I disliked." Interviewee no. 38 claimed, "I don't know what freedom is," and added, "I was just a simple farmer; they wouldn't let me in the Party"—an incomprehension that, earlier, had not prevented him from lauding the GVN milieu, where refugees from the NLF zone found "freedom to go wherever one wanted." Interviewee no. 20 pretended that he never talked to anyone, not even his own brothers, who were in the Front. Interviewee no. 137, who worked as a barber in the marketplace, where all the tendrils of the grapevine came together in a cacophony of hearsay and rumor, asserted that he had no idea what people thought about politics "because I never heard them say anything."[15]

Sometimes interviewers let these evasions pass without comment, and sometimes they hesitated when answers pressed against the limits of their preconceptions. "It required continuous pushing and rephrasing of questions in order to get the answers out of him," said interviewer no. 24 of the subject. "This was, perhaps, a result of his lack of intelligence rather than his intention to withhold information," a remark illustrating class bias overriding a glimmer of understanding that the informant might be seeking to mislead. Interviewee no. 122 was "simple and belonged to the poor farmers' class," but this time the staffer was more attuned to the deception: "Though he had tried hard to say only things which were contrary to his own thought, we could still perceive, here and there during the interview, that he had not been able to get rid of his communistic thoughts."[16]

Interviewers used the term "sincerity" to characterize subjects who said the right things about politics and the war, but even the most clueless sensed that "sincere" informants were sometimes being disingenuous. By contrast, the "insincere" interviewees, especially among the prisoners, tended to be the most helpful sources on "Viet Cong motivation and morale." Caught between their prejudices and their desire to learn, Rand staffers were in a double bind, one they could not help imposing on informants. Interviewee no. 9 "seemed very sincere and cooperative," noted the interviewer, who then added: "He showed sincere pro-GVN feelings. He deliberately used the designation 'VC' instead of 'the Front,' in each reply. In probing the subject's feelings, the interviewer occasionally gave the impression he did not credit some of the subject's replies. The subject reacted by showing his anger whenever this happened." No wonder the informant lost his temper. Obliged to parrot the Saigon party line, he took umbrage when this compliance was received with skepticism.[17]

In the same vein, interviewee no. 52, who admitted having been intimidated by a previous interrogator, "made a conspicuous effort to prove himself anti-VC and pro-GVN, and sometimes he overdid it." So did interviewee no. 129: "The subject was talkative and sincere. He seemed very eager to speak of his hatred towards the Front, perhaps thinking it was the best way to show how loyal he was to the new side he has just taken. Interviewed right after his coming to the Chieu Hoi Center, he was still afraid of being suspected by the officials." Interviewee no. 10 "was sincere and cooperative, but the interviewer felt that he dared not criticize the GVN officials or the GVN policy for fear of having trouble with Vietnamese authorities." In all these cases researchers could not avoid the impression that "sincere" answers did little to advance the understanding they wished to achieve.[18]

The opposite dynamic was at work with the "insincere" informants. In the words of his interrogator, interviewee no. 61, an unapologetic revolutionary who proved to be a knowledgeable source on the Front's inner workings, "has been indoctrinated for a long time. He was not sincere and cooperative." Another prisoner, interviewee no. 159, was a model of fearless honesty, which the Rand staffer could not parse: "The subject was not sincere at all. He tried to avoid answering the questions of the interviewer to the point. He refused to reveal anything about the high ranking cadres who he certainly knew. He liked to express his views boldly, and seemed to want to make propaganda for the Front. But he revealed his thoughts and showed that he was a hard core Front cadre." This interview is full of detail about the movement, the kind of information that offended the sensibilities of the researchers while helping them carry out the assignment they had been given.[19]

These and other citations illustrate both the bias and the professionalism of Rand staffers. Take, for example, interview no. 142, which ended with the following postscript:

[The interviewee] was typical of the Vietnamese peasantry, simple, sincere, credulous and grateful. The remarkable point about [him] was that although he had been heavily indoctrinated by the VC and intensively taught to hate the upper classes and to believe in the final victory of the NLFSVN [National Liberation Front of South Vietnam] in its struggle to liberate the proletariat—the class to which he belonged—[he] seems to have been enlightened more by his conversation with this interviewer than all these years of indoctrination. With an unaffected air, he expressed surprise and indignation over the fact he was so belated in realizing the lies and empty promises of the Front, regarding peace and happiness. [He] was of the opinion that the Nationalist cause will win over the Communist cause and he was happy about this because he believed under the Nationalist regime, peace will be durable, the people will prosper and the nation will become strong and powerful. [He] felt that the people and their happiness should come first. [His] cooperation with this interviewer developed as the interview progressed.

This smug and obtuse passage, which does not reflect credit on its author and makes the informant seem like a fool, comes to the reader in the form of an afterword. Perhaps in the chitchat surrounding the session the subject extolled the interviewer's evocation of GVN peace and prosperity and expressed "surprise and indignation" at "the lies and empty promises of the Front." But there is nothing of that sort in the transcript, where this veteran revolutionary comes across as a dignified and thoughtful man who, in a tactful way, remained true to his convictions.[20]

Elsewhere, when Rand personnel displayed a lack of discipline, informants politely but firmly stood their ground. Interviewee no. 153 was obliged to wrestle with such questions as "If peace can't be restored, in spite of the repeated peace offers by the GVN and the Free World, who will be responsible for the prolongation of the war?" and "Which do you think is better; the Communist regime or the free regime?"—a query followed by the helpful prod, "Please be frank." Trying his best to be "sincere," he declared, "When I was still in the Front, I didn't know much about the situation, but now that I've talked with you—and I believe what you tell me—I think that the Chinese are not like the Americans. The Americans who come here to help the GVN don't need us to feed them. On the contrary, they give the South a very generous economic and military aid, and they help the South from the point of view of manpower also." But when the interviewer continued to harp on Chinese perfidy, the subject suddenly abandoned caution. "Why don't the allies and the Free World attack China directly because China is the aggressor?" he demanded. "If the real aggressor is defeated, then the war will come to an end. If the war is switched to another country, then peace will come back to Vietnam. If the real aggressor—namely China—is defeated, then we'll have a long-lasting peace." In this session and others, interviewers tried to lead their subjects but also enabled readers to discern the resistance mounted from the other side of the table.[21]

The war itself reshaped the motivation and morale project. As bombing and shelling laid waste the countryside and U.S. and ARVN soldiers burned huts, plowed up rice paddies, and shot villagers, the costs of allied war making began to register in the transcripts. Perhaps interviewers hoped that evidence of mass suffering would reach well-meaning Americans who would then find ways to temper the excesses of their compatriots. Or maybe it was simply a matter of registering a statement, however muted and indirect, against a degree of violence that was difficult to justify on any grounds. Morale among Rand employees gradually faltered as officials in Saigon and Washington ignored the information they were gathering and continued to employ tactics that came to seem counterproductive and immoral. In that context one might guess that enthusiasm for intelligence gathering began to wane.

Whatever agendas they may have wished to pursue, interviewer and interviewee could not overlook the sinister drama unfolding all around them, one that seemed to override competing military strategies and party lines. The sense that they were witness to the destruction of rural society may have prompted Rand personnel to begin posing questions about a way of life that was seemingly on the verge of extinction. The result was a series of questions on religious and festive customs, household economies and survival strategies, relations between parents and children and between men and women. What might be called an ethnographic turn came late and never fully determined the thrust of the project, but for whatever reason, the interviews unmistakably took on a different tone and direction as war-related issues receded and attention shifted toward village life. It was as if interrogators stopped caring about who won and who lost and allowed themselves to be guided by sympathy for rural dwellers, including the revolutionaries among them, whose world was being torn apart. It is no doubt an exaggeration, but in making my way through the transcripts I more than once thought that interviewers were "defecting" from the U.S.-GVN war effort.[22]

The Rand prism distorted the text that might have emerged if NLF cadres had been questioned in less loaded circumstances. But Front discourse itself could not have served as a last word on the concerted uprising or the golden period and certainly not on the phase of escalating violence after 1965, when escalating warfare mocked all attempts to discern a meaning in events. Because of the compromised postures of the researchers and their subjects, some of the questions posed in the interviews remained unanswered. But that absence of closure also reflected the contradictions and confusions of the moment. Liberation Front militants were revolutionaries, and as in all revolutions, indeed in all human endeavors, a tension existed between the awareness and capacity of the protagonists and the circumstances they were endeavoring to control and change. The DT series throws light on their noble, unfinished effort to create a better world.

NOTES

1. A SOCIAL HISTORY OF THE VIETNAM WAR

1. Informants cited in this book commonly speak of the Republic of South Vietnam as the "GVN," a practice that I have followed. For the "concerted uprising," see chapter 3.

2. The origins and triumphs of the social history that I take as a starting point are analyzed in Geoff Eley, *A Crooked Line: From Cultural History to the History of Society* (Ann Arbor: University of Michigan Press, 2005). For more on the "motivation and morale" project, see Phillips Davison, *User's Guide to the Rand Interviews in Vietnam* (Santa Monica: Rand Corporation, 1972). "DT" stood for Dinh Tuong, the government designation for the province. It had gone under the name My Tho during the period of French domination and was still so known among inhabitants during the 1960s. After 1975 the province name was changed to Tien Giang.

3. See the appendix for a more extended discussion of the Rand materials. My initial attempt to draw on the interviews is elaborated in David Hunt, "Villagers at War: The National Liberation Front in My Tho Province, 1965–1967," in a double issue of *Radical America* 8, nos. 1–2 (1974): 3–184. See also my article "Gift of Food: The Provisioning of Troops during the American War in Vietnam," *Journal of the Historical Society* 2, no. 2 (2002): 125–43. This latter essay is about soldiers of the NLF, who are not much represented in the present book but whose stories I hope to address in a later work.

4. For extravagant praise of the NLF's "organizational weapon," which made the Front "a sputnik in the political sphere of the Cold War," see Douglas Pike, *Viet Cong: The Organization and Techniques of the National Liberation Front of South Vietnam* (Cambridge: MIT Press, 1968), 111. For constructions of the peasantry within Marxist discourse, see Esther Kingston-Mann, *Lenin and the Problem of Marxist Peasant Revolution* (New York: Oxford University Press, 1983).

5. David Elliott and W. A. Stewart, *Pacification and the Viet Cong System in Dinh Tuong: 1966–1967* (Santa Monica: Rand Corporation, 1969), 14; and David Elliott, *The Vietnamese War: Revolution and Social Change in the Mekong Delta, 1930–1975* (New York: Sharpe, 2003), xxii. Elliott's massive study is indispensable for anyone interested in My Tho and in the Vietnam War. My main criticisms, directed at Elliott's treatment of "social change," are spelled out in David Hunt, "Revolution in the Delta," *Critical Asian Studies* 35, no. 4 (2003): 599–620. Gabriel Kolko differs from Elliott on many points and frequently affirms that rural dwellers in southern Vietnam were more revolutionary than Communist Party leaders in Hanoi. But he too states, "The Communist Party is also the 'Revolution' in my lexicon." Gabriel Kolko, *Anatomy of a War: Vietnam, the United States, and the Modern Historical Experience* (New York: New Press, 1994), xi.

6. This solidarity is what E. P. Thompson had in mind when he spoke of the "moral economy," which at certain times and places in history has served as inspiration for "crowds" resisting messages from above and seeking to impose their own notions of how society ought to be organized. E. P. Thompson, "The Moral Economy of the English Crowd in the Eighteenth Century," *Past & Present* 50 (1971): 76–136. I owe a debt to Thompson and also to Raymond Williams for his complex meditation, always worth rereading,

on hegemony and counterhegemony, in *Marxism and Literature* (New York: Oxford University Press, 1977). Without the horizontal axis, the "moral economy" notion is an unrecognizable substitute for Thompson's conception; see David Hunt, "From the Millennial to the Everyday: James Scott's Search for the Essence of Peasant Politics," *Radical History Review* 42 (1988): 155–72. For a fresh assessment, with many references to the literature, see Pamela McElwee, "From the Moral Economy to the World Economy: Revisiting Vietnamese Peasants in a Globalizing Era," *Journal of Vietnamese Studies* 2, no. 2 (2007): 57–107.

7. On splits and confusing compromises among Communist Party leaders, see Robert Brigham, *Guerrilla Diplomacy: The NLF's Foreign Relations and the Viet Nam War* (Ithaca: Cornell University Press, 1999).

8. References throughout this book to Rand interviews are found in "Series DT: Activities of Viet Cong within Dinh Tuong Province" (AD 741305), in the Rand Vietnam Interview Series (Santa Monica: Rand Corporation, 1972). These interviews are cited many times in the pages that follow, and in order to save space and reduce clutter, I employ a simplified citation procedure. This quotation is in the DT series, interview no. 185, page 40, question 83: 185/40/83. Interviewee responses were translated and typed in haste and were not always rendered in correct English. In some instances I have taken the liberty of making minor, unsignaled changes in spelling and punctuation. In others, where problems are too substantial for silent correction and seem likely to confuse the reader, I have inserted adjustments in brackets. But mostly I have checked the impulse to intrude. I hope others will share my sense that a certain roughness in expression helps to convey the everyday character of testimonies offered by Rand informants.

9. On big landlords, see Elliott, *Vietnamese War*, 83; on the old power structure, 158; on destroying the entire socioeconomic elite, 439. Elliott cites estimates that 43,000 hectares (30 percent of the arable land) changed hands during the Resistance, and that after the GVN reversed many expropriations during the six years of peace, the NLF confiscated and redistributed 77 percent of the land in the province (122, 151, 445). He also notes that in the transcripts, only eleven out of the 129 landlords mentioned by name in the DT series were said to be living in the villages, and when they lingered on the scene, it was at the sufferance of the peasants (448). Contrasts between North (paternalist landlords/deferential peasants) and South (absentee landlords/revolutionary peasants) are developed in David Hunt, "U.S. Scholarship and the National Liberation Front," in *The American War in Vietnam*, ed. Jayne Werner and David Hunt (Ithaca: Southeast Asia Program, Cornell University, 1993), 94–97. Robert Sansom is close to Elliott when he declares that "the gradual retreat of landlords to the cities that had begun in the 1930s for reasons of role and preference, in the 1946–1948 period became a panic-stricken exodus to escape intimidation, assassination, or trial and probable execution by the Viet Minh." Sansom declares that landlords traveling in the delta were more at risk than Americans or government officials. Robert Sansom, *The Economics of Insurgency in the Mekong Delta of Vietnam* (Cambridge: MIT Press, 1970), 55 and 8, n. 13. Jeffrey Race argues that in Long An province the movement was more revolutionary than patriotic. "By bringing an antifeudal revolution to the countryside," he declares, the Viet Minh "motivated the peasantry to serve an anti-imperialist revolution as well." Jeffrey Race, *War Comes to Long An: Revolutionary Conflict in a Vietnamese Province* (Berkeley: University of California Press, 1972), 40. Local studies conducted in the North convey a very different impression. In John Kleinen, *Facing the Future, Reviving the*

Past: A Study of Social Change in a Northern Vietnamese Village (Singapore: Institute of Southeast Asian Studies, 1999), the theme of class struggle is absent from the chapters on the Resistance. In comparison to the "panic-stricken exodus" in the South, Hy Van Luong cites a local party member from Son Duong village who recalled that "former notables all wanted to join the Party." He adds that "the percentage of party members from landlord, rich, and upper middle peasant families well exceeded 46 percent." Hy Van Luong, *Revolution in the Village: Tradition and Transformation in North Vietnam, 1925–1988* (Honolulu: University of Hawaii Press, 1992), 157–58. Whereas southern peasants demanded land reform, northern cadres "complained of the difficulties they had in getting local farmers to recognize the true nature of the 'landlord class'"; Shaun Malarney, "Culture, Virtue, and Political Transformation in Contemporary Northern Viet Nam," *Journal of Asian Studies* 56 (1997): 910.

10. According to Hobsbawm, in the generation after 1945, literacy spread, advances in communication technology overcame constraints of time and space, and commodities generated by "a single, increasingly integrated and universal world economy" found buyers everywhere. The "disintegration of the old patterns of social relationships" created new risks and prospects for women and for young people of both sexes. In many regions, shifts in agricultural practice and out-migration from the countryside led to the "death of the peasantry." "For 80% of humanity," he concludes, "the Middle Ages ended suddenly in the 1950s." Among objections to this template, one might note that French colonialism and the Japanese occupation in Indochina are not well characterized as "medieval" phenomena and that the Vietnamese peasantry did not "die." But Hobsbawm's sketch of worldwide trends did open my mind to aspects not readily apparent when Vietnam's experience of the war is conceived as a singular, narrowly Vietnamese phenomenon. With respect to the peasant issue, Hobsbawm adds, "Only three regions of the globe remained essentially dominated by their villages and fields; sub-saharan Africa, South and continental South-east Asia, and China." Eric Hobsbawm, *Age of Extremes: A History of the World, 1914–1991* (New York: Pantheon, 1994), 15, 288, 289, 291.

11. On the "boon of continuity," see the great work of Eric Wolf, *Peasant Wars of the Twentieth Century* (New York: Harper & Row, 1968), 276.

12. Samuel Huntington, "The Bases of Accommodation," *Foreign Affairs* 46, no. 4 (1968): 652. Huntington performed a service by underscoring the link, repeatedly confirmed in history, between violence and what many define as progress. Hobsbawm was thinking globally and not just about South Vietnam when he declared that "the 1960s will probably go down as the most disastrous decade in the history of human urbanization" (*Age of Extremes*, 262). In drawing a distinction between "modernization" and "modernism," I am citing Marshall Berman's formulation in *All That Is Solid Melts into Air: The Experience of Modernity* (New York: Penguin, 1988), 16; see also David Harvey, *The Condition of Postmodernity* (Cambridge, Mass.: Blackwell, 1989). On U.S.-style "modernization," see Michael Latham, *Modernization as Ideology: American Social Science and "Nation Building" in the Kennedy Era* (Chapel Hill: University of North Carolina Press, 2000). Ngo Dinh Diem also saw himself as a modernizer, as noted in Philip Catton, *Diem's Final Failure: Prelude to America's War in Vietnam* (Lawrence: University Press of Kansas, 2002); and Edward Miller, "Vision, Power, and Agency: The Ascent of Ngo Dinh Diem, 1945–1954," in *Making Sense of the Vietnam Wars*, ed. Mark Bradley and Marilyn Young (New York: Oxford University Press, 2008), 135–69. If

the testimonies of Rand informants are to be credited, the "Personalism" sponsored by Diem and his brother Nhu found no audience in My Tho villages. For a general discussion of peasants and modernization, see Esther Kingston-Mann, *In Search of the True West: Culture, Economics, and Problems of Russian Development* (Princeton: Princeton University Press, 1999). The literature on "modernity" is vast; see the discussion and many references in Frederick Cooper, *Colonialism in Question: Theory, Knowledge, History* (Berkeley: University of California Press, 2005).

13. Many issues raised in the villages of My Tho in the 1960s had been addressed in the 1920s and 1930s. See David Marr, *Vietnamese Tradition on Trial, 1920–1945* (Berkeley: University of California Press, 1981); Hue-Tam Ho Tai, *Radicalism and the Origins of the Vietnamese Revolution* (Cambridge: Harvard University Press, 1992); and Nguyen Van Ky, *La société vietnamienne face à la modernité: le Tonkin de la fin du XIXe siècle à la seconde guerre mondiale* (Paris: Harmattan, 1995). One might wonder if the city-centered colloquy treated in these works was paralleled by similar debates in the countryside. Hue-Tam Ho Tai portrays interwar "radicalism" as an urban phenomenon, while Nguyen Van Ky, who concentrates on the same educated, urban-dwelling strata featured in the other books, occasionally pauses to note counterhegemonic tendencies within the village culture of the North. I believe David Marr when he affirms that the intelligentsia, "perhaps 10,000 in number," hoped "to fashion a new consciousness for themselves and for the Vietnamese people at large" (414, 9). Could it be that there were groups of peasants who also tried to achieve a "new consciousness" and who presumed to speak for "the Vietnamese people at large"?

2. AN ITINERANT PEASANTRY

1. This chapter is a revised version of David Hunt, "Taking Notice of the Everyday," in *Making Sense of the Vietnam Wars*, ed. Mark Bradley and Marilyn Young (New York: Oxford University Press, 2008), 171–97. In thinking about the issues laid out in the opening paragraph, I benefited from reading Karen Wigen, "Culture, Power, and Place: The New Landscapes of East Asian Regionalism," *American Historical Review* 104 (1999): 1183–1201. I am suggesting that the voyages of itinerant rural dwellers sketched the outlines of a new kind of urban-rural configuration, along the lines of the "pilgrimages" discussed in Benedict Anderson, *Imagined Communities: Reflections on the Origin and Spread of Nationalism* (London: Verso, 1983).

2. Fernand Braudel, *The Structures of Everyday Life*, trans. Sian Reynolds (Berkeley: University of California Press, 1992), 29.

3. 206/interviewer comment and 1/1; 178/1/1 and 4/5.

4. 49/annex 10, 14/43, and 2/5. My Tho residents were heavily involved in the 1940 "Nam Ky uprising" against the French. See also interviewee no. 193, who began by saying, "I have never left my village," then a moment later declared: "In 1957, I left my village for one year. I was then drafted by the GVN." He was sent to the Quang Trung Training Center near Saigon and later transferred to an ammunition depot at an unnamed place outside his home province (193/1/1 and 1/5).

5. 101/70/205. In the microfilm set of the DT series, which I purchased from the Rand Corporation in the early 1970s, almost all personal names were blocked out. Later on I was able to acquire unsanitized copies of about half the interviews. Knowing people's names helps make sense of the information they are providing, and identifying people by name

might seem a common courtesy. But there is a chance that doing so could lead to difficulties for those who are still alive and for their families in Vietnam. So personal names have been omitted in this text. Nevertheless, some of the informants come across so vividly and are so frequently cited that it seemed useful to give them some sort of name. I hope that readers will accept this as a respectful and not a presumptuous device.

6. The Platoon Leader tells his story in 101/1–3/1.

7. On the informant's father-in-law, see 101/65/191.

8. 101/29/93 and 68/197.

9. 271/1/3, 138/1/1, 230/1/1, 89/4/12. Interviewee no. 189 was orphaned at four, interviewee no. 175 and interviewee no. 208 at six, and interviewee no. 186 at eight; on the Khmer orphan, see 231/1/1; on the Binh Trung orphan, 180/1/2.

10. These cases are found in 77/1/1, 203/1/1, 198/1/1–3, 153/2/2, 252/1/1, and 290/1/1. See also 184/1/1, 243/1/1, 272/2/8, and 278/8/12.

11. 26/38 and 25, 108/78/162, 188/1/2, 128/1/1; see also 41/1/3.

12. 76/1/1, 100/1/2, 102/3/16, 22/3/10.

13. For the orphans, see 182/1/1, 213/1/1, and 263/1/3; for single-parent families, 164/1/3 and also 46/3/11, 65/3/9, 201/1/1, and 253/11/12; for refusals of arranged marriages, 263/1/4 and 141/1/1; for escape from mother-in-law, 65/8/25; for the fed-up daughter, 46/3/13. The only women who did not run away from home were interviewees no. 201 and no. 264. In the latter case, the marriage, which had taken place early in the twentieth century, almost certainly was arranged. Interviewee no. 65 estimated that in 1964–65 in Chau Thanh district, of the women who left their villages to follow the Front, about one-third "ran away from their families. The remaining two-thirds left their families with their parents' consent" (65/17/53).

14. Interviewer comments, no. 130 and no. 19.

15. 136/1/1 and 178/3/8.

16. 23/7/37, 81/1/1, 30/1 and 18, 57/15/99 and 16/101, 10/7/24, 152/1/1, 292/8/21.

17. 269/1/4, 66/2/9, 96/7/19, 148/61–62/119, 73/10/51, 11/57, and 4/18, 286/2/4.

18. 59/9/25 and 26, 201/3/5.

19. 82/1/1–2, 3/9, 6/11, 4–5/10–11, and 8/22.

20. 8/35/197, 159/25/56 and 20/41, 19/15/43. "Strategic hamlets" were inscribed in a history of government-imposed population relocations. Beginning in 1959, the GVN grouped villagers into "agrovilles" as part of a larger campaign to build a rural society in line with the "Personalism" favored by President Diem and his brother Nhu. In practice, these measures had more to do with isolating the Viet Cong than with winning hearts and minds, and a similar emphasis characterized "strategic hamlets," which succeeded agrovilles in 1962, and "new life hamlets" in the post-1965 period. On agrovilles and strategic hamlets, see Philip Catton, *Diem's Final Failure: Prelude to America's War in Vietnam* (Lawrence: University Press of Kansas, 2002), chaps. 3 and 4.

21. 57/15/100, 69/supplement 7/31, 80/2/7, 188/1–2/4, 128/1/2 and 2/9.

22. 107/1/1, 258/1–2/1 and 3/2, 224/1/2.

23. 144/28/82.

24. Philip Taylor, *Goddess on the Rise: Pilgrimage and Popular Religion in Vietnam* (Honolulu: University of Hawaii Press, 2004), 121–22; and Taylor, *Fragments of the Present: Searching for Modernity in Vietnam's South* (Honolulu: University of Hawaii Press, 2001), 160–61.

25. On the "golden period," see 203/60/88.

26. 111/1/2, 5–16, and 12/49.

27. 142/7–8/9.

28. 137/14/73 and 8/45. Other returning poor peasants included interviewee no. 178, who was frightened by the concerted uprising and fled to Saigon, where he worked as a bricklayer, then returned to Long Dinh village in 1962, in the middle of the golden period, because he was "unable to earn enough for my living" and was "homesick" (178/4/15); interviewee no. 167, who found a job in a Saigon textile factory, then retraced his steps "in order to add to the number of dependent exemptions in my family for the (VC) land reform program" (167/3/5); and interviewee no. 86, a member of the GVN Republican Youth, who took refuge in My Tho when the Front came to power, then joined the NLF a year later and eventually became a village-level cadre (86/2/6).

29. 150/23/80.

30. The Ethnographer tells his life story in 233/1–7/1.

31. 233/154–55/102 and 156–57/103.

32. 233/275–76/185. According to Gaston Bachelard, "the attainment of the superfluous causes greater spiritual excitement than the attainment of necessities"; cited in Braudel, *Structures of Everyday Life*, 186.

33. 233/277/185, 279/10/17, 281/15/20.

34. See 62/6/21, 135/180/387, 259/8–9/20, and 250/11/28; also 189/14/25.

35. 259/9/20, 251/7–8/19, 280/6/15, 257/15/19.

36. On first exposures to urban life and the resulting plasticity in self-awareness, see the very rich analysis in Dror Wahrman, *The Making of the Modern Self: Identity and Culture in Eighteenth-Century England* (New Haven: Yale University Press, 2004), 202.

37. 233/155/102, 14/12, 151 and 153/102, and interviewer comment.

38. 233/4/1, 278–79/185.

39. 233/279/185 and 315/222.

3. THE PEASANT REVOLT OF 1959–60

1. William Duiker, *The Communist Road to Power in Vietnam* (Boulder: Westview Press, 1981), 198. Duiker's formulation is cited in George Herring, *America's Longest War: The United States and Vietnam, 1950–1975* (New York: McGraw Hill, 2001), 80; and George Moss, *Vietnam: An American Ordeal* (Upper Saddle River, N.J.: Prentice-Hall, 1998), 106. The phrase is echoed elsewhere, as when Charles Neu writes, "It was an indigenous rebellion, but one shaped and directed from the north"; Charles Neu, *America's Lost War: Vietnam, 1945–1975* (Wheeling, Ill.: Harlan Davidson, 2005), 43.

2. 290/2/4. See also n. 16 below.

3. Accounts of the concerted uprising in Hoi Cu are found in interviews 109, 165, 166, 223, 278, and 290. The five other pathbreaker villages, where revolt began in 1959, were Dong Hoa (overture in June 1959, breaking the grip of the regime in March 1960); Binh Trung (overture at the end of 1959, liberation in January 1963); Duong Diem (overture, day/night dual power, and breaking the grip sometime in 1959, with the Front officially beginning to function in December 1960); Tam Hiep (overture and breaking the grip in 1959, several hamlets liberated by May 1960); and Phu Nhuan Dong (overture sometime in 1959, breaking the grip and liberation sometime in 1960).

4. David Elliott, *The Vietnamese War: Revolution and Social Change in the Mekong Delta, 1930–1975* (Armonk, N.Y.: Sharpe, 2003), 229. The Ethnographer said that news of the National Liberation Front reached district cadres in July 1961 and suggested that at the village level it was no more than a name. "Front Committees existed only at the district level in 1961," he said. "I don't know when Front Committees were organized at the village level. Actually, I don't even know if there are any village Front Committees at all!" (233/169/112). Perhaps it was a slip of the tongue or a typographical error, but interviewee no. 266 is recorded as stating that the NLF was proclaimed in My Long village on December 20, 1961 (266/6/10).

5. Ibid., 224–30.

6. Elliott, *Vietnamese War*, 250–51; 233/45/46. The boundaries of the 20/7 region were as follows: Route 4 in the north; Route 4, Phu An village, and the sector of Dong Hoa Hiep to the east of Cai Be town in the west; the Mekong River in the south; and Long Hung and Song Thuan villages in the east. Elliott's account draws on various official histories of the concerted uprising in My Tho.

7. For events in Hau My, see 280/4–5/7 and 64/2/5; My Hanh Trung, 238/3–4/9; My Duc Tay, 215/1–2/3; Long Hung, 134/5/8 and 226/3/11; My Long, 266/4/7; Ban Long, 230/5/9; Thanh Phu/CL, 229/12/23; Hoi Cu, 223/3/6. There were two villages called Thanh Phu in My Tho province, one in Cai Lay district (CL) and one in Chau Thanh district (CT). David Elliott explains, "Traditional decoratively carved hollow wooden tocsins used by Buddhist monks were called 'wooden fish'" (*Vietnamese War*, 32). The farther removed the official account, the less it has to teach us about local events. July 20 is not mentioned in the Military History Institute of Vietnam's version of the concerted uprising in the Mekong Delta. Its affirmation that "the people" in My Tho and other provinces "conducted simultaneous uprisings" on September 14, 1960, is not borne out by evidence in the DT series. See *Victory in Vietnam: The Official History of the People's Army of Vietnam, 1954–1975*, trans. Merle Pribbenow (Lawrence: University Press of Kansas, 2002), 65.

8. Elliott, *Vietnamese War*, 229; and see the glossary (1507) for Elliott's translation of "breaking the grip."

9. Ibid., 214–15.

10. See 135/204/440 and following for the Instigator's testimony.

11. Law 10/59 "widened the scope of political crimes from past affiliation with the Viet Minh to any political opposition, which was now labeled treason." As a result, "the range of political actions that were potential threats to 'national security' was almost unlimited." Elliott, *Vietnamese War*, 195.

12. Ibid., 230; see also Georges Lefebvre, *The Great Fear of 1789: Rural Panic in Revolutionary France*, trans. Joan White (New York: Pantheon, 1973); and Daniel Field, *Rebels in the Name of the Tsar* (Boston: Houghton Mifflin, 1976).

13. 216/8–9/23–25.

14. On Binh Ninh, see 58/2/11; on Nhi My, 144/10/37.

15. Cam Son, 236/7/33; Duong Diem, 194/21/40; Tra Cu, 231/2/3; Binh Trung, 199/4/6; Xuan Son, 249/3/5.

16. Vinh Kim, 188/9/25, and My Long, 266/6/10. Another witness from My Long called attention to the role of the "Liberation Army," but specified that the revolt was organized by "The Uprising Movement to Destroy the GVN Oppression" (204/9/13). Since the PLAF

did not begin to take shape until 1961, references to an "army" amounted to no more than a promise. Thus an informant from Long Khanh was told that "the Liberation Army would come to the hamlet," but in fact "no armed unit arrived" (161/12/29); see also Thanh Phu (CL) ("If the soldiers search your house and arrest us, the lives and the property of your family won't be protected by the Liberation Army," 203/9/17); Phu Nhuan Dong ("The Liberation Army of South Vietnam," 288/3/4); and Thanh Hoa (259/13/28). Other informants employed the term "Liberation Forces" (Binh Trung, 100/4/6; My Phuoc, 212/3/6; Tan Ly Dong, 233/8/31). The most common title was "Liberation Front," in Hoi Cu (165/13/30), Xuan Son (249/3/5), and Xuan Son (293/9/32); or variants, in Cam Son ("Liberation Front of the South," 236/7/33) and My Hanh Dong ("Village Liberation Front Committee," 237/8/16). For Rand informants, the "National Liberation Front" came later. Thus a man from Thanh Phu/CL made it seem as if the "National Liberation Front" played a role in the concerted uprising (203/3/7), then went on later in the interview to specify that "in April 1961, the name of National Liberation Front of South Vietnam was officially adopted" (203/74/103); see also Hiep Duc (159/8/17). In Vinh Long province, to the south of My Tho, local militants in early 1960 were calling themselves "the Revolutionary Movement of the South" or, more simply, "the Revolution": John Donoghue and Vo Hong-Phuc, *My Thuan: The Study of a Delta Village in South Vietnam* (Saigon: Michigan State University Advisory Group, 1961), 81, 83. In Thua Thien province in the Center, rebels claimed to speak for "the Liberation": James Walker Trullinger *Village at War: An Account of Revolution in Vietnam* (New York: Longman, 1980), 79, 91. For a different reading of this terminology, see Elliott, *Vietnamese War*, xviii–xix.

17. 160/3/8–9.

18. 160/3/8–9 and 1/1.

19. 160/1/4 and 4–5/14.

20. Xuan Son, 293/9/32; Ban Long, 239/17/35; Long Tien, 262/10/24; Hoi Cu, 117/24/27; Binh Duc, 175/3/8.

21. Long Hung, 185/3/11; Vinh Kim, 143/89/27; My Duc Tay, 215/1/2; Hoi Cu, 165/10/23.

22. 189/3–4/8.

23. Hiep Duc, 159/1/1 and 8/17; Hoi Cu, 223/3/6 and 7/13; Thanh Hung, 261/1/3; see also 285/1–2/2.

24. Long Hung, 182/13/54; Vinh Kim, 188/17/40; Tan Bin, 70/1/6. On Rand's awareness of the Front's "kidnap" ploy, see 22/2/7 and 48/3/12.

25. Vinh Kim, 143/5/15 and 17 (see also 11/6/19); Hoi Cu, 165/13/29; Phu Nhuan Dong, 288/2–3/3.

26. Vinh Kim, 188/17/40; Binh Trung, 199/10/16 (see also 180/5/15); Hau My, 192/7/19 and 141/15/46 (see also 208/7/13).

27. Thanh Phu/CL, 229/18/32 (see also 203/2/6); My Hanh Dong, 237/8/17; Xuan Son, 265/16/29 (see also 210/10/48 and 239/8/17).

28. 185/4/15 and 3/10.

29. Hau My, 64/2/6; Binh Trung, 199/8/13; Thanh Phu (CL), 203/8/17.

30. Long Hoa, 189/3/7; Xuan Son, 120/13/31, Cho Gao, 142/51/106; Chau Thanh, 135/209/455; Hoi Cu, 165/14/32; Thanh Phu (CL), 203/75/103.

31. Nhi Binh, 251/10/23; Binh Thanh Dong, 137/5/27; Tan Ly Dong, 233/176/117. On the "organizational weapon," see Douglas Pike, *Viet Cong: The Organization and Techniques of the*

National Liberation Front of South Vietnam (Cambridge: MIT Press, 1967). The Hanoi view of the relative importance of the popular movement on the one hand and NLF organizational structure on the other comes through in the account of a regroupee who recalled being told by DRV instructors in 1960 that because "the life of the people in the South was extremely miserable," the National Liberation Front had been formed "to lead the struggle against US-Diem. Because the people's forces were still weak, we had to go to the South to provide a framework for them" (101/24/70).

32. Hoi Cu, 223/6/12; Hau My, 64/2/6, Binh Trung, 199/8/13; Thanh Phu (CL), 203/8/16; My Tinh An, 139/7/33; Tan Phu Dong, 202/3/13; My Hanh Dong, 237/7/14; Duong Diem, 194/24/50.

33. Vinh Kim, 188/8/24; Hau My, 192/6/16.

34. Schematic views, which juxtapose order and revolution, miss the tension in all societies between the authorities and the unruly behavior they seek to contain and punish. For police forces, distinguishing real threats to public tranquillity from ephemeral gestures is an everyday preoccupation. My thinking about the issue has been stimulated by Arlette Farge, Subversive Words: Public Opinion in Eighteenth-Century France, trans. Rosemary Morris (University Park: Pennsylvania State University Press, 1994); and Jean Nicolas, La rébellion française: mouvements populaires et conscience sociale, 1661–1789 (Paris: Seuil, 2002).

35. 167/1/1.

36. 96/9–10/23; see also 219/19/19. Ngo Dinh Diem helped to propagate the view that communism "turned people into cogs in a machine and threatened to extinguish the national soul"; Philip Catton, Diem's Final Failure: Prelude to America's War in Vietnam (Lawrence: University Press of Kansas, 2002), 34.

37. 203/3/7 and 180/3/8. Wilfred Burchett was the first to note the Front's use of fake rifles ("mother carbines"), in Vietnam: Inside Story of the Guerrilla War (New York: International Publishers, 1965), 109. David Elliott coined the apt phrase "guerrilla theater" to describe such tactics in Vietnamese War, 386.

38. 109/26/118, 80/1/3, 215/1/2, 69/25/46, 285/1/2, 188/9/25, 7/5/28, 153/40/85, 189/17/31, 203/75/104, 223/33/36.

4. CONTESTED UNITIES OF THE GOLDEN PERIOD

1. 203/60/88 and 75/103, 150/23/80, 207/54/138.

2. 164/5/20, 261/2/4, 60/23/88, 239/30/60, 175/6/17, 275/13/36, 22326/46.

3. 215/32/54 and 29/48.

4. 135/77/173 and following. The Rand interviewer doubted this lurid claim, but the Instigator insisted on its veracity. Many other informants accused government soldiers of looting and brutality. Interviewee no. 65, a female prisoner whose testimony generally steered clear of melodrama, told a story about a village policeman who killed a youth, "cut out his bile and half of his liver," and made a meal of it, "mixed with chicken and duck" (65/2/5).

5. 135/207/450–51. Both the NLF and the GVN tinkered with district boundaries. The reference in this paragraph is to an enlarged Front version of Chau Thanh district, incorporating many villages that in other maps are located in Vinh Kim and Ben Tranh districts.

6. On well-off farmers, see 205/15/24; on flirting, 190/1/3; on adulterous relations, 189/4/9 (also 212/3/6); on the moneylender, 229/13/24. In the transcripts, "flirting" seems to function as a euphemism for more menacing approaches to women.

7. 89/5/13 and 288/4/5.

8. 194/21/40–41, 58/2/10, 181/4/10, 69 supplement/8/37.

9. 117/22–23/27, 239/5/11, 212/3/6, 216/8/23, 135/208/452, 69 supplement/8/38.

10. 105/2/4, 194/21/41, 146/19/24.

11. 203/74/103 and 290/3/4.

12. 210/7/37, 64/6/18, 78/4/14, 69/2/3 and 5/7, 185/3/12 and 4/14. The Self-Defense Corps (SDC) and the Civil Guards were GVN salaried militia.

13. In Hau My, one informant says that twenty villagers were killed; another reports that one person was killed in his hamlet; and a third also notes one victim in his hamlet (64/2/5, 68/2/3, 254/17/29). In Hoi Cu, one witness claims that "a few" were assassinated; another says that there were two in his hamlet and that he had heard of "many" elsewhere; a third claims that no one in his hamlet was killed but adds that two were executed in a neighboring hamlet; and one estimates that "over 30" perished, then offers another estimate, this time of eight victims, in a context in which it seems that GVN repression was responsible for a share of the mayhem (117/23/27, 278/17/34, 166/1/2, 223/3/7 and 6/12). A man from My Hanh Dong thought that "more than 20" were killed in his village (237/5/10). Someone from Long Hoa estimated a death toll of "more than 100," most of whom were "landlords and rich persons because during those six years of peace these two elements had been having big power and carrying out many relations with the GVN officials and troops. They had also indicated to the latter the hiding places of the Front's underground cadres." He adds that "the local cadres had gone too far" and that the organizer of the terror was later disciplined by the Front (189/4/9 and 20/42). The DT series does not include any other accounts from Long Hoa, which might be employed to check on this very high number. U.S./GVN sources estimated that the Viet Cong killed from 75 to 700 people in all of South Vietnam in 1957, 193 in 1958, and 233 in 1959 (Carlyle Thayer, *War by Other Means: National Liberation and Revolution in Viet-Nam, 1954–60* [Boston: Allen & Unwin, 1989], 144–45), and that 1,700 were assassinated in the 1957–1960 period as a whole (Douglas Pike, *The Viet-Cong Strategy of Terror* [Saigon: United States Mission, 1970], 82). If those figures are anywhere near correct, they indicate that in 1959–60 no one was killed in most of the three thousand–odd villages in South Vietnam and that double-digit village death tolls must have been exceedingly rare.

14. 109/139/56, 89/4/13, 229/13/24.

15. 87/19–20/50. These three assassinations were carried out in 1964–65 rather than during the concerted uprising.

16. 135/208/452, 68/2/3, 64/11/33, 107/22/64.

17. 203/4–5/8 and 184/2/4.

18. 203/4/8 and 98/17/72.

19. 121/4/5 and 98/17/72.

20. Frantz Fanon, *The Wretched of the Earth*, trans. Constance Farrington (New York: Grove Press, 1966), 73; Regina Janes, "Beheadings," *Representations* 35 (1991): 24.

21. 237/6/11. On virtual slavery, see Jeffrey Race, *War Comes to Long An: Revolutionary Conflict in a Vietnamese Province* (Berkeley: University of California Press, 1972), 7; on the landlord and the tenant, Robert Sansom, *The Economics of Insurgency in the Mekong Delta of Vietnam* (Cambridge: MIT Press, 1970), 29; see also Janes, "Beheadings"; William Beik, *Urban Protest in Seventeenth-Century France: The Culture of Retribution* (Cambridge: Cambridge

University Press, 1997); and Beik, "The Violence of the French Crowd from Charivari to Revolution," *Past & Present* 197 (2007): 75–110.

22. Gabriel Kolko, *Anatomy of a War: Vietnam, the United States, and the Modern Historical Experience* (New York: New Press, 1994), 129.

23. 144/67/214 and 257/23/29. Robert Sansom argues that NLF success was due not to terror but to "the sanction of implied force supported by the general will" (*Economics of Insurgency*, 65).

24. 168/6/16 and 4/10.

25. 64/2/5 and 5/13 and following.

26. 88/13/51, 244/2/5–6 and 10/32.

27. 189/1–2/3, 13/24, 25/62 and 64, 27/69.

28. 67/3/11 and 7/34, 114/11/41, 146/3/4.

29. 51/12/53, 13/56, 15/79, and 3/19.

30. 184/2/4 and 232/4/17.

31. 238/1/2, 4/10, and 11/29. In addition to the cases already cited, several other marginal "Viet Cong" also reported that a relative had been killed by the Front: interviewees no. 115 (a brother killed) and no. 121 (two uncles killed) were both village guerrillas for only a year; interviewee no. 290 served as a village guerrilla for two years (father shot by Viet Minh, uncle shot by Front); interviewee no. 47 belonged to the hamlet Farmers' Association for two years and was stirred by the Front's stand against the Americans and in favor of land reform (father killed) (47/5–6/14/15); interviewee no. 56 served as a hamlet militiaman for only a few months (two cousins beheaded); interviewee no. 89 was a squad leader in the 514th Battalion for one year (uncle killed) (89/4–5/13). Others went on to more substantial careers within the movement, such as interviewee no. 62, a cell leader in the 514th Battalion with four years of service before he was captured by the GVN (father and brother-in-law killed); and interviewee no. 198, an assistant squad leader who served in a main force unit for four years (brother killed) (198/6/5). See also references in the transcripts to individuals not interviewed by Rand, such as the man in Ngu Hiep, who was killed in 1961 with no announcement of the crime he had committed. This execution "caused a stir and a lot of speculation among the villagers" but did not prevent his two sons from later joining the Front (85/10/17); and the female cadre whose "father was killed by the VC in 1949" (133/29/169).

32. For more on restitution, see Hoenik Kwon's remarkable *After the Massacre: Commemoration and Consolation in Ha My and My Lai* (Berkeley: University of California Press, 2006).

33. 19/50, 10/5/14 and 17, 160/1/4.

34. 87/9/23, 206/3/10, 257/20/23, 265/3/4, 156/19/50 and 20/57.

35. 157/43/81, 146/25/37, 144/28/82.

36. 75/5/18, 99/25/75, 105/2/5, 112/15/31, 109/5/22, 135/150/325.

37. 159/13/33, 172/3/11, 289/8–9/32, 137/8/45.

38. 177/59/218 and 140/6/16.

39. 141/21/68, 190/6/18 and 3/6.

40. 204/4/5 and 153/40/85.

41. 63/14/78, 65/4/13, 161/10/21.

42. 226/77–78/106.

43. 122/27/56.

44. 62/11/33, 203/50/76 and 33/45.

45. 215/4/7, 101/17/50 and 14/38.

46. 7/17–18/84.

47. 195/2/5.

48. Kolko, *Anatomy of a War*, 104–6.

49. On "blueprint utopias," see Russell Jacoby, *Picture Imperfect: Utopian Thought for an Anti-Utopian Age* (New York: Columbia University Press, 2005), xiv; on "utopias of spatial form," David Harvey, *Spaces of Hope* (Berkeley: University of California Press, 2000), 173. "If we think of modernism as a struggle to make ourselves at home in a constantly changing world, we will realize that no mode of modernism can ever be definitive"; Marshall Berman, *All That Is Solid Melts into Air: The Experience of Modernity* (New York: Penguin, 1988), 6.

5. THE POPULAR MOVEMENT AND THE GENERATIONAL DIVIDE

1. 182/78–79/322. This and the following chapter elaborate on issues first explored in David Hunt, "Village Culture and the Vietnamese Revolution," *Past & Present* 94 (1982): 131–57.

2. 182/interviewer comment. For this informant's commentary on the Front's liaison network as a fully functioning postal service with regular and priority deliveries, see 182/42/16off.; on village medical services, including a "hospital," several medical stations, and a program in preventive medicine, 182/26/96ff.; on the school system, 182/24/88ff.

3. 182/12/51 and 50.

4. 182/2021/78.

5. 182/22/83.

6. 216/23/65, 217/10/20, 197/12–13/33 and 37.

7. 250/10/26, 274/14/25, 276/11/22 (this is the only passage in the transcripts where a French as well as a Chinese education is singled out for praise), 253/25/25, 259/11/23.

8. 253/14–15/18. A guerrilla in Binh Trung "is now aging—he is 40 years old," while another "was sympathetic, but because of his old age (he was forty years old), sometimes he was a difficult man" (100/8/11 and 10/15); a Tan Thuan Binh informant noted: "The Party members' morale has dropped and most of them are old. As a matter of fact half of them are over 40" (131/5/19).

9. 61/18/97–98, 251/7/19, 253/18/20.

10. 94/19/49.

11. 241/7/23, 257/16/19, 281/14–15/20, 254/12/16, 148/18/28.

12. 18/2/7 and 253/17/20. In his study of a village in Long An Province in the late 1950s, Gerald Hickey devotes many pages to such ceremonies, invariably organized by government officials and their landlord allies in consultation with trusted elders. The biggest of these festive occasions, which cost a lot of money and took months to organize, honored Nguyen Huynh Duc, an eighteenth-century general who fought against the Tay Son and who was the ancestor of a prominent local family, characterized by Hickey as part of "a relatively entrenched aristocracy"; Gerald Hickey, *Village in Vietnam* (New Haven: Yale University Press, 1967), 272. Other Saigon officials polluted the festival. "The Civil Guards and the SDC at that time were only interested in going to banquets, to drink wine and eat

dog's meat," asserted an informant from Kim Son. Villagers "had to invite the Village Council members and soldiers to the feast in order to be left alone. Then, all the SDC and Village Guards trooped in to eat and drink" (205/12/20). A hamlet chief in Thanh Phu (CL) employed similar tactics. "When there were wedding ceremonies, death anniversaries and other festivities in my hamlet," reported a rallier, "the hosts had to invite him. When he came to such events, he usually took the honor seat and talked vulgarly. If a host forgot to invite him, he would come to the house when all the guests were gathering and he would shout and charge all those persons of participating in an illegal meeting to discuss communist activities" (229/163/106). These testimonies indicate that before cultural revolutionaries turned their attention to the issue, GVN officials had politicized the festival by asserting that critics of their extortion were communists. In this last instance, they went out of their way to pick a fight with the elders by usurping their "honor seat."

13. 253/17–18/20, 265/11/20, 251/7/19, 259/9/20, 278/13/21.

14. 188/7/19, 259/8/20, 274/10–11/20.

15. 251/7/19, 259/9/20, 264/7/18.

16. 182/12/51 and following.

17. 182/13/54 and following. Considered the proper, "traditional" female garb, the *ao dai* style was created in the 1920s. Several Rand informants cited disapproval of the new marriage rituals. "Whenever two or three elders in Tan Binh Thanh "gathered around a pot of tea, they discussed the new custom and condemned it." In their view, "getting married the way the Front wants them to makes the wedding indecent and unofficial" (264/8/18). "If a couple really wanted to do away with the old custom," critics in Vinh Kim sarcastically affirmed, "it would be better for them just to move in and live together than to hold that ridiculous announcement ceremony" (188/40/122).

18. 43/14/93 and 57/10/56. For another reading of this interplay, see Nguyen Khac Vien, *Tradition and Revolution in Vietnam* (Berkeley: Indochina Resource Center, 1974).

19. 189/14/25, 140/57/123, 207/24/54, 223/14/24.

20. 135/180/386.

21. 197/14/39 and 253/15/18.

22. 142/64/163, 148/75/146, 204/77/91.

23. 130/25/41, 27/49 and 50, 185/25/56.

24. 233/277/185.

25. 250/11/28 and 257/15/19.

26. 153/41–42/89; a similar debate between youth and elders is recounted in 94/18–19/48.

27. 116/22/67.

28. 147/73/222. The "mercenary" characterization is in 147/interviewer comment.

29. 153/46/97 and 145/35/82.

30. 35/1/1.

31. 173/1/1, 12/41, 14/46, 16/49, 19/56, 48/126, and 47/123.

32. 230/7/18, 226/54/76 and 73/100.

33. 109/10/50.

34. 130/25/41.

35. 109/8/45 and 226/39/57. For more on this aspect, see 142/38/63 and 185/1/17. With reference to the government over which he nominally presided, Bao Dai affirmed that

what in Paris and Washington was called the "Bao Dai experiment" was really a "French experiment." Bao Dai, *Le dragon d'Annam* (Paris: Plon, 1980), 250.

36. 203/7/13, 207/15/32, 286/5/13, 177/24/104. See also 286/5/13, 266/6/10, 238/5/13.

37. 194/22/44 and 257/22/28. See 266/6/10 for another claim that the Viet Minh was more violent than the NLF. Several other informants, including two Viet Minh veterans, mention the "it is better to kill innocent people" slogan (173/6/23, 207/15/32, 226/39/58). One of the veterans adds that in 1948 "the Viet Minh revoked this policy" (226/39/58). Claims that the Front was more violent than the Viet Minh are rare, though one thirty-three-year-old cadre, whose brother had been in the Resistance but who himself did not become active until 1961, conceded that "the resistance cadres enjoyed more sympathy from the people than we do now, because most of the present cadres are inclined to use force to enforce the Front's instructions." For good measure he added, "Their behavior and their manner of speech are also cruder than that of the Resistances cadres" (143/12/36).

38. 109/8/45 and 142/39–40/64–65; see also 148/13/24.

39. 177/24/104 and 203/7/13.

40. 49 addendum/14 and 233/280/185.

41. 153/12/23; see also 109/10/49–50.

42. 109/10/49–50 and 9/48, 69/28/52.

43. 145/13/28.

44. 207/52/135.

45. Details in this section appear as follows: the Commander's half-Chinese background (116/3/5); his four wives and appointment as party secretary (4/5); cooperation with the French in order to have more freedom in order to escape (21/63); the cadre who killed out of personal hatred (26/75); his sojourn in France (26/76); his Catholic family (28/80); his move to Saigon after leaving the Front (32/90). The unflattering comments on his character and performance are in a supplement at the end of the interview.

46. Biographical details are found in 69/3–4/4–5.

6. MODERN GIRLS AND NEW WOMEN

1. 253/1/1, 18/20, and 36/44.

2. 258/39/44, 203/12/21, 259/9/20.

3. 182/12/51 and 20/76. In My Tho the term "feudal" was employed loosely and variously to stigmatize a variety of offenses, and in the midst of the cultural revolution, activists had a tendency to redefine the category to incorporate and condemn an increasing number of beliefs and practices. It was the same in the French Revolution, when the list of institutions branded as "feudal" continued to expand after 1789. See the brilliant analysis in John Markoff, *The Abolition of Feudalism: Peasants, Lords, and Legislators in the French Revolution* (University Park: Penn State University Press, 1996). My thinking about "patriarchy," another difficult and confusing concept, has been helped along by Carole Pateman, *The Sexual Contract* (Stanford: Stanford University Press, 1988).

4. Interviewees no. 46 and no. 273 were married, no. 164 was divorced, and no. 65 and no. 264 were widows; on the children of the widows, see 65/8/25 and 3/9, and 264/1/1. Female militants were outnumbered, no doubt by considerable margins, within the Front, but I do not think the disparity was as pronounced as it was in the Rand sample, in which

the fourteen women informants made up only 5 percent of the total. Eighty-five percent of Rand subjects were defectors, who had passed through the Chieu Hoi program, a route that men were more likely than women to choose. U.S. and GVN personnel eyed young men on the road or in the village with suspicion, while women in public spaces were less likely to be regarded as potential Viet Cong. As a result, a woman who resigned from the Front could more easily blend into the population and was less in need of the vetting procedure made available by the Chieu Hoi option. One of the selling points of the program was that it had the authority to issue government identification cards. Since the Front tactic of destroying cards was predominantly a ritual among young men, defection was, again, not so necessary for women as it was for men.

5. 259/9/20, 274/11/20, 257/15–16/19, 281/14/20.

6. 148/112/234 and 263/5/9.

7. 263/2/5.

8. 46/1/3. Two other female informants may also have been exposed to urban life: no. 201, whose mother moved from the village to work as a laborer; and no. 213, who apprenticed as a seamstress in her uncle's house.

9. 78/8/33. See also the sharecropper's daughter who "cherished the hope of coming and settling in the city some day" (201/3/5).

10. On liaison agents, see 107/36/101 (also 133/34/194, 182/20/232, 136/16/12). On intelligence work, 60/19/68 (also 206/23/58).

11. 253/40/48 and 117/38/28.

12. On boring liaison work, see 78/4/18.

13. 36/10/71 and 182/53/201.

14. 263/7/27 and 201/24/64.

15. 253/55/70, 52/62, and 44/53.

16. 65/9/25 and 11/30.

17. 233/280/185; see also 254/12/16.

18. 258/39/44; see also 278/12/20.

19. 264/7–8/18.

20. 239/12–13/71.

21. Both the Rebel and the Feminist reported that the rumor mill commonly portrayed female militants serving the Front as having run away with lovers (182/32/119, 253/20/21 and 57/71). On living unabashedly with the male cadres, see 259/9/20 (also 251/8/19 and 274/11/20); on not minding gossip, 274/11/20.

22. 182/71/288. On the blocking of marriages to GVN-connected partners, see the case of the Platoon Leader, cited in chapter 2.

23. 135/128/275 and 87/187.

24. 109/43/193–94.

25. 164/8/35, 184/9/26, 253/49/58.

26. 84/10/34, 88/9/35, 122/16/38, 142/61/150.

27. 43/16/104, 95/4/9–10, 252/8/13, 138/1/3; see also 142/14.

28. 148/35/49, 142/59/41, 49/16/51, 81/14/31; see also 184/9/26.

29. 122/12/34, 15/38, and 32/73, 148/11/24.

30. See also the case of the cadre and party member from Hoi Cu who rallied after being purged for having "illicit relations" (130/19/36); and the party secretary from Xuan

Dong Military Affairs Section, a married man who "seduced a guerrilla's widow," then "rallied to the GVN and brought his concubine along with him" (79/12/32).

31. 215/31/52.

32. 127/8/26, 51/2/12 and 17/64. Occasionally decisions made by women are incorporated into the narrative, as when an ex-cadre who had been expelled after taking a "concubine" was reported to be living "in dire conditions" and looking "very discouraged." His "two wives" had "let him down." The first refused to have anything to do with him "because of his concubine," and the second, who had been arrested during a GVN sweep, taken to town, and then released, "never came back to her husband" (138/1/3 and 3/9).

33. 253/49/58, 130/20/37, 103/14/53, 151/17/49.

34. 108/45/58, 135/177/380, 182/66/257–58. For examples of women militants as ciphers, see the case of a man attending a course for medics who reported a "love affair with a female trainee" (215/31/52); and a cadre who "met a woman during a meeting and had an affair with her" (81/14/31).

35. 108/44/58.

36. 91/5, 148/43/73, 142/11/11.

37. The closest approximation is the case of the leader of the Women's Association in Hau My who "got married a few months after her appointment. She then accompanied her husband and nobody knows where she is now living" (192/13/35).

38. 141/3/4 and 16–17/52.

39. 141/1/1 and 2–3/3.

40. 141/21–22/68–69 and 3/4.

41. 141/18/59 and 23/71–72.

42. 141/29–30/90–91.

43. 141/32–33/101 and 28/89.

44. 141/37/115.

45. 141/37/115.

46. 141/37–38/115 and 35/109.

47. 141/33/102.

48. 164/11/44 and 12/46; for an example of an unsuccessful male recruiter called to account, see 135/40/90.

49. 164/interviewer comment, 36/119, and 37/121.

50. 273/3/5.

51. 253/23/23, 11/12, and 1/1.

52. 253/18/20, 156/17/46, 278/8/20, 237/8/16.

53. 99/13–14/35 and 225/5/5; see also 65/17/53 and 89/6/17.

54. 146/29/43 and 27/41; see also 108/34/48, 119/3/9, 150/11/33.

55. 29/11/96 and 90/4/13. Other women recruits in the PLAF were assigned noncombat functions, such as "paper work, cooking, washing, vegetable planting and poultry rearing" (189/11/21). An officer in a rear service unit called attention to a platoon in his company "composed entirely of women" (205/49/105 and 50/108), and another informant declared that by 1967 the Front had transferred men out of specialized branches, which were "now filled with women" (246/3/11). See also 90/3/12.

56. 187/67/269, 97/5/10, 99/15/42, 65/17/54, 109/68/288; see also 90/3/12.

57. 213/11/25, 233/115/80, 154/16/53, 96/21–22/52.

58. 164/interviewer comment and 233/238/164.

7. ESCALATION AT GROUND LEVEL

1. For the Soldier's account, see 215/1/2, 11/19, 17/31 and 33, 23/39, 24–25/41.

2. For more on "dreams," see Richard Stites, *Revolutionary Dreams: Utopian Vision and Experimental Life in the Russian Revolution* (New York: Oxford University Press, 1989).

3. 151/21/57, 125/19/26, 123/4–5/19–20.

4. 159/27/59. Most advocates of U.S. escalation wanted nothing to do with Samuel Huntington's defense of "forced-draft urbanization" and denied that generating refugees was a policy. See, for example, letters to the editor by Robert Komer ("a vicious fabrication") and Edward Lansdale ("a blatantly Hanoi-based bit of propaganda") in the *Washington Post*, April 18, 1975. The Rand materials on My Tho underscore the futility of these protestations. As David Elliott puts it, "the results were the same whether or not the intention was deliberate." He goes on to cite evidence that General William Westmoreland, commander of U.S. military operations in Vietnam, approved of forcible relocations; David Elliott, *The Vietnamese War: Revolution and Social Change in the Mekong Delta, 1930–1975* (New York: Sharpe, 2003), 619 and 1133.

5. 16/2 and 273/9/19.

6. 145/34/60, 226/11/20, 16/2, 144/29/59, 15/3/6, 186/29/59, 273/9/18.

7. 233/196–98/125.

8. 285/25–26/55–56 and 266/22/43; see also 107/44/139, 286/17/43, 142/68/170, 259/2/3.

9. 49/22/66, 207/17/34, 264/15/38, 159/13/31, 274/21/42; see also Hoa Dinh, 148/119/247.

10. 273/10/20.

11. 194/42/97, 50/3/15, 83/6/51, 235/3/5.

12. 264/3/6 and 141/48/147.

13. 130/15–16/29 and 251/3/8.

14. 120/40/118 and 24/63, 175/14/45, 154/1/2, 140/54/117.

15. 248/9/11, 275/2/4, 50/3/14; see also 23/14/84 and 54/11/44. According to their own account, U.S. troops claimed license to fire on Vietnamese "taking evasive action" or dressed in "black pajamas"; see David Hackworth, *Steel My Soldiers' Hearts: The Hopeless to Hardcore Transformation of the Fourth Battalion, 39th Infantry, United States Army, Vietnam* (New York: Touchstone, 2002), 320–24. Hackworth was the commander of the Fourth Battalion in the U.S. Ninth Division, stationed in My Tho. On "black pajamas," see Lady Borton, *After Sorrow: An American among the Vietnamese* (New York: Viking, 1995), 28. Borton's reports on postwar discussions with women from Ban Long village are filled with detail about everyday village life during and after the war.

16. 278/10/16, 104/2/3, 64/12/40, 63/9/51, 291/4/11, 204/50/63, 69/24–25/46.

17. 141/51–52/156–158. In the period before the Tet Offensive, B-52s also bombed My Loi and perhaps other villages. Elliott, *Vietnamese War*, 1162.

18. 147/91/279 and 281, 144/73/231–32. A "cong" equals one-tenth of a hectare.

19. 110/17/44, 8/19/197, 141/39/116, 69/24/45 and 9/19. Along with Cam Son, Binh Ninh and Hau My were also Front bastions.

20. On Thanh Hoa, see 253/6/5; My Duc Dong, 82/1/3; Tan Binh Thanh, 264/2/4. For more on groups working in the fields, see Cam Son (69/9/18), Duong Diem (177/119/83), and Quon Long (275/2/4); on weddings and funerals, 142/65/165; see also 181/28/74; on soccer games, 217/9/18, and basketball games, 144/65/207.

21. On My Long, see 266/9/18; Tan Binh Thanh, 264/6/15; Thanh Phu (CL), 123/1/3; Xuan Son, 114/7/22, 265/9/17, 276/9–10/17; My Phuoc, 212/15/39–40; Binh Trung, 284/6/15; Diem Hy, 151/12/35; Hoi Cu, 227/8/9–10/16; Hau My, 64/14/48; Cam Son, 286/19/47; Hoa Dinh, 122/5/16; Quon Long, 112/28/62; Tan Ly Dong, 233/207/137; Vinh Kim, 99/17/48; and Phu Phong, 153/49/102.

22. 63/1/1 and 5, 114/1/1, 131/1/2, 122/23/41 and 46/132, 20/5/42, 157/23/23–24, 286/17/42, 270/2/6, 152/4/8, 55/7/27.

23. 55/8/31.

24. On Cam Son, see 69/24/45; Vinh Kim, 99/23/64–66; Hoa Dinh, 148/57/103; Long Trung, 66/2/13; Quon Long, 112/3/6; Dong Hoa Hiep, 3/10/63; Huu Dao, 20/5/39 and 42; Binh Trung, 63/1/5 and 7/40; Binh Thanh Dong, 89/3/6; and Hoi Cu, 117/29/27. On civilian casualties, see Elliott, *Vietnamese War*, 1387.

25. On Binh Ninh, see 63/7/40 and 9/50; Hau My, 64/12/40 and 115/5/16; My Hanh Trung, 61/11/58; Xuan Son, 120/10/24; My Long, 40/1/3; My Phuoc Tay, 98/5/22 and 6/27.

26. On Phu An, see 57/6/29; Thanh Phu (CL), 1/4/24 and 29/1; Trung An, 78/2/9; and Thanh Hoa, 259/22/62.

27. On Hiep Duc, see 159/27/59; Hau My, 141/48/147 and 49/150; Nhi My, 144/65/208; Song Thuan, 169/3/9; Tan Thuan Binh, 131/3/11; Vinh Kim, 111/9/32; and Tan Binh Thanh, 264/15/38.

28. 223/30/56.

29. 84/3/9, 99/23/67, 82/2/5.

30. 140/46–47/100 and 179/26/49.

31. 84/3/9, 179/26/49, 89/2/6, 130/18/34, 93/2/8, 204/62/74.

32. 30/5, 80/2/5, 92/3/11, 88/4/12.

33. 151/5/9, 130/15/28, 38/5/31.

34. On My Hanh Trung, see 61/11/61; Hiep Duc, 159/27/59; Hoa Dinh, 84/14/51; My Long, 40/1/3; Long Trung, 41/4/10 and 43/15/100.

35. 144/64/205 and 66/211, 231/73.

36. 46/2/7.

37. On Diem Hy, see 289/2/4; My Long, 266/9/17; An Thai Dong, 87/4/13; Binh Phuc Nhi, 72/1/2; and Vinh Kim, 111/10/36. In this context, "strategic hamlet" and "new life hamlet" are terms for the same kind of place, a settlement putatively under government control and therefore relatively safe from bombing and shelling by US/GVN forces.

38. 69/24/45, 78/2/9, 169/3/10. Nguyen Van Thieu served as president and Nguyen Cao Ky as prime minister of the Republic of South Vietnam.

39. 204/58/70, 215/34/57, 72/1/2, 49/7/14; see also 210/14/66.

40. 8/4/25. For cases in which government personnel made explicit their determination to kill "innocent people" in response to Viet Cong provocations, see reports from My Thinh An (142/65/165) and Phu My (179/26/49).

41. 101/40/125.

42. 63/8/45–46, 208/11/21, 36/3/20, 16/3; see also the Midwife's detailed report on the Hau My situation (141/50/152).

43. 204/58/69, 99/22/66, 181/25/66, 259/8/20, 11/4/10, 77/17/49.

44. 272/6/26, 82/1/3, 153/18/35, 233/138/93, 55/7/27.

45. 135/138–39/302.

46. 187/8/49 and 95/12/30. The interviewer in another session, who still had not caught on, asked: "How will you give security to the people? What can the GVN do to help those poor people?" Could a way be found to "force the fish (Front) to leave the water (people)?" Turning the metaphor right side up, the subject answered, "If you want all the people to move out here, then attack them with air and artillery, especially the F-105's, the jets and 250lb. bombs" (187/11/61).

47. 122/23/43 and 165/19/42.

8. MAPPING THE EXODUS

1. On Hau My, see 64/9/28, 192/1–2/3, 254/5/5; Thanh Phu (CL), 1/3/18, 123/1/3, 203/71/101, 229/46/78; Hung Thanh, 76/1/4, 104/1/2, 129/1/2; Phu My, 171/4/8 and 179/3/5.

2. On Nhi Binh, see 207/2/4 and 31/81, 226/2/3, 235/1/2, 244/7/22, 274/4/6; Long Dinh, 178/9–10/46; Tam Hiep, 247/16/46.

3. On Binh Ninh, see 63/1/1 and 74/5/19; Hoa Dinh, 108/86/113 and 268/4/6.

4. On Binh Duc, see 162/3/6 and 164/7/30; Thanh Phu, 172/1/1 and 9/26, 182/49/183; Ap Cho, 273/8/18.

5. On Binh Trung, see 83/6/14 and 284/17/50; Long Hung, 185/13/41, 190/7/21 and 11/33; Phu Phong, 89/18/51; Ban Long, 239/38/82; Song Thuan, 169/2/6; Vinh Kim, 97/12/21 and 99/1/1.

6. On Long Trung, see 145/7/12 and 66/5/30; Long Khanh, 24/10; Long Tien, 89/18/51 and 262/7/17.

7. On Hoi Son, see 145/7/12; Cam Son, 145/7/12, 270/9/20, 105/9–10/39, 69/9/19, 106/2/2, 236/14/71; My Long, 204/3/4; Xuan Son, 114/1/1, 120/1/1, 63/5/20, 265/3/5, 293/1/1.

8. See the table on village population movements in David Elliott, *The Vietnamese War: Revolution and Social Change in the Mekong Delta, 1930–1975* (New York: Sharpe, 2003), 1418.

9. 105/2/7.

10. 123/1/3.

11. 141/39/116.

12. 188/14/36, 159/20/42, 148/7/17, 205/73/146, 207/16/33, 275/13/35, 271/5/15.

13. 173/23/66; see also 108/95/131.

14. 130/34/65, 132/1/1, 141/49/151, 197/6/17.

15. 204/96–97/119, 286/17/41, 188/41/125; see also 61/10/54.

16. 112/24/52, 124/5/14 and 1/3.

17. 124/5/16 and 1/2, 112/18/37, 276/4/7.

18. 180/23/64, 229/16/27, 282/4/7; see also 223/30/55.

19. 180/27/73, 268/1–2/2, 262/14/40.

20. 192/2/5, 257/5/8, 218/11/18, 130/14/27.

21. 83/5/12, 253/8–9/9, 233/221/149, 181/33/87, 19/12/39.

22. 34/6/39, 131/1/2, 70/14/74, 138/9/35.

23. 35/8/47 and 117/41/29.

24. 10/8/28, 236/9/46, 90/10/43, 86/22/58, 103/3/11, 109/105/394.

25. 42/10/32, 145/7–8/12, 210/21/99, 120/3/7, 153/48/101, 122/4/9, 149/20/42, 207/55/142.

26. 149/20/42, 99/34/103, 24/7, and 148/110/230.

27. 115/4/13, 254/7/7, 84/1/3, 148/110/230, 117/38/28, 165/21/47.

28. 174/6/18, 262/9/22, 233/224/149, 253/9/9, 181/33/87.

29. 68/36/82 and 99/33/102–3.

30. 239/11/24, 177/20/85, 171/14/45, 253/9/9; see also 284/3/8.

31. 147/116/359.

32. 200/7/35–36.

33. 69/38–39/68–69.

34. 69/39/69, 77/11/27, 216/2/5, 83/13/36.

35. 275/4/9 and 15/42, 124/5/16, 276/4/7 and 5/9.

36. 224/20/38.

37. 224/1/1.

9. THE AMERICAN OTHER

1. 108/10/21, 149/79/164, 68/18/45, 58/13/64, 69/13/23, 120/2878, 97/4/9 and 10/19.

2. 180/26/71, 146/23/33, 136/36/30, 135/150/325.

3. 149/91/92. See David Hunt, "The My Tho Grapevine and the Sino-Soviet Split," in A Companion to the Vietnam War, ed. Marilyn Young and Robert Buzzanco (Malden, Mass.: Blackwell, 2002), 79–92.

4. 88/8/30, 97/12/22, 108/61/76, 7/21/96; see also 143/22/61, 107/34/98, 147/37/90. On the "hinge year," see David Elliott, The Vietnamese War: Revolution and Social Change in the Mekong Delta, 1930–1975 (New York: Sharpe, 2003), 736.

5. 1/15/81 and 99/37/115.

6. 142/33–34/42. According to the Communist Party schema, the NLF was engaged in a "special war" in 1960–1965, when Washington sent advisers and equipment to help the GVN, and spoke of "limited war" after 1965, when U.S. combat elements took over primary responsibility for the fighting.

7. 69/11–13/23 and 33/53, 68/19–20/48.

8. 135/52/122, 140/36/81, 145/6/11.

9. 140/16/39, 65/15/49, 87/23/63, 88/14/58.

10. 61/21/117 and 89/22/72. Choosing from many recent treatments, one might begin with the very different interpretations found in Fredrik Logevall, Choosing War: The Lost Chance for Peace and the Escalation of War in Vietnam (Berkeley: University of California Press, 1999); Robert Dean, Imperial Brotherhood: Gender and the Making of Cold War Foreign Policy (Amherst: University of Massachusetts Press, 2001); and Gareth Porter, Perils of Dominance: Imbalance of Power and the Road to War in Vietnam (Berkeley: University of California Press, 2005). Logevall argues that Washington policymakers knew from the start that the chance of success in Vietnam was minimal, and so does H. R. McMaster, Dereliction of Duty: Lyndon Johnson, Robert McNamara, the Joint Chiefs of Staff, and the Lies That Led to Vietnam (New York: Harper Collins, 1997).

11. 142/49/98, 123/11/51, 145/34/81 and 34/79, 49/13/41; see also 120/26/72. On the way some Rand interviewers introduced themselves to their subjects, see Phillips Davison, *User's Guide to the Rand Interviews in Vietnam* (Santa Monica: Rand Corporation, 1972), 33. On the Hung Thanh My battle, see Elliott, *Vietnamese War*, 394.

12. 137/23/115, 122/47/136, 147/117/363, 101/74/213; see also 101/74/214, 139/1/89, 143/35/95, 147/117/363.

13. 175/15/49–50.

14. 199/74/90.

15. 87/24/63 and 205/46/97.

16. 153/45/93, 164/27/96, 169/4/14.

17. 182/46/176 and 47/177.

18. 182/47–48/178 and 180.

19. To someone unfamiliar with her overall presentation in the interview, which conveys an impression of sharp intelligence, the Rebel's way of telling these stories might seem naïve. I prefer to think that she purposely adopted an ingenuous tone as a cover for inserting into the transcripts a lot of disturbing testimony, albeit with obligatory happy endings tacked on for the edification of her interrogator.

20. 182/46/175 and 271/6/20; see also 169/4/13, 210/14/66, 236/8/38.

21. 188/24/63 and 20/49.

22. 218/7/7 and 181/34/90; see also 200/20/95 and 206/1/3.

23. 192/22/64, 218/6/7, 148/6/15, 183/4/6.

24. 190/interviewer comment, 262/16/47, 275/17/48.

25. Elliott, *Vietnamese War*, 1126–27.

26. 177/58–59/216–217.

27. 65/3/7.

28. 169/5/15.

29. 154/3/13, 182/49/182, 164/24/83, 174/6/17 and 8/22; see also 155/3/7. *Dong tam* means "with one accord."

30. 164/22/72 and 74 and 3/4.

31. 162/6/16, 154/3/13, 155/3/7, 158/4/20, 162/6/16, 163/4/22 and 24, 164/24/84, 168/9/27, 172/9/28, 174/8/23 and 25.

32. 162/6/15.

33. 164/24/84.

34. 154/3–4/13, 155/3/5, 162/3/7, 163/4/23, 168/4/7, 172/1/2–3, 180/26/73.

35. Samuel Huntington, "The Bases of Accommodation," *Foreign Affairs* 46 (1968): 652, 648. A similar adjustment was imposed in Russia during the 1990s, after the dissolution of the Soviet Union. See Esther Kingston-Mann, "Transforming Peasants in the Twentieth Century: Dilemmas of Russian, Soviet, and Post-Soviet Development," in *The Cambridge History of Russia*, vol. 3, *The Twentieth Century*, ed. Ronald Grigor Suny (Cambridge: Cambridge University Press, 2006), 411–39.

36. 155/3/6 and 162/7/19.

37. 162/7/15 and 172/1/2. No attempt was made by DT interviewers to raise the subject of the sex industry in My Tho. David Hackworth's treatment, with its jocular indulgence toward GIs with "drippy dicks" (venereal disease) and contempt for Vietnamese women and their male relatives, is painful to read. But at least he talks about prostitution around

the base, a topic Rand declined to address. See David Hackworth, *Steel My Soldiers' Hearts: The Hopeless to Hardcore Transformation of Fourth Battalion, 39th Infantry, United States Army, Vietnam* (New York: Touchstone, 2002), chap. 17.

38. 180/26/73.

39. 180/26/73–74 and 1/2 and 3 and 4/13.

40. 44/12/86, 69/12/23, 144/74/236, 87/24/65; see also 80/20/62.

41. 79/25/75; see also 70/50/217.

42. 135/149/324 and 99/40/122. The Instigator's choice of words is congruent with his general approach to sexual issues; see chapter 6.

10. FATE OF THE LIBERATED ZONE

1. 251/1–2/4. If the Americans and the Saigon authorities had defeated the Front, postwar wreckage might have come to seem a form of "creative destruction," opening the way for the most enterprising among uprooted families, each with "two or three thousand piasters" in startup funds, to take the lead in forging a capitalist economy of a modern type. According to one account, something of the sort happened in South Korea after the Korean War; see Bruce Cumings, *Korea's Place in the Sun: A Modern History* (New York: Norton, 2005).

2. David Harvey, *The Condition of Postmodernity: An Enquiry into the Origins of Cultural Change* (Cambridge, Mass.: Basil Blackwell, 1990), 11.

3. James William Gibson's analysis has been important in shaping my thinking about U.S. intervention; see James William Gibson, *The Perfect War: The War We Couldn't Lose and How We Did* (New York: Vintage, 1986), 19, 22.

4. David Hackworth, *Steel My Soldiers' Heart: The Hopeless to Hardcore Transformation of the U.S. Army, Fourth Battalion, 39th Infantry, Vietnam* (New York: Touchstone, 2003). In *The Perfect War*, Gibson shows how "technowar" encouraged Pentagon planners to imagine Vietnam as an empty space, without inhabitants embedded in their own social and historical circumstances.

5. 187/50/217, 155/9/20, 210/37/149.

6. 236/13/66 and 16/75.

7. 101/38/120 and 152/24/56.

8. 152/4/7.

9. 117/25/27 and 229/11/22. On "soundscapes," see Richard Rath, *How Early America Sounded* (Ithaca: Cornell University Press, 2003).

10. 110/40/120.

11. 134/9/16 and 8/16, 11/19, and 8/14. No doubt these various usages were continuations and modifications of local custom.

12. 275/15/40, 49/6/11, 61/12/66, 63/7/37–38.

13. 264/13/30, 203/14/23, 185/2/9, 130/23/38, 106/2/5, 237/22/38. Cadres on mission in "contested" and dangerous Tan My Chanh warned villagers to get rid of their dogs and later shot two barking canines (73/1/2); see also 122/17/38 and 212/3/6. In prerevolutionary Vinh Kim, peasants "never dared to set foot in the houses of the rich people. Usually they had extremely fierce dogs to guard their houses. Most of the time when a poor person came to their gates, they just let the dogs bark furiously and didn't bother to chase them away or welcome the poor visitor" (260/7/26).

14. 99/28/84, 60/2/5–6, 78/7/28, 65/3/7.

15. 227/4/9 and 87/19/49–50.

16. 54/3/12.

17. 179/30/55, 181/27/72, 193/14/51, 207/28/71.

18. 177/29/124; see also 293/8/28.

19. On parents in Vinh Kim, see 197/9/27; on children of cadres, 175/1/1, 207/14/31, 267/1/1, 279/9/13, 165/3/5. As one might expect, relatively prosperous families were especially likely to send children away to school (176/7/17, 178/7/30, 190/10/27, 192/17/50, 194/37/81).

20. 178/7/33 and 274/9–10/18; see also 217/6–7/10.

21. 185/21–22/51, 229/40/67–68, 193/10–11/35, 200/10/51, 180/21/58, 181/25/66, 239/24/50, 197/8/25; see also 210/1/4 and 279/16/20.

22. 55/5/19, 61/14/75, 7/17/84.

23. On visiting relatives, see 74/8/21; also 23/14/84, 25/9, 164/31/106, 173/17/49; on going to market, 44/11/74; on tramping villagers, 34/11/80; on heading to a wedding, 51/17/68; on the boat captain, 8/32/184; on replacing lost papers, 120/40/116; on missions, 149/127/260; see also 200/21/98.

24. On socializing, see 19/8/20 and 10/7/24; on festive occasions, 181/27/72; on letters, 223/28/50; on news and newspapers, 75/8/28, 3/7/42, 17/8, 38/12/74.

25. 121/4/8 and 179/32–33/47; see also 86/22/56 and 96/19–20/30.

26. On Miss S.D., see 36/6/44 and 7/47; on buying food, 140/48/103; firecracker powder, 81/9/19; fabrics, 133/18/109; medicines, 97/17/30, and also 87/15/38, 157/45/86, 185/21/51; on going to market, 68/18/45.

27. On inciting opinion, see 109/111/403; on villagers coming back from market, 97/26/47 and also 26/19, 29/20, 122/10/7; on letting slip the wrong word, 85/14/28; on visiting a brother, 54/9/35.

28. 69/37/67 and 133/18/109.

29. 141/8/20 and 22 and 41/121.

30. On the fruit seller, see 41/8/35; on women going to district town, 90/9/37; see also 26/4 and 83/11/27; on the woman and the rallier, 99/40–41/122.

31. 53/12/51–55, 76/8/35, 60/26/97; see also 83/13/35.

32. 73/10/51, 188/5/15, 84/12/45, 126/9.

33. On Lambretta drivers, see 34/11/77, 52/22/132, 53/12/51; on bus drivers, 40/11/42.

34. 99/15/41, 199/58–59/66, 231/7/13.

35. 14/18/36, 41/8/36, 25/9, 181/26/69, 125/36/61, 89/21/66, 102/4/22, 8/32/182.

36. 132/74/131, 44/11/73–74, 8/35/196.

37. 164/31–32/106. The eighteen-year-old defector mentioned rumors having reached her family that, on her way to the Chieu Hoi Center, she had been forced to work as a porter and had been beaten by soldiers, claims she (not very emphatically) denied to the Rand interviewer.

38. 89/21/66; see also 74/8/24.

39. 49 addendum/12.

40. 233/186/120 and 107/17/43.

41. 173/30–31/85, 142/22/22, 209/2/4.

42. 157/17/10, 166/4/13, 207/17/36; see also 235/1/1.

43. 142/22/22.

44. 157/27/30, 139/12/56, 176/12–13/27.

45. 137/20/105, 160/11/39, 278/5/5, 166/5/18, and also 173/33/93.

46. 166/4/14.

47. On Hau My, see 192/17–18/52; My Long, 204/71/86; Long Hung, 206/19/50; My Hanh Dong, 237/22/38; My Hanh Trung, 238/15/38; Duong Diem, 194/38/83.

48. On bicycles before 1965, see 195/6/20, 227/14/39, and also 178/7/34; on the end of bicycle use, 236/9/45, 179/14/31, and also 197/10–11/30; on destroying every road and bridge, 197/9/28; see also 180/22/60 and 192/17/51.

49. 28/3/8, 218/3/3, 247/15/43. A passage in David Hackworth's book indicates that U.S. soldiers took tu dia warnings, along with cooking smells and well-worn paths as indications that the Viet Cong were nearby, implying that they hastened to enter rather than avoid "deadly places." Hackworth, Steel My Soldiers' Hearts, 325.

50. 195/6/25, 247/16/45, 140/53/113.

51. 157/14/9, 159/19/38, 104/3/13.

52. 212/9/22 and 188/19/46.

53. On all the canals and roads, see 140/53/113; on Hau My, 192/17–18/52; on My Hanh Dong, 237/22/38; on My Long, 266/21/39 and also 204/71/56; on owning sampans, 179/13/31, 195/6/26, 178/7/38.

54. Michel de Certeau, The Practice of Everyday Life, trans. Steven Rendall (Berkeley: University of California Press, 1988), xix, 37.

55. 239/30/60, 73/3/15, 70/4/48.

11. "LIVE HOUR, LIVE MINUTE"

1. 149/126/260 and 155/6/14.

2. 125/37/62, 164/1/2 and 26/89.

3. 154/6/17, 204/82/101, 182/25/92.

4. 147/47/129, 190/23–24/57, 215/6/10, 231/13/27, 170/7/15.

5. 211/5/7 and 13/22.

6. 195/19/80 and 78, 194/15/25.

7. 182/51/190 and 213/9/20.

8. 117/10/20, 182/61/236, 186/20/36, 273/5–6/9–10.

9. 97/15/24, 172/15/52, 88/5/19.

10. 144/58–59/86.

11. 209/6/18 and 193/20/75; see also 206/23/157 and 257/29/37. On the two calendars, see the insightful commentary in Patricia Pelley, Postcolonial Vietnam: New Histories of the National Past (Durham: Duke University Press, 2002), chap. 4.

12. On the inauspicious day, see 205/4/5; on the God of Agriculture, 179/30/55; on the village spirit, 181/27/72, 193/14/51, 204/75/90; on Buddhist worshippers, 178/10/51, 179/31, 193/14/51, 250/2/3, 259/7/17; on the Nui Nua sect, 280/4/13.

13. 141/11/29, 130/30/53, 134/2/3 and 17/34.

14. 148/116/241, 130/32/59, 151/26/76, 141/10/26.

15. Some military maneuvers had to be pegged to the lunar calendar: see the demolition unit that "did not operate from the 13th day to the 18th day of the lunar month when the moon was up in the sky at night" (147/76/232); and the saboteurs mining rivers who

needed to keep track of "the 15th and 30th of the lunar months" in order to gauge the tides (157/221/19). For other examples of out-of-synch lunar references, note the Viet Minh attack on a post in "the 10th month of the lunar calendar" in 1953 (241/1/1); the defection "on the 6th of the sixth month (lunar year)" (51/17/66); the cadre who said that "each month on the 15th lunar day I filed a report to the Village and District Propaganda, Culture and Education Sections" (134/14/28).

16. 130/29/51.

17. 130/28/51. Development specialists often affirm that subsistence agriculture, with its irregular labor demands, perpetuates underemployment in the countryside. Given such a view, one could argue that the southern revolution drew on and eliminated downtime in the villages by encouraging peasants to "invest" surplus labor time in politics.

18. 182/52/196, 165/42/107, 100/7/10–11.

19. On 1960, see 141/17/54; 1961, 241/18/60; 1962, 140/36/70 and 278/23/46; 1963, 210/36/148; 1964, 246/1/2; 1965, 164/4–5/20.

20. 168/2/4, 164/27/94, 182/75/307, 187/12/67, 269/6/13.

21. 165/52/135 and 200/14/68; see also 182/74/303.

22. 204/24/36 and 135/184/393; see also 59/23/83 and 165/44/110.

23. 285/8/15 and 22/47.

24. 204/5–6/7, 145/28/64, 142/79/199; see also 131/12/37.

25. 210/13/63 and 216/4/11.

26. 281/18/26, 165/54/142, 190/8/23; see also 153/31/59.

27. 190/10/30.

28. 253/19–21/20–21.

29. 280/8/22, 164/9/38 and 10/40, 252/13/19; see also 168/8/23.

30. 188/29/70, 165/49/126, 207/43/13.

31. 146/72/125 and 140/10/30. Robert Brigham demonstrates that the Saigon government's draft policy, which by 1975 had drawn one-sixth of the male population into the armed forces, crippled household-based agriculture, thereby threatening "to destroy the social fabric of rural South Vietnam." But I am not convinced by the adjoining argument, suggesting that the NLF somehow found a way to reconcile the competing demands of the PLAF and the agricultural sector. Robert Brigham, ARVN: Life and Death in the South Vietnamese Army (Lawrence: University Press of Kansas, 2006), 1, 73, 50.

32. 200/10/54, 156/17/44, 154/6/18–19.

33. 227/25/75, 257/45/53, 173/17–18/51.

34. 65/4/11, 165/1/4, 178/3/13; see also 200/1/1.

35. 130/28/51, 175/11/33, 157/39/70, 275/16/43.

36. 117/8/14, 140/55/118, 49 addendum/9, 227/5/10; see also 278/5/6.

37. 269/5/13, 229/47/80, 210/13/62; see also 209/4/10.

38. 179/10/20, 257/4/4, 253/3/3.

39. 144/79/245, 239/36/79, 175/14/45, 194/42/97, 238/10/26.

40. 188/14/36 and 149/47/97.

41. 264/1–2/3 and 249/17/31.

42. 253/17/20, 180/23/64, 274/12/21.

43. 188/33/91, 247/11/29, 183/9/13.

44. 208/15/29, 172/13/43 and 20–21/67, 229/43/73.

45. 250/12/29 and 251/8–9/19.

46. 282/1/1.

12. THE TET OFFENSIVE

1. David Harvey, *The Condition of Postmodernity: An Enquiry into the Origins of Cultural Change* (Cambridge, Mass.: Blackwell, 1989), 44.

2. 274/11/20.

3. 166/5–6/21.

4. 208/17/35. On connections between "festival and revolt," see Yves-Marie Bercé, *Fête et révolte: les mentalités populaires du XVIe au XVIIIe siècle* (Paris: Hachette, 1994); and Maurice Agulhon, *Le République au village: les populations du Var de la Révolution à la Seconde République* (Paris: Seuil, 1979). For more on Agulhon, whose example I try to follow, see David Hunt, "Working People of France and Their Historians," *Radical History Review* 28–30 (1984): 45–65.

5. Gabriel Kolko thinks that planning for the offensive began in January 1967 and that orders were dispatched to the South in September; Gabriel Kolko, *Anatomy of a War: Vietnam, the United States, and the Modern Historical Experience* (New York: New Press, 1994), 303 and 305. My understanding of Communist Party objectives owes much to Kolko's treatment. Also essential on that aspect and on the Tet Offensive more generally is Ngo Vinh Long, "The Tet Offensive and Its Aftermath," in *The American War in Vietnam*, ed. Jayne Werner and David Hunt (Ithaca: Southeast Asia Program, Cornell University, 1993), 23–45.

6. On the final stages of preparation for the offensive, see David Elliott, *The Vietnamese War: Revolution and Social Change in the Mekong Delta, 1930–1975* (New York: Sharpe, 2003), 1063 and 1055–56; on the nature of the Tet decision, 1056; on the November 22 order, 1077; on hearing news over the radio, 1053. Recalling the offensive years later, women in Ban Long declared: "We knew only to prepare for an offensive. We thought it would be local. We had no idea until we listened to the radio. Not just our uprising at Vinh Kim Market, but a hundred cities and towns all across the entire country!" Cited in Lady Borton, *After Sorrow: An American among the Vietnamese* (New York: Viking, 1995), 114.

7. On the eight battalions, see Elliott, *Vietnamese War*, 1090; on damage in My Tho, 1037; on main force losses, 1116; on massive firepower, 1119; on civilian casualties, 1126; on posts and watchtowers, 366; on the revolution at its lowest ebb, 1126. The My Tho story fits into the larger history of the Tet Offensive in South Vietnam, where PLAF units found their way into cities that were then "saved" by bombing and shelling, and the NLF absorbed a terrible pounding. According to Gabriel Kolko, "the U.S. estimate that up to one-half of the Revolution's southern born armed forces were lost during 1968 is probably as accurate as any." Kolko, *Anatomy of a War*, 371.

8. The DRV official is cited in a dispatch by Jacques Decornoy, *Le Monde*, March 1, 1968. For an authoritative treatment of the offensive, with up-to-date references to Vietnamese- and English-language sources, see the new edition of William Turley, *The Second Indochina War: A Concise Political and Military History* (Lanham, Md.: Rowman and Littlefield, 2008), chap. 6.

9. For this account, see 192/21/59.

10. 226/72/99 and 196/6/9.

11. 213/14/36 and 2/3.

12. 213/5/9.

13. 213/16/43 and 13/31.

14. 181/9/22 and 257/40–41/46.

15. 216/5/14.

16. For this account, see 269/6/13ff. and 8/22ff.

17. 269/9/24–25.

18. 291/3/8. See also the reference to "an opportunity that only occurred once in a thousand years," cited in Elliott, *Vietnamese War*, 1084.

19. On "something big," see Elliott, *Vietnamese War*, 1071; on *dut dien*, 1088; on rice collection, 1070; on taxes in Phu Phong, 1104; on the Tet Offensive as a "rural uprising," 1044; on the jubilant idiom of the revolt and many examples of mass participation, 1101 and following. For more on the "apocalyptic discourse" sometimes heard in peasant revolts, see Lynne Viola, *Peasant Rebels under Stalin: Collectivization and the Culture of Peasant Resistance* (New York: Oxford University Press, 1996).

20. Unable to let go of a view that assigns agency only to the Communist Party, scholars make it seem as if this mood was created by "overeager cadres" who "exceeded their mandate by giving the villagers the impression that this would be the final major push of the war" (Elliott, *Vietnamese War*, 1082); by leaders who "asked the vast bulk of those who were to act to take unlimited risks to produce a victory of the proportions the Politburo thought possible but unlikely" (Kolko, *Anatomy of a War*, 333–34). Villagers who shrank from the specter of protracted war did not have to be instructed to think in an apocalyptic register about the Tet Offensive.

21. Elliott, *Vietnamese War*, 1050, 1293, and 1371. Other local studies agree on the persistence of the NLF; see Eric Bergerud, *The Dynamics of Defeat: The Vietnam War in Hau Nghia Province* (Boulder: Westview Press, 1991), 205, 305, 311, 318; on the situation in Phuoc Tuy province, Frank Frost, *Australia's War in Vietnam* (Boston: Allen and Unwin, 1987), 161–62; and also references in David Hunt, "U.S. Scholarship and the National Liberation Front," in Werner and Hunt, *The American War in Vietnam*, 104–7.

22. In the 1990s, informants in Vinh Kim put forward a strange version of the war in which "village intellectuals" figured prominently and peasant revolutionaries were invisible; cited in Philip Taylor, *Fragments of the Present: Searching for Modernity in Vietnam's South* (Honolulu: University of Hawaii Press, 2001), chap. 5. Movement feminism also does not register in recent work; see Jayne Werner and Daniele Belanger, eds., *Gender, Household, State: Doi Moi in Viet Nam* (Ithaca: Southeast Asia Program, Cornell University, 2002); and Ashley Pettus, *Between Sacrifice and Desire: National Identity and the Governing of Femininity in Vietnam* (New York: Routledge, 2003). The Werner and Belanger collection includes a detailed review of the literature (13–28). When questioned by Lady Borton after the war, women veterans of the Liberation Front in Ban Long remembered their resistance to the repression visited on the province by the Saigon government, but said nothing about the generational and gender conflicts that emerge so vividly from the testimonies gathered by Rand. "Don't you understand," one said to Borton, "gesturing toward the creek and her house with its ladder of light lying on the fresh water urns under the thatch eaves. 'This is all we wanted'" (cited in Borton, *After Sorrow*, 132). Contributors to Hue-Tam Ho Tai, ed., *The Country of Memory: Remaking the Past in Late Socialist Vietnam* (Berkeley: University of

California Press, 2001) establish a critical perspective on the construction of memory and try to bring forgotten aspects to light. The book analyzes memorializings sponsored by the Communist Party but has nothing to say about the Liberation Front.

23. Mandy Thomas, "Needlepoints of Labour: Vietnamese Women, the Garment Industry, and Transnational Space," in *Gender Practices in Contemporary Vietnam*, ed. Lisa Drummond and Helle Rydstrom (Singapore: NIAS Press, 2004), 240.

1. For a brief history of the project, see Phillips Davison, *User's Guide to the Rand Interviews in Vietnam* (Santa Monica: Rand Corporation, 1972).

2. Ibid., 33. Davison also raises the possibility that interview rooms were bugged (22, 30). The other citations in this paragraph are from the comments at the end of interviews 81, 144, 57, and 81 again.

3. For prisoners who claimed to have left the NLF, see 67/3/15 and 144/54; for those disillusioned with the Front, 61/5/31, 62/11/32, 63/1/4, 153/46/97, 2095/15, 239/38/83, and 272/4/16; recollections of the informant who had been imprisoned under the Diem regime are in 226/26/46.

4. On being detained, see 12/10/27, 43/22/143, 260/24/69; also 80/19/56, 85/30–31/77, 271/9/29.

5. Davison, *User's Guide*, 33–34; 187/72/276 and 73/280, 51/11/50; see also 126/interviewer comment.

6. 91/interviewer comment, 216/interviewer comment, 271/4–5/14, 101/70/204; on NLF spies in Chieu Hoi Centers, see also 126/interviewer comment and 136/interviewer comment.

7. David Elliott, *The Vietnamese War: Revolution and Social Change in the Mekong Delta, 1930–1975* (New York: Sharpe, 2003), 1159 and 761 (see also 754); 50/19/101 and 241/interviewer comment.

8. 208/interviewer comment; see also 137/interviewer comment; Davison, *User's Guide*, 33.

9. Davison, *User's Guide*, 15; 171/interviewer comment and 15/interviewer comment. Davison states that the thirty-six Vietnamese interviewers associated with the motivation and morale project were "city people" and that twenty-two were born in North Vietnam. It would be interesting to know which interviews were conducted by the nine women on the team (15–16).

10. Interviewer comments at end of interviews 45, 161, 230, and 134.

11. A sense of the interview methodology comes through when interviewer no. 25 expresses appreciation for the cooperative attitude of the subject, who "made a voluntary and deliberate effort to slow down and to enable the interviewer to record his 'dictation.'" In explaining why he came to trust his Rand interlocutor, interviewee no. 101 stated: "I saw that you have gone to all the trouble of writing down everything I have said. At first I thought that you were writing everything down so carefully to crosscheck me on whether or not I was telling the truth when you asked a second time, but I see that you have not gone back to the old questions, so that I have concluded that you are writing everything down so that one day you may pull it all together in a recapitulation of what goes on with the other (VC) side. The reason that I think you are doing this is that you have a printed

questionnaire" (101/70/205). Davison indicates that some interviews were taped (*User's Guide* 34) and that interviewers "edited" transcripts (43). For his remark about the possibility that interviewers were placed under surveillance, see 22.

12. The image of informants "pushing back" is found in Sherry Ortner, "Resistance and the Problem of Ethnographic Refusal," in *The Historic Turn in the Human Sciences*, ed. Terrence McDonald (Ann Arbor: University of Michigan Press, 1999), 298.

13. On "Orientalist" travel literature, see Mark Bradley, *Imagining Vietnam and America: The Making of a Postcolonial Vietnam, 1919–1950* (Chapel Hill: University of North Carolina Press, 2000). John Mecklin, a U.S. adviser to the Vietnamese in the early 1960s, declared that the peasants of Vietnam were hobbled by a vocabulary of only "a few hundred words," in *Mission in Torment: An Intimate Account of the U.S. Role in Vietnam* (Garden City, N.Y.: Doubleday, 1965), 76. Interviewer comments are from interviews 247, 67, and 18.

14. 69/36/63, 43/33/215, 153/49/103; see also 40/13.

15. 14/10/19, 17/8, 34/7/47, 38/9/59, 10/66, and 4/24, 20/7/55ff., 137/4/23.

16. Interviewer comments and the end of interviews 24 and 122.

17. 9/interviewer comment.

18. Interviewer comments and the end of interviews 52, 129, and 10.

19. Interviewer comments at the end of interviews 61 and 159. In the latter session the interviewer was reduced to petulant outbursts, asking, for instance, "Why is killing such a trifle to the NLF?" (159/6/11). See also interview no. 195, in which a dignified and unrepentant prisoner frustrated the questioner to the point where he lost his temper: "In the future, where will the NLF cadres go if there are no people in their areas? Will you depart for North Vietnam and live there with Mr. Ho? As a matter of fact, if you don't come over to the GVN side, you will have no people to support you" (195/21/92).

20. 142/interviewer comment.

21. 153/34/70, 35/73, and 37/78–79.

22. On the growing suspicion that officials in Saigon and Washington were not interested in Rand reports, see Davison, *User's Guide*, 20.

INDEX

DAVID HUNT was born in Buffalo and grew up in Rochester, New York, and earned degrees from Haverford College and Harvard University. His career at the University of Massachusetts Boston, where he is now professor of history, began in 1969. His teaching won awards in 1986 and 2002. He is the author of *Parents and Children: The Psychology of Family Life in Early Modern France*; he co-edited and contributed to *The American War in Vietnam*; and he has written articles and chapters on the French Revolution and French social history and on Vietnam and the Vietnam War. He lives in Boston with his wife and daughter.